Clamor

Praise for this book

'This is a beautifully written account of one of the most horrific chapters in recent global history. It will ensure it will never be forgotten. While communicating the extreme cruelty of South America's military dictatorships, it juxtaposes this with the solidarity, self sacrifice and meticulous efforts of Clamor's volunteers, its allies and activist victims to record and resist it.'

Professor Jenny Pearce

'In the darkest days of the military dictatorships of South America, a small group of activists brought a ray of hope to victims of human rights violations. Jan Rocha recounts a true story of daring and courage, to reveal the chilling reality of the death camps, the thousands of people who "disappeared" at the hands of the military and the heart-breaking search of the "Grandmothers of the Plaza de Mayo" to trace the babies and children torn from their families. It is a tale of tenacity, resilience and the commitment to justice: and a testimony to how truth and determination can eventually triumph over evil.'

Clare Dixon, Regional Manager Latin America and Caribbean at CAFOD

'This book reveals the close collaboration between the dictatorships in South America in the late 1970s and 1980s, little known at the time to those of us reporting from the region. It also tells the tale of how a small, poorly funded human rights organisation, Clamor, based in Brazil, was able to play a key role in tracking down children, born in prison to left-wing activists and then illegally adopted by government supporters, often military officers. A fascinating tale.'

Sue Branford, a journalist reporting for the Financial Times
from Brazil during the 1970s

'In the midst of the dictatorship, when they called us madwomen, one of our first destinations abroad was Brazil, to visit *Clamor*, where we immediately felt shielded and helped.

Thanks to Clamor, which collected the testimonies of the survivors of the genocide in Argentina, we could confirm the birth in captivity of various of our grandchildren.

Besides proving the coordination of the South American dictatorships, we discovered an enormous regional solidarity, ignoring frontiers, between victims, their families and people committed to justice and human dignity. And all this was due to a great extent to that first contact with Clamor.'

Estela Barnes de Carlotto, president of the Grandmothers of the
Plaza de Mayo, Buenos Aires

Clamor

The search for the disappeared of the South American dictatorships

Jan Rocha

This book is dedicated to the courageous grandmothers of Argentina, Uruguay and other South American countries who, even in the darkest days of violence and repression, never gave up the search for their missing children and grandchildren.

Published by Practical Action Publishing Ltd
and Latin America Bureau

Practical Action Publishing Ltd
25 Albert Street, Rugby,
Warwickshire, CV21 2SD, UK
www.practicalactionpublishing.com

Latin America Bureau (Research & Action) Ltd
Enfield House, Castle Street, Clun,
Shropshire, SY7 8JU, UK
www.lab.org.uk

First published under the title *Solidariedade Não Tem Fronteiras*, by Editora Expressão Popular, 2018

A catalogue record for this book is available from the British Library.

ISBN 978-1-90901-492-3 Paperback
ISBN 978-1-90901-429-9 Hardback
ISBN 978-1-90901-430-5 Electronic book

Rocha, J. (2023) *Clamor: The search for the disappeared of the South American dictatorships*, Rugby, UK: Practical Action Publishing and Latin America Bureau <http://doi.org/10.3362/9781909014305>.

Since 1974, Practical Action Publishing has published and disseminated books and information in support of international development work throughout the world. Practical Action Publishing is a trading name of Practical Action Publishing Ltd (Company Reg. No. 1159018), the wholly owned publishing company of Practical Action. Practical Action Publishing trades only in support of its parent charity objectives and any profits are covenanted back to Practical Action (Charity Reg. No. 247257, Group VAT Registration No. 880 9924 76).

Latin America Bureau (Research and Action) Limited is a UK registered charity (no. 1113039). Since 1977 LAB has been publishing books, news, analysis and information about Latin America, reporting consistently from the perspective of the region's poor, oppressed or marginalized communities, and social movements. In 2015 LAB entered into a publishing partnership with Practical Action Publishing.

Original cover Clamor bulletin, No. 16, November 1984. this edition by Katarzyna Markowska, Practical Action Publishing
Typeset by vPrompt eServices, India

Contents

Part 2: Light at the end of the tunnel (1983-1989)

List of acronyms

AALA	Associação de Advogados Latinoamericanos (Association of Latin American Lawyers)
APDH	Asamblea Permanente por los Derechos Humanos (Permanent Assembly for Human Rights)
CADHU	Comisión Argentina de Derechos Humanos (Argentine Human Rights Commission)
CAFOD	Catholic Agency for Overseas Development
CBA	Comitê Brasileiro de Anistia (Brazilian Amnesty Committee)
CBS	Comitê Brasileiro de Solidariedade (Brazilian Solidarity Committee)
CELAM	Consejo Episcopal Latinoamericano (Episcopal Council of Latin America)
CELS	Centro de Estudios Legales y Sociales (Centre for Legal and Social Studies)
CNI	Central Nacional de Informaciones (National Intelligence Centre)
CNT	Confederación Nacional de Trabajadores de Chile (National Confederation of Chilean Workers)
COB	Central Obrero Boliviano (Bolivian Workers' Federation)
CONADE	Comité Nacional de Defensa de la Democracia (National Committee for the Defence of Democracy)
CONADEP	Comisión Nacional sobre la Desaparición de Personas (National Commission on the Disappearance of Persons)
COPACHI	Comité de Cooperación para la Paz en Chile (Committee of Cooperation for Peace in Chile)
CPI	Comissão Parlamentar de Inquérito (Parliamentary Commission of Inquiry)
DINA	Dirección de Inteligencia Nacional (National Intelligence Directorate)
DOPS	Departamento de Ordem Política e Social (Department for Political and Social Order)
ERP	Ejército Revolucionario del Pueblo (Revolutionary People's Army)
ESMA	Escuela Superior de Mecánica de la Armada (Higher School of Mechanics of the Navy)
FASIC	Fundación de Ayuda Social de las Iglesias Cristianas (Social Aid Foundation of Christian Churches)

FEDEFAM	Federación Latinoamericana de Asociaciones de Familiares de Detenidos-Desaparecidos (Latin American Federation of Associations of Relatives of the Detained-Disappeared)
FPMR	Frente Patriótico Manuel Rodríguez (Manuel Rodríguez Patriotic Front)
GAA	Grupo de Acción Anticomunista (Anti-Communist Action Group)
JOC	Juventude Operária Católica (Young Christian Workers)
MDB	Movimento Democratico Brasileiro (Brazilian Democratic Movement)
MDP	Movimiento Democrático Popular (People's Democratic Movement)
MIR	Movimiento de Izquierda Revolucionaria (Revolutionary Left Movement)
MLN	Movimiento de Liberación Nacional (National Liberation Movement)
OAB	Ordem dos Advogados do Brasil (Brazilian Bar Association)
OAS	Organization of American States
OCOA	Organismo Coordinador de Operaciones Antisubversivas (Coordinating Organization for Anti-Subversive Operations)
OPM	Organización Politico Militar (Political Military Organization)
PVP	Partido por la Victoria del Pueblo (Party for the Victory of the People)
SERPAJ	Servicio Paz y Justicia (Service for Peace and Justice)
SIDE	Secretaría de Inteligencia del Estado (Secretariat of State Intelligence)
SIJAU	Secretariado Internacional de Juristas por la Amnistía en Uruguay (Secretariat of Jurists for Amnesty in Uruguay)
WCC	World Council of Churches

Acknowledgements

I would like to thank LAB for sponsoring the publication of this book, especially Mike Gatehouse and Sue Branford, and the staff at Practical Action Publications, especially Rosanna Denning and Chloe Callan-Foster, for their efficient and good natured collaboration. I am grateful to Louise Byrne for doing a first edit and to Keiran MacDonald for his meticulous proof reading.

During the several years when I researched the CLAMOR archive at the documentation centre CEDIC, in São Paulo, I was given generous help and support by the staff, especially Professor Heloisa de Faria Cruz and historian Ana Celia Navarro de Andrade. My daughter Ali helped me organise the huge amount of material I had to deal with, besides giving me constant encouragement to carry on.

My thanks also go to all the people I interviewed, including former refugees and members of solidarity and human rights organisations, in Brazil, Argentina, Uruguay, Paraguay, Chile and Bolivia, and fellow Clamor members, reviving often painful memories.

And finally, I want to thank my family, Plauto, Camilo, Ali and Bruna who for years co-existed with CLAMOR activities, urgent meetings in the sitting room, mysterious phone calls in the middle of the night, distraught strangers appearing on the doorstep and staying the night. Thank you all and anyone else I might have overlooked.

Foreword

Jan Rocha, who was the BBC World Service's first correspondent in Brazil and, from 1984, the Brazil correspondent for the *Guardian* newspaper, has written a lively and engrossing book about Clamor, the human rights NGO she co-founded, which was dedicated to defending human rights in the countries of the Southern Cone. Within these pages, Jan charts the organization's eventful history from 1977 until its dissolution in 1991.

After the Cuban Revolution, the US government became ever more determined to prevent the spread of Soviet-inspired ideology and activism on its doorstep, and to that end it encouraged, enabled, or tolerated a series of coups against democratic governments in South America. With their anti-communist rhetoric, military governments in South America aligned themselves with the Cold War priorities of their powerful northern neighbour. Apart from generous funding, via the CIA and the State Department, of right-wing elites, the US government also provided intensive training for the region's military and intelligence services. This had dire consequences, as one by one democratic governments were ousted, freedom of expression was suppressed, and thousands of opponents of the regimes were imprisoned, tortured, and killed. By 1976, all but two countries in South America were ruled by dictatorships. It was against this backdrop that Clamor came into being.

Clamor had the distinction of being one of the earliest regional human rights NGOs in South America. Among its unique features was the fact that its founders had first-hand experience of state repression: Jaime Wright was a Presbyterian minister whose brother, Paulo, a political activist, had 'disappeared' three years before, while Luiz Eduardo Greenhalgh was one of the few lawyers willing to defend political prisoners. As a journalist, Jan had filed numerous reports about life under Brazil's military dictatorships and had interviewed many victims of the repression and their families (in 2021, a selection of her reports was published in Portuguese). In 1975, Jan's friend and former BBC colleague, Vladimir Herzog, died as a result of torture in DOI-CODI, the headquarters of military intelligence in São Paulo, a few hours after presenting himself voluntarily for questioning about his alleged links with the banned Communist Party. Herzog's death, which triggered a wave of protests in Brazil, overshadowed President Geisel's state visit to the UK in May 1976.

Jan, despite the risk of working under the shadow of the dictatorship's repressive legislation, was in regular contact with Amnesty International, providing crucial information about political prisoners to the International

Secretariat in London. I first got to know her when I was the researcher responsible for Amnesty's work on Southern Cone countries, including Brazil and Argentina. I valued her initially as a reliable source, and later as a personal friend. Brazil's military government, infuriated by Amnesty's 1972 *Report on Allegations of Torture in Brazil*, had refused to allow the organization to conduct in-country investigations. But because most flights from London to the Southern Cone were routed via Rio de Janeiro or São Paulo (their airports were regional hubs), these stopovers provided the perfect cover for meetings, and so I had the opportunity to get to know Jan, her family, and the Clamor team. I was immediately struck by Jan's warmth, generosity, and sense of humour, as well as her commitment to human rights.

A factor that contributed to Clamor's effectiveness was its location. Based in São Paulo, it was well placed to gather testimonies from hundreds of refugees arriving mainly from Argentina, who passed through en route to exile in Europe or North America, or made Brazil their temporary home. As Jan explains, 'The military were still in charge in Brazil and democracy was but a distant dream there, yet for the thousands of Argentines fleeing the reign of terror unleashed in Brazil's southern neighbour, it had become a haven.'

Clamor's founding members, through their professional work, had extensive national and international contacts, including with the Catholic Agency for Overseas Development and the highly influential World Council of Churches, which provided funding to Clamor. In the uncertain political climate in Brazil, Clamor benefited greatly from having the endorsement of Cardinal Paulo Evaristo Arns, the archbishop of São Paulo. The archbishop's offices became an unofficial centre for Latin American refugees. As Jan acknowledges, 'None of our achievements would have been possible without the uncompromising support at all times of Dom Paulo, Cardinal Arns, the archbishop of São Paulo.'

At the end of 1978, Sister Michael Mary Nolan, an indomitable American nun, and Father Roberto Grandmaison, a Canadian priest from Quebec, joined Clamor. The two missionaries, who worked in poor neighbourhoods in São Paulo's sprawling *periferia*, used their Church contacts to provide shelter and other assistance to the families of undocumented political refugees remaining illegally in Brazil. At a swanky lunch in honour of Canadian prime minister Pierre Trudeau, the self-effacing Roberto, out of place at the lavish event, even managed to dodge past Trudeau's protection officers and hand over a letter from Clamor asking Canada to accept more refugees.

Clamor's small, flexible structure, unburdened by bureaucratic policies and procedures, enabled it to work in an unorthodox way. Its freewheeling methodology had grown out of the founding members' experience of repression in Brazil – their guiding principle, articulated by Jaime Wright, was to use any opportunity, however unconventional, that could benefit the people they were fighting for. Clamor's modus operandi could at times entail risks for some of its collaborators, however: in 1979, Ricardo Carvalho, a well-meaning journalist, somewhat blithely agreed to travel to Montevideo to make contact with the paternal grandmother of two children who had been discovered living in Chile under false identities, and it was only after completing his tasks that the perilous nature of the enterprise dawned on him.

With the help of volunteers, Clamor built an impressive documentation centre using the testimonies of political refugees, many of whom had been held in secret detention camps and tortured. This archive later proved an invaluable resource for Argentine NGOs and in particular for the Abuelas de Plaza de Mayo, the organization of grandmothers searching for children who had disappeared after being abducted with their parents or who were born in captivity during Argentina's 'Dirty War'.

Unlike Amnesty and other organizations based in the northern hemisphere, Clamor could react rapidly to human rights emergencies on Brazil's borders or in neighbouring countries. One chapter describes in vivid detail the abduction in 1978 of Lilián Celiberti, a Uruguayan exile living legally in Porto Alegre with her family. Clamor, after getting a tip-off, contacted an intrepid local lawyer, Omar Ferri, to check on their well-being. His timely intervention and persistence not only saved her life and prevented her children from being stolen, but also exposed to the Brazilian public, and the world, the clandestine collaboration between Brazilian and Uruguayan security forces. The following year, Sigifredo Arostegui, a Uruguayan human rights defender, disappeared after taking a bus from Foz do Iguaçu to Buenos Aires. Plauto Rocha, a lawyer, travelled with the missing man's father to find out what had happened. On making inquiries about Sigifredo's whereabouts, they were immediately arrested by Argentine border guards. Plauto, armed with a letter authorizing him to act on behalf of Cardinal Arns, faced down this hostile reception and forced the authorities to acknowledge Arostegui's detention. Without Clamor's intervention he would have entered the ranks of the disappeared.

Other chapters relate how, with its increasingly high profile, Clamor became a magnet for defectors from the Uruguayan army and navy who made their way to São Paulo. They provided sensitive information that corroborated the joint operations of the region's security forces against *subversivos* (dissidents), and the grisly fate that awaited them.

The existence of a coordinated, cross-border system of repression was a subject of speculation for many years in the specialist press, such as the usually well-informed *Latin America Newsletter*. In 1975 the intelligence chiefs of Argentina, Bolivia, Chile, Paraguay, and Uruguay agreed to establish Operation Condor, the code name for the collection, exchange, and storage of intelligence data concerning 'leftists, communists, and Marxists'. Brazil joined Condor a year later. This secret alliance between South American dictatorships set up a rendition and repression programme to track down and eliminate perceived enemies of the military regimes. Condor involved the formation of special teams from member countries prepared to travel anywhere in the world to carry out assassinations. According to declassified US State Department files, Amnesty leaders in London were also potential targets.

While none of us were aware of the full extent of Operation Condor, both Amnesty and Clamor were trying to deal with its devastating impact. Buenos Aires, traditionally a safe haven for the region's political exiles, had become a hunting ground: opponents of the regimes in Chile, Uruguay, Bolivia, and Paraguay were kidnapped, tortured, and killed. Many of the refugees were seized in broad daylight from centres supposedly under the protection of the Office of the United Nations High Commissioner for Refugees (UNHCR). In May 1976, the prominent Uruguayan politicians Zelmar Michelini and Héctor Gutiérrez Ruiz were abducted from their homes in central Buenos Aires. Their bodies were later found in a car, handcuffed and riddled with bullets. Wilson Ferreira Aldunarte, the leader of the Uruguayan Blanco Party, with help from Amnesty International and UNHCR, narrowly escaped the same fate. In late 1976, as a member of an official Amnesty delegation investigating human rights violations in Argentina, I had several frightening encounters with plain-clothes security patrols. On a visit to a UNHCR refugee centre in Buenos Aires, I noticed with alarm that the car we were travelling in was being tailed by a posse of armed men in unmarked Ford Falcons, the abduction squads' trademark vehicle – a gesture obviously intended to intimidate the delegation.

According to Oxford University's Database on South America's Transnational Human Rights Violations, at the height of Operation Condor's criminal activities, between 1976 and 1978, there were 382 cases of illegal detention and torture, 367 instances of murder and enforced disappearance, and 25 cases of kidnapped children. Argentina and Uruguay experienced the greatest number of atrocities attributed to the Condor programme.

Without a doubt, Clamor's most significant contribution to human rights in the Southern Cone was its long-lasting collaboration with the Abuelas de Plaza de Mayo, in their efforts to track down stolen children. Some of the most compelling parts of this book relate how Clamor, often on the basis of leads provided by whistle-blowers, helped trace some of these children. The discovery in 1979 of Anatole and Victoria Julien Grissonas in Chile was the first indication that children who had disappeared or been born in captivity in Argentina's secret camps could still be alive. This vindicated the claims of the grandparents, and from that moment the search for the missing children became Clamor's top priority.

Displaying amazing courage and resourcefulness, Clamor – with support from lawyers, journalists, churches, political activists, and trade unions – not only exposed the egregious crimes of the military governments' war against subversion but also, through its mixture of quick reaction and painstaking investigation, helped to save many lives and reunite families torn apart by state-sponsored terror.

Clamor closed down in 1990. As Jan writes, in that year,

> the last of the Southern Cone dictatorships, Chile, inaugurated a civilian president, and the years of military rule that had blighted

the region, killing, torturing, and disappearing thousands, sending hundreds of thousands into exile, ruining economies, and mutilating societies, came to an end. Democracy, however limited and imperfect, had been restored, and therefore the raison d'être for Clamor's existence had disappeared.

Even though Clamor no longer exists, its mission remains relevant. President Bolsonaro's troubling support for dictatorship, his attacks on the Supreme Court and other civil institutions, and his questioning of the country's electronic voting system make many Brazilians fearful of a return to the horrors of the past. This book is a timely reminder of what may be at stake, the importance of taking a stand, and the need for international solidarity.

In the pages that follow, Jan convincingly captures the mood of the period of *abertura* (opening up) in Brazil – its tensions and setbacks amid growing pressure for a restoration of the rule of law. Her invigorating chronicle of Clamor's often-hair-raising exploits across the countries of the Southern Cone is a testament to the major contribution that this small organization was able to make to human rights in South America.

Tricia Feeney,
Oxford, 8 September 2022

Tricia Feeney worked for Amnesty International, Oxfam, and UNESCO before setting up an NGO, Rights and Accountability in Development (RAID), in 1998. She is currently a senior adviser for the US SAGE Fund.

Introduction

In the 1970s, thousands of refugees arrived in Brazil. They were fleeing the right-wing dictatorships installed in neighbouring countries after civic–military coups overthrew democratically elected governments. They described how state-sponsored terror regimes were 'disappearing' thousands of people, who were then tortured and murdered in clandestine prison camps. Brazil was still a military dictatorship, but after years of repression, some freedoms were gradually being restored.

In São Paulo a handful of people listened to these stories, at first with incredulity, then deciding they had to act. In 1978 they formed a group, which took the name Clamor, and with the enthusiastic support of the then archbishop of São Paulo, Cardinal Paulo Evaristo Arns, they rapidly became a vital lifeline for the families and human rights organizations who courageously resisted terror within the dictatorships.

Funded by the WCC, along with Catholic and Protestant churches and organizations in the US, Canada, and Europe, Clamor was ecumenical and international: it included a Brazilian Presbyterian minister, a French Canadian Catholic priest, an American Catholic nun, a Brazilian lawyer, and a British journalist. The group soon began receiving scores of letters from desperate family members denouncing the forced disappearance or imprisonment of sons, daughters, grandchildren, wives, and husbands. They came mostly from Argentina, but also from Chile, Paraguay, Uruguay, and Bolivia.

Over the next decade, Clamor became an important source of information for international human rights organizations, like Amnesty International, through its bulletins, published in three languages: Portuguese, Spanish, and English. In 1978 it was one of the first organizations to denounce the existence of concentration camps in Argentina, from which prisoners were taken on death flights or killed and their bodies burned. The same year, in a response to Operation Condor, an international state terror organization set up by the South American dictatorships which involved cross-border collaboration between their security forces, Clamor adopted the motto 'Solidarity knows no frontiers'.

In 1979, Clamor located the first 'disappeared' children ever to be found. The young brother and sister had been kidnapped in Argentina three years before, and then abandoned hundreds of miles away in Chile to prevent their families from ever finding them. A year later the organization launched a campaign to publicize the large numbers of children and babies who had disappeared in Argentina after the coup, producing special calendars with their photographs to draw attention to the issue. In 1982 Clamor compiled the biggest list up to that date of the disappeared in Argentina, and in 1983 it organized the first meeting of survivors from a clandestine camp. Clamor members carried out sometimes risky investigative missions to Paraguay, Chile, Bolivia, and Uruguay, collecting information, visiting prisoners, and bringing solidarity.

Clamor finally closed its doors in 1991 when the last of the military dictators, General Pinochet of Chile, reluctantly handed over power to an elected president. Thirty years later, few people remember or even know about its existence. As one of the founder members, I decided it was time to tell the story of Clamor.

PART 1
Five terrible years (1977–1982)

CHAPTER 1
The house on Turiassu Street

November 1977: it was raining as I made my way to São Paulo's Avenida Paulista, a wide street once lined with the mansions of wealthy coffee barons, now taken over by banks and shopping malls. I was heading for the Top Center shopping mall, not to shop, but for a rendezvous with an Argentine refugee. The military were still in charge in Brazil and democracy was but a distant dream there, yet for the thousands of Argentines fleeing the reign of terror unleashed in Brazil's southern neighbour, it had become a haven. They arrived desperate to denounce to the wider world what was happening, many of the children traumatized by the horrors they had seen. Some of us wanted to find ways to help them.

Stories had appeared in the papers when the armed forces seized power the year before on 24 March 1976, overthrowing unpopular president Isabelita Perón, the widow of Juan Perón – but it seemed like just another military coup, all too familiar in South America. Soon, it was reckoned, democracy of some sort would be restored.

The refugees told a different story. They told of things so hard to believe that most people did not. They talked about the disappearances. Thousands had been disappeared, abducted in broad daylight or dragged from their homes at night and never heard from again. Sometimes the refugees were talking about their own wives or husbands. And in low voices, hesitantly, as though they hardly believed it themselves, they mentioned the existence of clandestine detention camps where thousands of men and women were held in inhuman conditions, tortured and killed.

When we became convinced that they were telling the truth, I wrote a joint story with fellow journalist Sue Branford, based on interviews with some of the refugees, and sent it to the *Guardian*. The editor of the foreign desk also found it hard to believe and insisted on adding another section about the crimes of the left-wing guerrilla organization, the Montoneros, for 'balance'. When it was finally published in the newspaper in May 1977, halfway down an inside page, I received a letter from a colleague at the BBC in London saying that many people simply could not accept that our story was true – it was too far-fetched.

The contact in the Top Center had been set up by an exiled union leader known simply as Pedro, after many conversations in a rambling house on Rua Votuporanga, in São Paulo's Sumaré district. The house, rented by a group of English journalists, including Sue Branford and my brother Nick Terdre, had also become home to a group of refugee families.

In the cloak-and-dagger style that was second nature to the Argentines, many of them former members of the armed left-wing organizations which had been ruthlessly hunted down by the security forces, nobody used their real names and everyone took elaborate security precautions, because even in Brazil they were still afraid. So I had no idea whom I was actually meeting or where we would be going.

Consequently, it nearly went wrong. At 7 p.m. I arrived at the Top Center, and among the crowds of window-shoppers, I recognized an Argentine refugee couple I already vaguely knew. Anxious to avoid them seeing me, I hurried further inside, but they caught up with me.

'Jan, wait!' said the man, Juan. He continued quietly, 'We are your contact. Come with us – we have to get a bus.'

By now it was dark. When we got to the bus stop, the woman, Claudia, said, 'Don't look to see which bus we are taking.'

On the crowded bus, we stood strap-hanging in silence. After 20 minutes or so, they told me we had reached our stop. We walked up a dimly lit street and stopped outside a small terraced house. Juan rang the bell, and immediately the door was opened by a tall man with a large moustache. 'Entra, entra' – come in, come in. He led me down a corridor into a room lined with bookcases.

Somebody was already there. I recognized Luiz Eduardo Greenhalgh, one of the few lawyers who defended political prisoners in the Brazilian courts. I had been to his office several times in search of information about prisoners and trials. Luiz had also been sought out by Argentine exiles desperate to do something about the situation in their country, and to help the many now arriving in Brazil, practically destitute.

We talked about what we could do and began to think of others who might be willing to join us. I remembered Jaime Wright, a Presbyterian minister; I had recently interviewed him about his brother, Paulo Wright, a political activist who had disappeared three years before. In October 1975 Jaime had co-celebrated an ecumenical mass held in the packed Sé Cathedral for an ex-BBC journalist, Vladimir Herzog, murdered by the military. He had stood in front of the altar with São Paulo's Catholic archbishop, Cardinal Paulo Evaristo Arns, and the archbishop of Recife, Helder Camara, branded the 'red bishop' by the military because he preached that poverty was the worst violence. Beside them stood Rabbi Henry Sobel, who had refused to bury the Jewish Herzog as a 'suicide'. It was an open act of defiance against the dictatorship.

Jaime seemed a good bet.

We left the house, which I later discovered was located on Turiassu Street, under cover of darkness and went our separate ways. A few days later I went to see Jaime and he immediately agreed to join us.

The next step was to create some sort of organization. We left behind the clandestine methods of the Argentines and began meeting at a college run by a liberal-minded nun, Mother Cristina, who provided space for human rights groups to meet.

First, we had to find a name. We did not want to be just another 'committee'. We wanted something which would have more impact, like Amnesty International, known worldwide simply as Amnesty. On the blackboard in the classroom where we met, we chalked up possible names and acronyms, and from the alphabet soup, Clamor emerged.

It was a name that included 'LA' for Latin America, and 'amor', or love – love your neighbour, which seemed appropriate. Jaime immediately came up with a Biblical reference, 'I heard the clamour of your people' (Psalms 88:2), which became the group's motto.

He also suggested that the next step should be to talk to Charles (or Chuck) Harper, the World Council of Churches' (WCC) coordinator for Latin America. A lifelong friend of the Wright family, he was also, like Jaime, a Presbyterian minister, born in Brazil, the son of Protestant missionaries.

The WCC was already heavily involved in helping Latin American refugees. Chuck liked the idea of Clamor, and from then on the WCC became an ally and funder.

Both Jaime and Chuck suggested that we should get the blessing of Dom Paulo, São Paulo's archbishop, for the proposed organization and place ourselves, as it were, under his 'umbrella'. The cardinal had already become known for his courageous stand on human rights, demanding explanations about the disappeared and protesting the torture of prisoners. In reprisal, the archdiocesan radio station, 9 de Julho, had been closed down, and the weekly newspaper, *O São Paulo*, was subject to heavy censorship.

By 1978, the Brazilian military had been in power for 14 years. General had succeeded general as president. Elections were cancelled, and the existing political parties were banned and replaced with two tame parties – the so-called 'yes' party and 'yes, sir' party. Strikes were forbidden and censorship was rigorous. Thousands of Brazilians suspected of 'subversion' – a vague, all-embracing term – had been tortured and imprisoned, many killed. The attempts by small left-wing groups at armed resistance had been crushed.

The archbishop's offices, known as the Curia, had become an unofficial centre for Latin American refugees. Before the Argentines and the Uruguayans, Chileans fleeing the 1973 coup that brought General Pinochet to power and Paraguayans escaping the repression of dictator Alfredo Stroessner, in power since 1954, had also sought refuge in Brazil.

The Curia, a large, double-fronted mansion located in one of São Paulo's middle-class districts, was home to the Justice and Peace Commission and the Archdiocesan Committee for the Human Rights of the Marginalized, which did their best for the refugees who turned up on their doorstep. But their priority was the many Brazilians who were victims of human rights abuses, torture and imprisonment, both political prisoners and the many innocent victims murdered by police death squads. It was difficult to find time and resources to deal with the growing number of refugees from other countries.

So we went to see the archbishop, clutching the single piece of paper on which we had typed out our aims. We were going to defend human rights in the countries of the Southern Cone, collect and publish denunciations in a monthly bulletin – *Clamor Bulletin*, also known simply as *Clamor* – and provide assistance to the refugees. We would be politically independent – an ecumenical, Christian group with humanitarian motives.

Dom Paulo welcomed our proposal with open arms. To sponsor an organization dedicated to helping left-wing political refugees and denouncing the crimes of right-wing generals, in a region they ruled with an iron fist, might have seemed audacious, but Dom Paulo was enthusiastic and encouraging.

So there we were, the three of us, with a name, a proposal, and the support of the leading human rights champion in Brazil. Like the three musketeers, we were ready to start fighting – not with swords or pistols, but with words. We decided to publish *Clamor Bulletin* to coincide with the World Cup about to be held in Argentina. For a month the eyes of the world would be on Argentina, and we needed to show what was really happening outside the stadiums, away from the cheering crowds.

Time was short. I invited several of the refugees to help prepare the first *Bulletin*. We met at my house, and the dining room table disappeared under piles of documents and papers written in Spanish, Portuguese, and English, as articles were written, translated, and revised on my small typewriter, an Olivetti 22. In the midst of this chaotic scene my two young children, Camilo and Ali, ate their lunch and dinner, surrounded by strangers talking Spanish.

Clamor Bulletin No. 1 had only four pages. The cover page showed the logo we had chosen – a candle with a flickering flame against a black background with prison bars, the design of political prisoner Manoel Cyrillo de Oliveira Neto, which in its turn was inspired by Amnesty International's logo.

The *Bulletin* carried eyewitness accounts of secret detention camps and disappearances, provided by refugees or taken from letters received from family members. The originals were mimeographed and posted to every organization we could think of in Brazil, Latin America, Europe, and North America.

By the end of 1978 our group had grown with the addition of Sister Michael Mary Nolan, an American nun, and Father Roberto Grandmaison, a French Canadian priest. Both had come to Brazil in the late 1960s as part of the influx of progressive missionaries from the 'First' to the 'Third' World, which followed the Second Vatican Council's decision to bring the Church up to date – Pope John XXIII's *aggiornamento*.

When Clamor began, we had little idea of what a huge undertaking it would be. As our existence became known, letters and reports began to pour in, revealing the depths of the human suffering and pain that was being inflicted on the populations of the Southern Cone countries by the cynical dictatorships that had overthrown elected governments across the region in the name of democracy and Christian values.

We were all volunteers with other commitments, jobs, professions, and families, but gradually Clamor took over more and more of our time. There was no way we could ignore the desperate pleas for help, for solidarity, that reached us. We listened with horror to stories of unbelievable cruelty, and with amazement and humility to accounts of unbelievable courage. We came to deeply admire the many men and women who refused to be silenced and risked their lives to denounce the dictators. We had to help them, whatever the risk.

CHAPTER 2
The refugees

When Eduardo tried to stop his wife being dragged away by the group of armed men who had broken down the door of their apartment in Buenos Aires, they threw him over the balcony into the courtyard below, while their two small sons watched in terror. He survived the fall and fled to Brazil with his children. He never heard from his wife again. She became one of the disappeared.

Isabel, a chubby middle-aged woman, was a union official in Buenos Aires. When she heard they were looking for her, she fled with only the clothes on her back, not daring to go home. She turned up on my doorstep one day, distraught and exhausted.

Elida, a young, extremely pale, thin student had spent three days hiding in a park in Buenos Aires, waiting for friends to arrange false papers for her to escape over the border.

Marcela, fearing arrest, fled without her children. She was desperate to bring them to Brazil, but she dared not go back to Argentina to fetch them. (Months later Sue Branford and Rosario Roman made a daring and risky trip to Argentina to rescue the children and bring them back to their mother in Brazil, armed only with a document concocted by lawyer Plauto Rocha and validated by a São Paulo notary.)

Alcira, a lawyer, and Luiz, a journalist, had been disappeared for four months, held and tortured in a clandestine camp. They arrived with their two small sons, who clung to their parents, fearful of losing them again.

Many of the children who arrived were deeply traumatized by what they had been through. In an article for the weekly alternative paper *Movimento*, I described the scene at a children's party organized by the refugees:

> Balloons, presents, a cake with candles, noise and music. It seems normal, but some of the children are too aggressive, they hit or scratch each other. In the kitchen a small girl screams hysterically. They are the children of Argentine exiles, deeply affected by the experiences they have been through. Before arriving in Brazil, most of them have spent months in hiding, moving from house to house. Sometimes with their parents, other times with relatives, or friends of their parents, leaving behind toys and clothes, fleeing inside their own country. The father of two girls, aged three and four, said: 'After their mother was kidnapped, we moved from house to house. In three or four months, we moved 23 times.

> Once there were 15 of us in one room, men, women and children.
> There were guns everywhere. We took turns, keeping watch from
> the window.'

The younger daughter of this left-wing militant had convulsions every time
she heard a police siren. This went on for months, even after they arrived
in Brazil.

A psychologist diagnosed the little girl in the kitchen as profoundly
disturbed. Her father, a student activist, was shot dead by the soldiers who
invaded their home. Her mother, Raquel, tells how it happened:

> It was in September 1977. My husband was looking after our
> six-month-old baby. I wasn't there, I had taken our daughter to
> visit my mother. After they killed my husband, they were there for
> three or four hours. They took the baby and left him in a hospital.
> From there he was sent to another hospital. My mother took a
> week to get him back. He had been well looked after, but the baby
> is backward for his age, and withdrawn.

Those were just some of the refugees who arrived in São Paulo from Argentina,
traumatized by what they had seen and suffered, desperate to find out what
had happened to missing family members.

Brazil became the principal destination for the refugees after the 1976 coup
in Argentina. At the time of the coup, Argentina harboured thousands of
exiles from Uruguay – in the three years between the 1973 coup in Uruguay
and the 1976 coup in Argentina, over 350,000 Uruguayans were believed to
have crossed the River Plate for political or economic reasons. They joined
the Chileans who fled after the 1973 coup, an estimated 15,000, and a large
number of Paraguayans, including all the leaders of the anti-Stroessner parties
and organizations.

Traditionally, foreign dissidents were left untroubled by internal coups –
but in the 1970s, under the US-inspired doctrine of national security and
the setting up of the cross-border collaboration known as Operation Condor,
things were different. In Argentina, nobody was safe from being disappeared.
Even those recognized by UNHCR and accepted for asylum in other countries
were not safe. UNHCR's offices in Buenos Aires were broken into and lists of
refugees were stolen soon after the 1976 coup.

Brazil had been the scene of the first national security coup in 1964,
but by 1974, all the armed guerrilla groups had been wiped out, and a very
cautious programme of *abertura* (opening up) began. It went in fits and starts,
but compared to the terror unleashed in Argentina, Brazil seemed a haven of
relative normality and safety.

The diaspora of Latin Americans in the 1970s was huge. The UN calculated
that in 1980 over a million people in the region were either refugees or
displaced. The greatest numbers came from Argentina, Uruguay, and Chile,
fleeing for both political and economic motives.

The exodus of this army of mostly young, qualified men and women was a brain drain that deprived the countries that drove them out not only of their talents, but also of their idealism. While solidarity became a dirty word, individualism, consumerism, and corruption thrived.

In Brazil the majority settled in Rio or São Paulo, but many Uruguayans preferred to stay closer to the border with their country, in Porto Alegre, while Paraguayans often remained in Foz do Iguaçu, just across the river from Paraguay.

Most of them arrived in Brazil by bus, crossing the border in Chuí, Uruguaiana, or Foz do Iguaçu, pretending to be tourists. To travel between the countries of the Southern Cone, an identity document was enough; passports were not needed. Those who had been members of armed organizations travelled with false documents. Almost all the Uruguayans came from Montevideo, but the Argentines came from a variety of cities besides Buenos Aires, such as Córdoba and Tucumán in the north and Bahia Blanca in the south.

The political refugees fell into two groups. The first group contacted UNHCR as soon as they arrived, anxious to acquire official refugee status. This gave them the right to receive a monthly subsidy while they waited for a third country to grant them asylum, a process that usually took several months. The second group avoided UNHCR because they wanted to stay in Brazil, even if it meant becoming illegal.

In May 1977, as the numbers of refugees grew, Brazil's military government reluctantly allowed the UN to open an office in Rio, where UNHCR interviewed refugees and then set about finding countries that would offer them permanent asylum. Brazil was merely a country of transit because the military did not want refugees, many of them from left-wing organizations, to settle there. European countries, led by Sweden, took most of them; the UK took some Chileans but no Argentines or Uruguayans.

The Archdiocese of Rio, under Cardinal Eugênio Sales, a conservative, decided to provide assistance for the growing numbers of refugees. Cândido da Ponte Neto, who was secretary to Cardinal Salles, remembers that Dom Eugênio 'picked up the red telephone on his desk and asked to speak to General Sylvio Frota, Commander of the First Army in Rio'. He said, 'Frota, if you hear that I am sheltering communists in the São Joaquim Palace, it is true. I am responsible and I don't want to be troubled.' Known as a radical anti-communist, Dom Eugênio was therefore trusted by the military, in contrast to his fellow cardinal in São Paulo, Dom Paulo, whose relations with the military were far from cordial.

Clamor's priority was the group of refugees who did not, or could not, claim UN status. An unofficial solidarity network had grown up among Brazilians who became aware of the plight of the refugees, and many took them into their own homes. A group of psychologists and doctors offered free treatment, while some school directors overlooked the lack of documents to give children school places.

The churches who worked in periphery areas played an important part. Sister Michael Mary Nolan remembers how the nuns of the Santa Cruz congregation called a meeting and decided they had to offer shelter to refugees; other congregations did the same. Parish priests like Father Roberto Grandmaison found places for families to stay. Creative solutions were found for the lack of documents. Baptisms were arranged to provide children with a baptismal certificate, which, in the absence of any other document, became their identity document.

In 1980, uneasy about the large number of refugees who had arrived in Brazil in the previous three years, and under pressure from the other governments of Operation Condor, especially Argentina, the Brazilian government decided to introduce a new, much tougher Foreigners' Law. It came into effect on 19 August 1980, just a few days before the official visit of the Argentine dictator, General Rafael Videla, causing panic and anxiety among the large Argentine community, who feared that there could be attempts to arrest and even abduct those wanted in their country of origin. Ten human rights organizations set up an emergency legal clinic to avoid such actions. In the end, no attempts were made.

CHAPTER 3
Coups and Operation Condor

When Clamor came into existence in 1978, every single country in the Southern Cone of South America was being run by right-wing generals who had seized power in civic–military coups.

Latin America was no stranger to coups. Ever since the different countries of the region had gained independence from Spain or Portugal in the nineteenth century, military coups had been the normal engine of political change in many countries, rather than elections. Bolivia was the record holder with 193 coups and rebellions since independence in 1825, but every other country in the region had undergone coups, rebellions, and revolts. Traditionally the groups who were overthrown sought asylum in neighbouring countries, beginning a life of political exile that could last months or even years.

But the Cold War, which had divided the world into opposing ideological camps after the Second World War, brought a different sort of coup. The US had no intention of allowing its 'backyard', Latin America, to follow the path of Cuba and fall into communist hands. Populist governments that promised an end to the region's huge social inequality and its extreme concentration of land and income also threatened America's commercial interests. US companies had to be saved from nationalization so that their profits would continue to flow home. The mass movements demanding social reforms, land reform, and educational reform were dangerous and had to be crushed.

Left-leaning governments, even when they had been democratically elected in legitimate elections, therefore had to be overthrown. The threat of communism, whether real or imaginary, provided a convenient excuse for closing the door on social reforms.

In South America, the series of Cold War coups began in Brazil on 31 March 1964. President João Goulart, far from being a communist, was a wealthy landowner, but he had nevertheless promised the reforms demanded by the unions, peasant leagues, and intellectuals, and was therefore dangerous. He was overthrown by an alliance between a sector of the armed forces, a vociferous right-wing press, the conservative wing of the Catholic Church, and the middle classes. The ousting of the democratically elected president was actively encouraged and financed by the US government, to avoid what they claimed was an imminent communist takeover of Brazil. A fleet of US warships was stationed off the Brazilian coast ready to intervene with troops if needed. To avoid the bloodshed of civil war, Goulart flew into exile in Uruguay.

In 1971 General Hugo Banzer overthrew the elected president of Bolivia, Juan José Torres, who went into exile in Argentina. Banzer remained in power until 1979, when he was ousted by a popular movement of the miners' unions, indigenous organizations, and women's movements, who staged hunger strikes.

In July 1973, the military seized power in Uruguay, under the pretext of fighting the left-wing National Liberation Movement (Movimiento de Liberación Nacional, MLN), known as the Tupamaros. In fact, they had already killed or imprisoned most of its leaders. They kept the civilian president, Juan María Bordaberry, in power as head of a puppet government until 1976.

Three months later, on 11 September 1973, the Chilean armed forces staged a coup which was actively supported and financed by the US. Elected president Salvador Allende, a socialist who had introduced agrarian and other reforms, committed suicide when Chilean Air Force planes bombed the presidential palace. General Augusto Pinochet became president and unleashed a wave of terror.

On 24 March 1976, the Argentine armed forces overthrew Isabelita Perón, the vice president and widow of elected president Juan Perón, who had died a year after returning from exile in 1974. The left-wing armed guerrilla groups, the People's Revolutionary Army (Ejército Revolucionario del Pueblo, ERP) and the Montoneros, had already been largely defeated. General Jorge Videla became head of a three-man military junta.

On 17 July 1980, the Bolivian armed forces staged a bloody coup to prevent elections which the left was expected to win, overthrowing the incumbent president Lydia Gueiler. Argentina provided arms and advisers. General Garcia Meza became president.

Paraguay had been run as a personal fiefdom by General Alfredo Stroessner since 1954, when he defeated a rival military faction. Stroessner adopted a strong anti-communist rhetoric, which ensured US support and funding.

What united all of these military dictators was their allegiance to the new Cold War doctrine of 'national security'. No longer did the threat come from invasion by foreign powers or hostile neighbours. Instead, the armed forces were retrained to face a new threat, the 'internal enemy'. Thousands of police and military officers from all over Latin America were sent to the US School of the Americas in Panama to learn their new role. French counter-insurgency techniques, including interrogation methods, developed in Algeria during the war of independence there, were also taught. The doctrine of national security became the bible of the military regimes that had taken power; under it, the security forces classified and targeted people based on their political ideas rather than any illegal acts they may have committed.

National security now meant defending the country against internal threats. The armed forces stopped being professional forces who were trained to defend their countries from an external enemy, as the Falklands War showed all too clearly in the case of Argentina. Instead, they became politicized forces, spying and gathering intelligence on their own populations and attacking civilian targets, whether armed or unarmed. The laws were ignored. Hundreds of thousands were imprisoned and tortured, and thousands were killed. A section of the population had become the enemy, which had to be not only defeated, but destroyed.

Under the doctrine of national security, the erstwhile democracies of the Southern Cone were plunged into a long night of repression: parliaments were closed, political parties abolished, strikes banned, and censorship imposed. Thousands fled; many others went into hiding or lived in fear of midnight raids and mass arrests.

The repression was not haphazard, but part of a plan to change the course of history in South America by eliminating every organization, party, or group, whether armed or not, that could be seen as communist, socialist, or just left-wing, and by extension every person who defended the democratic right to have different ideas from those in power. Solidarity became subversive. General Ibérico Saint-Jean, an Argentine general, defined the new state terrorism in brutal terms: 'First, we are going to kill all the subversives; then their collaborators; then their sympathisers; afterwards the indifferent, and finally, the timid.'

What began as an anti-communist crusade became a crusade against the principles and institutions of democracy and against progressive and liberal as well as revolutionary forces, and was used to justify the institutionalization of state terrorism. And although it had helped to install regimes that had adopted state terrorism as a way of government, rather than the democracy it advocated for the world, the US government backed the generals with money, equipment, and intelligence, turning a blind eye to their methods, corruption, and incompetence.

Soon, the Southern Cone regimes were not content with wiping out subversion within their own frontiers but decided they had to eliminate opposition wherever it raised its head – even in other countries. Operation Condor, a new concept of 'hemispheric defence defined by ideological frontiers',[1] was born.

Operation Condor was in effect an international state terrorist organization sanctioned by the governments of Chile, Argentina, Uruguay, Paraguay, Brazil, and the US, officially created in November 1975 at a secret meeting in Santiago, Chile. Ostensibly set up to exchange intelligence on subversives living in each other's countries, its activities included the employment of hit squads to kill dissidents. Salvador Allende's foreign minister, Orlando Letelier, killed by a bomb in Washington in 1976, was its most notorious target. The bomb was placed by Chileans with the help of the CIA. The long arm of Condor also reached into Brazil, hunting down Uruguayan and Argentine opponents.

When the members of Clamor began their ambitious task of documenting and denouncing the violations of human rights being committed by neighbouring regimes, they had little idea that they would also uncover an international terrorist organization.

Note

1.   McSherry, J. P. (2012) *Predatory States: Operation Condor and Covert War in Latin America*, Lanham, MD: Rowman & Littlefield.

CHAPTER 4

The 1978 World Cup in Argentina

Having got the go-ahead from Dom Paulo, the Clamor team rushed to get their first *Bulletin* out in time for the 1978 World Cup, knowing that the eyes of the world would be on Argentina. The introduction explained: 'Coming out on the eve of the World Cup, when the attention of the world is upon Argentina, this first number is dedicated exclusively to that country.'

The World Cup had become a controversial issue. In Europe, human rights groups, exiles, and some French intellectuals had launched a movement to boycott the tournament in protest at the Argentine junta's violations of human rights. Some European football associations threatened to withdraw from the competition, but the leaders of the French and Italian communist parties resisted the idea, fearing it would set a precedent for the 1980 Olympic Games in Moscow. The boycott failed, but the attempt drew attention to the situation.

There were concerns about the safety of the players and the fans, in a country where, allegedly, left-wing guerrillas were still active. In 1976 the president of the organizing committee for the World Cup, retired general Omar Carlos Actis, had been assassinated on his way to give a press conference about the preparations in Buenos Aires. The Montoneros were blamed, but later it emerged that he had been killed on the orders of junta member Admiral Emilio Massera, who wanted to place a naval man in the prestigious position. Rear Admiral Carlos A. Lacoste became president and also a member of the international football governing body FIFA.

For the Argentine government, the World Cup was a propaganda gift – a chance to clean up the junta's tarnished image and convince the world that the reports of atrocities were untrue. They spared no expense: new stadiums, airports, and roads were built, and the introduction of colour TV was rushed forward.

The junta, sitting on a pile of corpses, hired one of America's best-known advertising agencies, the New York-based firm Burson-Marsteller, at a cost of US$1 million, to help whitewash their image. As *Clamor Bulletin* No. 2 noted at the time:

> The company accepted the military junta government of General Jorge Videla as a client with the full knowledge of and advice from the U.S. State Department, and the remit of attracting industrial investment, marketing Argentine bonds, promoting Argentine products, mainly wine, and improving the image of the dicta-torship around the world. In doing so the company produced press

kits and direct mailings, arranged for journalists to visit Argentina,
and held lunches with business groups and financial seminars.

Staging the tournament cost Argentina an estimated $700 million, or four
times what West Germany spent in 1974, as Clamor noted in its *Bulletin* No. 2,
published after the World Cup. 'Criticised as excessive and inflationary, for
the Junta it had been a well calculated political investment to improve its
image abroad.'

No chances were taken. Not only was the press banned from publishing
stories about the human rights situation, but the sporting press was even
forbidden to criticize the Argentine football coach Cesar Luis Menotti.

In the stadiums, thousands of plain-clothes security officers mingled with
spectators, ready to deal with any suspect act. (At the 1974 World Cup in
Germany, Brazilian exiles held up large banners demanding an amnesty
for political prisoners, knowing they would be seen on Brazilian TV.)
Prohibitively expensive ticket prices prevented the largely impoverished
working class from attending the games. Instead the crowds were mostly
middle-class people, some of whom had never been to a soccer match before.
Security agents and their families, given free tickets, filled the seats behind
the presidential tribunal.

The junta scored another public relations triumph when former US
secretary of state Henry Kissinger, a keen football fan, came to watch the
final. In October 1976, during his last months in office before the Jimmy
Carter administration took over, Kissinger had expressed his support for the
coup at a secret meeting with the junta's foreign minister, Admiral César
Augusto Guzzetti. Appearing at the World Cup final at the side of General
Jorge Videla, he was making a public statement that the regime still had
supporters in the US.

These efforts were successful, and many foreigners came away impressed by
the smooth organization, the well-dressed crowds in the stadiums, the polite
policemen. The World Cup was a PR triumph.

Behind the scenes, the junta took other measures.

In Córdoba, hundreds of signs reading 'Military zone – Do not advance or
you will be shot' were removed. Some 200 political prisoners were reportedly
moved to an unknown destination, to be held as hostages against any attempt
to sabotage the games.

A telegram dated 21 June 1978 from the US embassy in Buenos Aires to
Secretary of State Cyrus Vance revealed more of the junta's efforts to mask
reality: 'Police and military forces in Argentina have been under strict orders
to avoid reactions or incidents which would give foreign visitors and press
fuel for criticizing the country's security practices.' So, during the World Cup
there had been fewer government arrests and an increase in the number of
prisoners being released and deported.

But less than a mile from the River Plate stadium where the final was played,
hooded and chained prisoners were being held at the clandestine detention
camp inside ESMA, the naval mechanics school. Very few of them would

survive. In the clandestine camp known as La Cacha, in La Plata, the guards had the radio on full blast and noisily celebrated each goal by Argentina. All over Argentina, while the World Cup was being played, thousands of prisoners were being held in secret detention camps.

The international press largely accepted the misleading vocabulary of the junta. This was a 'dirty war' where 'excesses' had been committed, and the women wearing white headscarves who walked in circles in front of the Casa Rosada every Thursday afternoon to denounce the disappearance of their children were 'locas' – 'mad women'.

Journalist Richard Gott wrote a story[1] entitled 'Will Generals and Guerrillas Defeat the World Cup?', in which he considered that the greatest danger to be faced in Argentina was kidnapping by left-wing guerrillas. But by 1978 the guerrillas had been decimated, and thanks to their reign of terror, the military were completely in charge.

Even so, outwitting the heavy security, the Montoneros held a secret press conference for selected foreign journalists. The organization's political secretary, journalist Norberto Habegger, gave them details of the murders, disappearances, and prison conditions. A month later Habegger disappeared at Rio de Janeiro International Airport, a victim of Operation Condor.

The human rights groups did their best to call attention to the real situation. In the two years since the 1976 coup, thousands had been detained and disappeared and hundreds more were imprisoned under the drastic powers of the National Process of Reorganization, without trial or sentence. On 17 May, the organizations placed a full-page ad in *La Prensa*, with a list of over 2,500 names of people who had disappeared.

Clamor received a copy of a letter sent, on the eve of the World Cup, by the so-called 'locas', the Mothers of Plaza de Mayo (Madres de Plaza de Mayo), to each member of the Argentine squad, appealing for help in finding their missing children. The letter began by congratulating the players on having been chosen to play for the team, and then said that the Madres supported the World Cup being held in Argentina, but feared that a distorted image of reality was being shown to the world:

> Thousands of young people like you have disappeared in similar conditions: armed civilians who sometimes say they are police break into homes and carry off their victims. ... Human rights organizations in Argentina have computed 2,536 cases, just of disappeared, not counting political prisoners, who number over 3,000 according to official lists.

> We ask for the list of disappeared to be made public, that political prisoners without accusation or trial be released and that the situation of repression and intimidation that is maintained through continual disappearances be ended.

The Madres wrote that the authorities refused to reply to their requests for information. They blamed the government's silence for the campaign being waged abroad against the World Cup. They continued: 'We feel obliged to inform you, a star figure in 1978 before the World, that the country has another, very sad face and we want to say that the glory of the matches should not blind the men who compete in them, much less when they represent Argentina.'

The World Cup ended with victory for the Argentine team, who reached the final after a controversial 6-0 victory over Peru; Argentina was later accused of match fixing. In the final, Argentina beat the Netherlands 3-1, but the Dutch team spoiled Videla's triumph by refusing to receive their runner-up medals from his hands, in protest at the human rights situation. Instead, they went to the Plaza de Mayo to take part in the Madres' weekly protest. The Swedish delegation did the same, in a show of solidarity.

Note

1. Gott, R. (1978) 'Will Generals and Guerrillas Defeat the World Cup?', *The Guardian*, 14 January.

CHAPTER 5
The disappeared

The sinister word 'disappeared' had begun to appear more and more in documents, letters and newspaper reports, and on the lips of the refugees themselves.

As Clamor became better known in Argentina, we began receiving letters from relatives describing how their sons and daughters, their wives and husbands, had been 'disappeared'. Some had been abducted in the street or at work. Most were seized from their homes in the middle of the night by groups of heavily armed men in plain clothes. They were beaten, hooded, and dragged away, often in front of their terrified partners or children, then thrown into the boots of Ford Falcons, a type of car that became synonymous with fear.

One man, poet Claudio Nicolas Grandi, seized at home in June 1976 while his baby daughter Yamila slept in her cot, had somehow managed to scrawl a message on the door before he was bundled off: 'Te Quiero Mucho, Yamila, Y a Tu Mama La amo' (I love you very much, Yamila, and I love your mother). But most had no chance to say farewell to their families before they disappeared forever.

Nearly all the letters Clamor received were handwritten, some laboriously, some eloquently. But they all conveyed the anguish and suffering of people struggling to understand the inexplicable disappearance of family or friends – where were they, why had they been taken, when would their families see them again?

A tsunami of pain and perplexity reached São Paulo via the letters, the interviews, and the testimonies of the refugees.

From La Plata, Efraim Ford wrote about his son, 20-year-old Alejandro Efraim Ford, kidnapped on 11 May 1977 with his equally young wife, 19-year-old Monica Edith de Olaso. 'Until he was seized, I had never been separated from him, therefore I know he wasn't involved in terrorism.'

A mother, Laura Azurmendi, whose daughter and son-in-law had disappeared, leaving behind two small children, wrote that 'the older child, aged 4, cries for her parents'. Another mother, whose son had disappeared, wrote that when he was seized his flat had been looted: 'They took everything including the front door.'

The father of Hernan Maria Ramirez, a mechanical engineer, described how on 2 June 1978, he went to his son's home to find out why he had not been to work. When he entered the house where Hernan lived with his wife, Elza Martinez, he found everything smashed and broken, papers scattered around. The TV, radio, camera, and the couple's more expensive clothes were missing, as well as their car. In the kitchen he found a salad ready to serve, next to broken glasses.

Many of the forcibly disappeared were people who held leadership positions in their professions. Beatriz Perozi, abducted from her place of work by an armed group on 8 August 1978, was the president of the Argentine Psychologists Association. Carlos Mariano Zamorano was vice president of the Argentine League of Human Rights and disappeared from within the prison at Rawson. Adan Pedrini, ex-president of the Chaco Province Legislature, was abducted from his home by a group of armed men on 14 July 1978.

Not all the disappeared were young. A refugee in Rio sent us a letter asking for help to find his 60-year-old mother, Elvira Garaycoche de Ortaegui, who had disappeared in Villa Bosch.

The families tried every measure they could think of to find out where their missing relatives had been taken by the unidentified men who had seized them. The obvious place to start was the courts, to present writs of habeas corpus. Between 1976 and 1980, thousands of writs were presented. Not one was accepted. Instead, the judges washed their hands, like so many Pontius Pilates, with the excuse that as there was no official record of an arrest, the people in question were not officially detained, and therefore there was nothing to be done.

The human rights organizations that already existed in Argentina were inundated with pleas from desperate people. Soon the families themselves formed new organizations – Families of the Detained-Disappeared, Mothers of Plaza de Mayo, Grandmothers of Plaza de Mayo. They prepared lists and published announcements asking 'Where Are They?', pleading for information on their missing sons, daughters, husbands, and grandchildren. They appealed to international organizations like Amnesty International, the WCC, and the Jewish Council, along with human rights groups in other countries – and, increasingly, Clamor.

After being rejected by the courts, many families also turned to the Catholic Church for help. The hierarchy had supported the coup, applauding its proclaimed Western, Christian values and the declared aim of wiping out communist subversion, and they had good relations with the junta – but they too washed their hands. Only a handful of bishops and priests dared to defy not only the junta, but their own superiors.

The families turned to the archbishop of São Paulo, Dom Paulo. In September 1978 the Mothers of Plaza de Mayo appealed to him to raise the question of the disappeared at the meeting of the Episcopal Council of Latin America (Consejo Episcopal Latinoamericano, CELAM), due to be held at Puebla, Mexico, in October that year. After the sudden death of João Paulo I, the council was delayed to January 1979.

The junta had successfully spread the idea, taken up by much of the international press, that Argentina was engaged in a 'dirty war' where left-wing terrorism had to be countered with a strong arm, even using irregular methods.

The disappeared were all terrorists, and many were probably in hiding, or had gone abroad, where they lived a life of luxury while their families grieved. The Mothers of Plaza de Mayo were 'locas' – mad women who were responsible for not bringing up their children properly.

So, who were the disappeared? Headlines from *Clamor Bulletin* No. 2, published in July 1978, provide some answers. 'Scientists and Academics Continue to Be Disappeared'. 'Soccer Referee Abducted'. 'Nursing Director and Professor Disappear'. 'Mother Seeks Her Steelworker Son'. 'Son Seeks Disappeared Parents'. 'Mother Seeks Catechist Daughter' … A grandmother wrote: 'My daughter, Silvina Monica Parodi de Orozci, was six months pregnant when she disappeared, now the child would be about 18 months old. That is why I appeal to you to help me find them, in order to discover what happened to the baby, because I am that child's grandmother. At least, let the child stay with me until their parents can be located and set free.'

Journalists were among those most targeted. *Bulletin* No. 2 reported that more than 40 had been abducted since the 1976 coup.

Two years after the coup, they were still disappearing. *Bulletin* No. 3, published in October 1978, reported the disappearance of Enrique Esteban, the *Clarín* correspondent in Neuquen, abducted on 23 July 1978. 'The week before he disappeared, Esteban interviewed the minister of the interior, General Hardinguey, and asked him about political prisoners. The minister reacted angrily, asking him to prove the existence of political prisoners, saying that if they existed, he would have them freed.'

Four days later, two more journalists, Luis Pablo Córdoba and his wife Alcira Ríos, were abducted by a group of armed men after leaving their home in Santa Fé. They both worked for the local daily, *El Litoral*.

The list of the disappeared in *Bulletin* No. 3 also includes a bank employee, a domestic servant, a lecturer, a dietician, a textile factory worker, a lawyer, a stonemason, a nursemaid, a teacher, and a nuclear physics student. In other words, anyone could be taken.

Bulletin No. 3 carried an article entitled 'The Anguish of the Families'. It read:

> Disappearances continue. Almost every day the press reports a new case. Amnesty International estimates that between June and August of 1978, seventy people disappeared. President Videla recently admitted there had been 'excesses of repression'. It is now clear, however, that these abductions are not 'excesses' but a regular weapon in a war of terror against the population. Otherwise, the desperate attempts by thousands of families to obtain news of their missing members would not be met by a wall of silence, cynicism, or threats.
>
> This war of terror has left thousands of families living in the daily anguish of not knowing whether a mother, father, wife, husband, son, or daughter is alive or dead. Hundreds of small children are

being brought up by grandparents, not knowing whether they are orphans or not.

In *Bulletin* No. 5, published in May 1979, Clamor reported on the many attempts by the families to obtain information about their missing members:

> On November 27, 1978, a petition signed by 1,221 relatives assisted by 12 lawyers was presented to the Supreme Court, asking the whereabouts of 1,542 disappeared men and women. In a historic ruling, the Supreme Court exhorted the government to 'take the necessary measures that will permit the judiciary to fulfil its commitment to safeguarding individual freedom as guaranteed under the national constitution'.

This to and fro between the powers did not, however, produce any concrete results. A month later, Clamor reported, a delegation from the Permanent Assembly for Human Rights (Asamblea Permanente por los Derechos Humanos, APDH) had handed in a petition, signed by 37,000 people, to the presidential palace in Buenos Aires. 'In it they appealed for the disappeared and political detainees and asked for a gesture of justice and humanity from President Videla.'

In January 1979, a further 142 documents with 4,550 signatures were sent to President Videla by the APDH. The organization also sent Videla a letter asking about recent cases of unidentified corpses found in different places, like the 17 bodies found on the Atlantic coast near Santa Teresita.

Bulletin No. 5 also contained a section entitled 'Where Are They?' On the list was the name of Elba Lucia Gándara Castromán, abducted on 18 February 1977 from her home in Florencio Varela. She lived there with her husband, their three children aged 13, 8, and 4, and their baby of three weeks. The *Bulletin* reported on what happened to Elba and her family at 4 o'clock that morning:

> Breaking down the door with shouts and blows, a group of about 12 people occupied the house. They began hitting the couple (Elba and her husband Juan Enrique Velasquez Rossano) with their weapons in front of the children ... with the children terrified, they are beaten and their heads submerged in cans of water ... they take the baby by its feet, upside down and hit it ... After six hours in these conditions, they take the parents away, tied up, in the boots of their cars. ... After being kept in places of torture where he saw his wife three times the husband is freed with the 'recommendation' to leave the country, otherwise next time they will kill him.

> The children and their father now live in exile in Europe, but all attempts to find their mother in the two years since she was abducted have failed.

As the clamour for information about the disappeared grew along with their numbers, the Argentine junta tried to mislead public opinion by publishing lists of 'reappeared'. One such list, published in August 1978, contained 201 names, without any information about where they were being held, or why. After examining the list, human rights organizations discovered that none of the 201 names appeared on their lists of disappeared. They concluded that the 'reappeared' list was a red herring designed to appease the growing pressure from international organizations and the government of Jimmy Carter, elected US president in November 1976.

Ten months after Carter took office, he sent Secretary of State Cyrus Vance on a visit to Argentina. Vance carried with him a list of 7,500 names of disappeared people, for whom he demanded explanations. Earlier in the year the US Congress, under intense pressure from the leaders of Catholic and Protestant churches and Jewish organizations, had passed a bill to end all military aid to Argentina, because of human rights abuses. Together with Uruguay and Ethiopia, Argentina had become one of the three countries targeted for action because of the level of violations.

Vance said that the American Embassy in Buenos Aires would ask the Argentine government for case-by-case reports on all 7,500 cases. After Vance, the US undersecretary of state for human rights, Patricia Derian, made several visits to Argentina, meeting with human rights organizations. Not even the Americans obtained any answers.

As they grappled with the flood of heart-rending letters from families, the members of Clamor also asked themselves, why? Why was the junta 'disappearing' so many? Where were they? Were they still alive? Disappearances were not unknown in Brazil; the Brazilian Amnesty Committee had a list of at least 150 people who had not been heard of since their arrest. But in Argentina the numbers of forced disappearances were in the thousands.

The families eventually concluded that the disappearances were not sporadic, or the work of rogue elements in the so-called 'dirty war', but rather a 'plan of the Argentine military to exterminate a generation of activists, thinking that, with their death, the questioning of a system in crisis would disappear'.[1]

At the UN Commission on Human Rights meeting in Geneva in early 1980, the WCC made a statement expressing the belief that forced disappearance was being used to avoid leaving evidence of human rights abuses and so avoid condemnation – or as a fictional detective might say: 'No body, no crime.' The WCC stated:

> The unexplained disappearance of people, carried out by security forces of a given government, can be said to be, in a real way, the subtle accommodation of those governments to international – and national – expressions of concern for human rights. Whereas most other means of repression affect victims who constitute evidence of human rights violations, disappearance does not constitute evidence. Clearly, in the words of a church official, disappearance is tidier than torture.

We have already heard here that offending governments deny knowledge or blame for the institutional practice of disappearance, ascribing such practices to political parties, marginal movements or delinquent groups.

The practice of arbitrary abduction and subsequent disappearance is most often used against real or imagined political opponents of a particular regime, but it is also [used] against those opposed to repression as such and who act out of non-political, humanitarian, or religious motivation. ... Disappearances represent, in the final analysis, the ultimate negation of the individual human identity.

For the families, the disappearance of a loved one was the cruellest possible torture – not knowing what had happened to them or if they were still alive, not knowing what to tell their children, not knowing whether to hope or despair. Some parents committed suicide or entered a state of depression, unable to cope with the anguish. But many reacted with courage and determination to find the truth, to demand justice.

But what had happened to the disappeared?

Clues had begun to appear. Towards the end of 1979, Clamor received an anonymous letter, handwritten, about bodies with their hands and feet tied being washed up in the coastal waters near Buenos Aires: 'From 1976 up until the present date, on the coast of the municipality of De La Costa, in the zones of Las Toninas and Mar del Tuyú, 45 bodies were found. All were bound hand and feet, and many had bullet wounds.' These bodies always appeared in the spring, in October and November. The latest, two women and five men, had appeared in the early hours of the date of the letter, 10 October 1979. All were found by fishermen. They were handed over to the National Maritime Authority and placed in white plastic body bags. The naval authority said they had been brought by the current from the Uruguayan side of the river, but the fishermen say that this current only exists in summer and autumn. The bodies were buried in collective graves. The author of the letter had drawn a map on the back of it to show exactly where they were buried.

Note

1. Familiares de Desaparecidos-Detenidos por Razones Politicas. (1984) *Testimonios sobre la Represion y la Tortura* 6.

CHAPTER 6
The secret camps

The refugees had told us about the existence of secret or clandestine detention centres in Argentina. What they told us was so gruesome and terrible that at first it was hard to believe that such atrocities could be happening on the other side of the border.

The refugees called them concentration camps. Amnesty International called them secret detention camps, while others called them clandestine detention centres. Whatever their name, these were the places where the disappeared were taken. People were detained by members of the security forces, usually in plain clothes but backed up by police or army vehicles; then they just vanished. Officially, they no longer existed – the courts said they knew nothing about their detention, the judges rejected the thousands of writs of habeas corpus presented by their families. They had disappeared.

In reality the armed forces knew exactly who had been arrested and where they were held, but they deliberately denied this information to the families and to the human rights organizations. The aim was to create a climate of terror in the Argentine population and to hide the evidence that they were detaining, torturing, and killing so many people.

In *Clamor Bulletin* No. 1 of June 1978, we reported what we knew about the clandestine detention centres, based on the information supplied by refugees and exiles. The centres were believed to number up to 60, and they were located all over the country. The *Bulletin* noted:

> The main ones are located inside military bases. Some of the best known are the Campo de Mayo and Regimento de Palermo, in Buenos Aires; the Campo de la Rivera and Campo de La Perla, in Cordoba; Campo de Arana, in La Plata; the Arsenal Militar Miguel de Azcuenago, on Ruta 9, near Tucuman (all Army bases); and the Escuela Mecanica de la Armada, the Navy base in Buenos Aires.

> Other camps are located in disused warehouses and plantations, like the Ingenio Baviera in Famailla, near Tucuman, a disused sugar mill. Some ranches are reported to have been taken over. Smaller houses are used as clandestine torture centres and temporary prisons.

> Lastly, in ordinary prisons like the Carcel Penitenciário in San Martín, Cordoba, people are held in separate blocks or under false

names, so even the prison director may not know who his inmates really are.

Clamor's second *Bulletin*, published the following month, carried an editorial on the clandestine detention camps in Argentina and Uruguay, comparing their horrors to the concentration camps of the Second World War:

> As a result of the recent discovery and arrest in Brazil of a Nazi war criminal [Gustav Wagner], accused of the mass killing of Jews, thousands of words have been written about the horrors of the concentration camps of the Second World War. Once again, people ask themselves how such things could happen in civilized countries. And some still prefer to believe that they did not happen.
>
> Now there is concrete evidence that equally horrible and unbelievable things are happening in countries much nearer to us. Argentina and Uruguay, two of the most developed countries in Latin America, are accused of acts of savagery and cruelty which rival those of the Nazis.
>
> The obsessive persecution of the 'subversives', which began with the armed groups, has ended up including all the opposition, critics, independent thinkers, and even different religions.
>
> As in the Soviet Union, defence of human rights has become treachery.
>
> But what is happening in Uruguay and Argentina is not happening in another continent or forty years ago, it is happening here and now.

The *Bulletin* also included a long report from a prisoner who had been held in a clandestine camp in Uruguay, known El Infierno, between 1975 and 1976. He described how prisoners, both men and women, were given a number and tied to chairs where they remained day and night, blindfolded and unable to move. Loud music blared non-stop from speakers. They were given little food or water and were only released for torture sessions, which included being hung up by the wrists for hours at a time, being forced to stand in the same position for hours or even days, and having their heads submerged in buckets of water, urine, and excrement. Electric shocks were also applied. A doctor was present to monitor the prisoners' state – not to stop the torture, but to say whether it could continue without killing the prisoner. Nevertheless, some people died.

A pregnant prisoner, tortured to find out where her husband was, had a miscarriage. One night dogs were brought in to where three prisoners, two men and a woman, were hung up. When one of the men was cut down, the dogs savaged and killed him.

When he was eventually released, the former El Infierno prisoner said he was given a paper to sign which read 'I declare that while I was here, I was not tortured and I was properly fed.'

Most of the secret camps were in Argentina. The military had coined a special term for those they kidnapped; they were the *chupados* (the sucked-up). They were taken to *chupaderos*, the secret detention centres.

In the early months of Clamor's existence, many refugees wrote down what they knew about the camps or gave taped interviews. Because of the fear that still enveloped them, they often did not give their proper names.

One who did was Rafael Videla, who with his wife and six children was given asylum in Sweden in 1978. Nicknamed Grillo (Cricket) because of his small stature and cheerful face, it was hard to imagine the appalling ordeal he and his family had been through.

Grillo had been a local government employee in Bahia Blanca, a port city in the south of Argentina. A fervent Peronista, he was detained on the eve of the 1976 coup, together with his wife, who was eight and a half months pregnant, after the entire block where they lived had been attacked with mortars and several houses had been destroyed. When they were arrested, their five children were left behind in the house. Grillo recalled:

> We were taken to the Fifth Army Corps Regimental barracks and held in a shed next to the building with pigs and the horses of the Cavalry. I knew by the smell. We were hooded, handcuffed, and chained to the walls, lying on beds without mattresses. There were about 30 men in the shed and we were given numbers, but we could identify each other by our voices. Nestor Farias had been badly hurt, but he was a very strong man; he shouted out his name. He shouted 'Viva la patria! They are going to kill me but they can never kill a patriot', and 'If you survive, raise my flag.'

> Farias and another man called Pelado Repeto were killed. Then the military did what they called 'television', putting Nestor's head inside Pelado Repeto's stomach and making all of us look at it.

> Their families didn't know how they had died – after they disappeared, newspapers in Bahia Blanca and the national paper *La Nación* published the official version, which was that they were killed in a shootout between security forces and four terrorists.

Grillo was tortured for 45 days with electric shocks all over his body – his genitals, anus, mouth, eyes – sometimes while he was suspended 20 or 30 centimetres above the ground. A weight was hung from his testicles. They urinated on him to wet his body, which made the shocks worse. His head was dipped in buckets of excrement and water. But he said the worst torture was hearing his wife crying: 'I suffered more than anything, more than the torture, hearing my wife crying for her children, a model mother. I don't know how it didn't make me go mad. I wanted to die; really, I didn't care about anything any more.'

He continued:

> For five days I was left in a dark dungeon one metre square, without food, hands tied to the wall, so weak that I could not raise my arms or walk or even drag myself around or talk. I concentrated on breathing. I could only breathe very slowly; I had to concentrate on making my body breathe. I lived because God gave me the force to live. I wanted to live, and yet I didn't want to. I don't know how the human body can resist so much.

The couple's baby was born by Caesarean section, but the man who brought the baby to his mother deliberately squeezed its head. Later the child was slow to walk and talk. After three months, Grillo's wife was released, but was told that if she talked, they would kill her children.

'After 45 days I was transferred to a boat, where conditions were better; it was only psychological torture', Grillo said. 'After six months I was set free. But I was re-arrested again several times to be questioned about my *companeros*. Sometimes I would arrive home to find men who I knew were torturers playing with my children. They would tell me that they would come for me on Friday, and to be there, otherwise they would take one of the children.'

Grillo was left with severe health problems as a result of the torture: he lost 50 per cent of his sight, could no longer read, and lost the hearing in his left ear. He became impotent. The child born in the camp suffered from impaired development.

Another refugee who told me personally about his experience in a camp was a 38-year-old mechanic from Tucumán, nicknamed Negro because he was dark-complexioned, like many Argentines from the north.

Negro and his wife Maria Angela were kidnapped in January 1976, three months before the coup. Negro had been confused with another man who was wanted for involvement in an armed attack; at the time, the left-wing guerrilla group, the ERP, was very strong in Tucumán. Negro and his wife were taken to a secret detention camp in a former sugar mill called Ingenio Baviera, in Famailla, and also held for periods at the Military Arsenal Miguel de Azcuénaga on Highway 6 and at the Central Police Department.

Negro said he was kept blindfolded all the time, with his hands tied behind his back, wearing the same clothes. Maria Angela said her dress rotted under her arms, but the only shower they got was when the guards could not bear the stink any more and hosed them down. Some people's clothes had rotted away completely, and they were left naked. They had to eat with their hands from unwashed tins or plates. The food was usually polenta, which had often gone bad. Sometimes insects had fallen into the food, but the prisoners could not see them because of the blindfolds. The prisoners were kept in large sheds subdivided into stalls; there were no beds so they had to sleep on the ground, and there were no toilets, just buckets.

Three-metre-high wire fences had been erected around the camp, which was guarded by members of the national gendarmerie. The guards came from other provinces and changed every three months. They wore plain clothes inside the camp.

Negro was beaten with iron bars and given electric shocks all over his body until he lost sensitivity, then to his mouth and nose. He was hung from a tree in blazing sunshine and buried up to his waist in the ground.

He saw a young prisoner buried up to his neck, naked, for two days after being beaten. This prisoner became very weak, and his wounds got infected; a military doctor gave him some aspirin, but he died. His body was left for a whole day until the stench became too much, then they cut off his head and took his body away.

Many prisoners became ill with infections. Doctors only gave them aspirin and accused them of complaining over nothing. After torture sessions they were given showers. Some had skin falling off their bodies when they washed.

The prisoners were forbidden to speak to each other. Loud music was played.

Negro showed me the marks of torture on his back and chest. He was released after two months with Maria Angela, and they were left near their home. He thinks the security forces realized that they had got the wrong man, but there was also pressure from his family connections.

The sugar mill camp was still being used a year later. Negro had heard of another survivor, a 58-year-old woman who was detained and taken there in January 1977, together with her husband and son. The security forces were looking for her nephew.

She said that when her blindfold got loose, she saw six or seven heads sticking out of the ground. At first she thought they were dead, but then she realized they were alive. Later she learned they were prisoners considered to be dangerous, or who had dared to complain about the conditions. One survived the torture and was carried back to the shed, with part of his left shoulder rotting away and his face unrecognizable after being exposed to the weather for several days running. He was 19 years old. In April 1977 he was known to be still alive.

The woman said that at night, the guards took prisoners away. They heard the noise of machine guns and believed these prisoners were being executed. When eventually she and her husband were released, he had a heart attack and she needed psychiatric treatment. Their son was not freed and remains disappeared.

Most of the disappeared were young people, but when the security forces did not find the person they were looking for, very often they took members of the family instead. One refugee from Buenos Aires told Clamor what had happened to his family:

> They went to my parents' home at 5 o'clock in the morning, army and police together. They made everyone lie on the floor. They were looking for me but instead they took my father, mother,

and 18-year-old sister. They stole lots of things – a TV set, two cars, everything they could carry away.

[My parents] don't know exactly where they were kept. They were hooded with hoods made from their own sheets, they had to sleep on the ground with their hands and feet chained, and they could only go to the toilet once a day; otherwise there was only a bucket. They had one sandwich a day to eat and a small Coca-Cola bottle of water. They reckon there were about 50 prisoners there, all hooded, day and night. They think they were held in an army barracks because they heard marching, and they managed to see the boots and trousers of the guards.

There was a climate of terror, with loud music, the screams of people being tortured, the blows of the guards. They were forbidden to speak to each other and there was a permanent climate of humiliation; all their values were turned upside down. All that mattered was to survive. The moment of going to the toilet or getting the water ration became all-important. [My parents] were interrogated and beaten, and my sister was tortured with electric shocks in front of them.

His parents were released after 25 days, but his sister was held for another 30 days and only released after pressure from the family's influential connections. They suffered the after-effects for a long time: 'After being blindfolded for so long they had bad conjunctivitis. My mother would start screaming if she heard a police siren or someone spoke to her in the street.'

While most of the survivors said they had been held in sheds or buildings, a student who was kidnapped in December 1976 reported being held in a corral in the open air. He was taken to the army barracks at Campo de Mayo in Buenos Aires. He told his story to one of the refugees who came to São Paulo, who related it to Clamor: 'After being tortured for three days he was taken to a sort of corral not much bigger than a room with about 30 people in it, men and women. They had to eat with their hands and relieve themselves there. About once a month they turned a hose on them and washed them down.'

The stories we heard from the refugees in 1977 and 1978 were corroborated by other survivors who gave their testimonies to international organizations in Paris and Madrid.

In 1979, Amnesty International published a report entitled *Testimony on Secret Detention Camps in Argentina*. In November 1980, the organization added the testimony of three young refugees who had fled to Brazil and, via UNHCR, been given asylum in Holland. One of them, 22-year-old Pablo Alejandro Jurkiewicz, had been kidnapped from his grandmother's house and taken to the camp known as El Banco. His 72-year-old grandmother was also detained.

'On arrival I was stripped and given a number, 183. The first thing they did was to take me to my grandmother. ... [I]n tears she said to me: "tell them to stop hitting me" and "they want to take out my pacemaker." My grandmother was given the number 182. The second time I saw her she was lying in a cell. ... [T]he walls and the floor of the cell were soaking wet.'

The security forces were looking for Pablo's mother, Maria del Carmen Judith Artero, a union leader, who later disappeared. When Pablo was released and returned to his grandmother's house, she told him that all her personal possessions, mementos, and furniture had been looted.

Graciela Geuna was one of the few survivors of the secret detention camp called La Perla, near Córdoba. She gave her testimony to the Argentine Human Rights Commission (Comisión Argentina de Derechos Humanos, CADHU) in Madrid in 1980.

Both the La Perla and La Ribera camps were located inside the military area of the Third Army, which was commanded by General Benjamin Menendez. It is believed that between 1,500 and 2,000 prisoners passed through these camps, and most of them were killed. Groups of prisoners would be called by their numbers and taken in lorries to a field near the camp. They were blindfolded, gagged, and handcuffed. Pits had already been dug. They were forced to kneel down in front of the pits and shot. The bodies were covered with tar and burned. Menendez took part personally in some of the executions, as did the son of President Videla, Lieutenant Jorge Rafael Videla, and all the other officers in Third Army. It was a blood pact, involving them all in the murder of political prisoners, so they would not talk about it.

The prisoners were executed without trial, without the right to defend themselves, at the whim of those who ran the camps. The survivor who gave her testimony to CADHU in Madrid described a woman who was arrested by mistake; she knew nothing about armed or resistance groups, and she had nothing to do with any form of opposition. But after being held in La Perla for a while, they decided she could not be freed because she had seen too much. She had to be executed.

In La Perla, about 40 to 70 prisoners, men and women, were held in a shed, about 40 metres by 15 metres, lying on thin pallets of straw, blindfolded, forbidden to talk to each other. In the winter it was very cold, and they didn't have warm clothing.

In her testimony, Graciela recalled: 'Between July and August 1976 about 60 secondary school students, aged 16 to 18, some of them still beardless, were brought there. The other prisoners thought they would be released, as their only crime was student politics. But one of the guards said, "We must kill them when they are young chicks because it is best not to let those who have social concerns grow up."'

Everyone was tortured, some until they died. On Christmas Eve, one young woman was tortured for hours with electric shocks to make her reveal her husband's whereabouts, but she refused to say anything, even her own name.

'The torturers became impatient because they wanted to eat their Christmas dinner. Finally, they left her, mutilated and covered in wounds, naked and alone, to bleed to death, tied to the metal bed. The next day a prisoner sent to clean the room found her body covered in flies.'

Graciela's testimony was corroborated by one of the refugees in São Paulo, who said he had heard of an Air Force chaplain in Córdoba who was called to give extreme unction to Catholics who were about to be shot. Although a conservative, the chaplain was so shocked by what he saw that he told many people. He said there was a large group of prisoners – he thought several hundred, but this might be an exaggeration – lined up in a field. After he had given the last rites to the Catholics they were shot, then earth-moving machines buried them in mass graves.

Outside the clandestine detention camps, life went on as normal. Like Germans living near concentration camps in the Second World War, most Argentines had no idea what was going on in their own country, sometimes quite near them. In 1978, while the disappeared were living and dying in the secret detention camps, the football stadiums were crowded with delirious crowds cheering the Argentine team's triumphant progress to victory in the World Cup. Among the illustrious guests was Henry Kissinger, the former US secretary of state who had given the junta the go-ahead for the elimination of 'terrorists'. Did he know about the camps?

Alfredo Eduardo Peña, another refugee who survived after being held in a secret camp because he was transferred into the legal system, told Clamor that he could hear the traffic on the highway nearby and the noise of trains passing. A factory worker, he was seized as he left work on 7 August 1978 and taken to a clandestine camp next to the highway Autopista General Ricchieri, near Puente 12, at the General Guemes Provincial Police School.

'We could not lie down because of the chains, and we were confined in dog kennels with three prisoners piled up in each compartment', he recalled. He said prisoners were also shut into cement bunkers with closed lids, completely isolated and very cold.

Inside the camps, once the prisoners had been tortured and information had been extracted from them, or they had resisted the torture and given nothing away, or they had been found to have no information to give but were still not going to be released, the question was what to do with them.

The solutions varied. One of the refugees told me that a friend who had served as a conscript in the army had reluctantly revealed to him what he had seen at the army HQ at Campo de Mayo in Buenos Aires:

> It was June, the coldest time of the year. A group of soldiers came back with two men in a lorry. They were left in the lorry for a week, tied hand and foot, hooded, wearing just shirts and trousers in a temperature of zero degrees, with nothing to eat. Some soldiers smuggled *mate* tea to them. After a week one of them died: they took him to the ditch where they burn bodies. It's near the firing range. There they'd pour in a tank of aviation fuel and burn the

people they'd shot or who had died under torture. The stench of burning flesh was so strong we all felt sick. I don't know what happened to the other man. I don't know how many bodies were burnt but it happened all the time.

The term used by the authorities for their planned killings was *traslado*, or transfer. Prisoners were told they were being transferred to another place of detention, but in reality, they were being taken to their deaths. Some were buried in unmarked graves in fields or cemeteries, but many hundreds were thrown drugged but alive into the South Atlantic from aeroplanes – the so-called 'death flights', later confirmed by naval officer Adolfo Scilingo.

According to testimony given to CADHU in 1979:

At ESMA [Escuela Superior de Mecánica de la Armada, the Higher School of Mechanics of the Navy], the *traslados* always took place on Wednesdays, very rarely on Thursdays. At first they told us that the prisoners were being taken to other places or to the work camps which they said they had near the Rawson prison. It took us a long time to convince ourselves that in reality the '*traslado*' led to death.

On the day of the *traslado* the climate was tense. We prisoners did not know if this would be our day or not. The guards were much more strict than usual. We could not go to the lavatory. Each one had to remain rigorously in their place, hooded and handcuffed, without looking to see what was happening. There was no talking or calling the guards.

At about 5 o'clock they began to call the prisoners by their numbers. They put them in single file, holding onto each other's shoulder, as they were hooded and handcuffed. We heard the sound of the chains as they walked to the door, which opened and shut immediately.

They were taken to the infirmary, where the male nurse gave them an injection to put them to sleep, without killing them. Still alive, they were taken out by the side door and put into a lorry. Half asleep they were taken to the airport [Aeroparque Jorge Newberry] and put aboard a plane which flew south, over the ocean, into which they were thrown alive.

We never heard again from the thousands of prisoners who were taken on these collective *traslados*. Often we found the clothes they were wearing on the day of the *traslado* in the storeroom where they put the clothes used by the prisoners.

… [I]n the hours following a *traslado* our anxiety got worse. On the one hand we had another week of life, on the other hand we were discovering which companion they had taken, from the mattresses which were now empty. And then we wept for them in a mixture of grief, impotence, and anger.

From what we could gather, ESMA was designated as the place where the detained were brought together, that is to say the place where prisoners were concentrated for their later *traslado*.

Some 5,000 prisoners are said to have passed through the ESMA secret detention camp, and up to 2,000 through La Perla. Hundreds of others died in scores of other camps up and down the country. Almost all of them were young people, some only teenagers. They were executed without a chance to say goodbye to their families, who were deprived of the right even to know where their bodies were. Of the 30,000 people that the human rights organizations estimate to have been forcibly disappeared in Argentina, the remains of most of them have never been found.

The groups of armed men who raided homes to kidnap men and women also helped themselves to whatever they liked from those homes. At ESMA, a survivor reported seeing a room full of *botín de guerra* (war booty) in 1977: 'Inside it smelt of death. There were two big piles of clothes, of all sorts, four metres wide by three metres high. These were the dresses, trousers, shirts of thousands of disappeared. The rest of the "loot" was perfectly organized and classified: fridges, stoves, heaters, furniture, etc.' All these objects had been stolen from the homes of the disappeared. According to the 1979 testimony given to CADHU:

There were so many looted homes that at the end of 1978 they set up a real estate office to sell the properties of the kidnapped. For this they forged all the necessary documents. Involved in this business, among others, were naval captain Jorge E. Acosta, Lieutenant Savio, Captain Paso and a civilian called 'Vaca' who was said to be a lawyer or a judge, or maybe the son of a judge.

CHAPTER 7

Kidnapped in Porto Alegre: Condor in Brazil

One Friday afternoon in November 1978, I arrived at the Curia to go to Clamor's office, now located in the basement of the large mansion. As I approached the room, a young woman with shoulder-length fair hair stopped me. I had never seen her before. She seemed nervous, worried. She said, 'We need your help.'

She told me her name was Maria, and she was a Uruguayan exile. She said she was very worried about a comrade called Lilián Celiberti, who lived in Porto Alegre, the capital of Brazil's southernmost state, Rio Grande do Sul. The mother of two small children, Lilián shared a flat with another Uruguayan exile, medical student Universindo Díaz.

Lilián was in Brazil legally. She had moved here following four years in Italy after being expelled from Uruguay in 1974 because of her activities in the teachers' union, for which she had been imprisoned. The last time Lilián called her comrades in Paris, she had sounded strange, saying things that did not make sense. Maria was afraid that something had happened to Lilián.

She asked if Clamor could find someone in Porto Alegre to go to Lilián's flat and check out the situation. I remembered a lawyer called Omar Ferri, a fervent supporter of exiled political leader Leonel Brizola, who had impressed me as an impassioned, fearless person.

As soon as could, I called him and outlined the problem. Probably there was nothing to it, just a bit of overanxiety on the part of the Uruguayans, but could he possibly go there and check?

I gave him Lilián's address. He said he could go there after the court session that afternoon, when he was defending a man being tried for armed robbery. In the first of many coincidences, this fact was to play a part in the drama that was about to unfold.

The next day, Ferri called. He had been to the flat at about 9 o'clock the night before, but there had been no answer when he had rung the bell and knocked on the door. On the way out he had found the janitor and asked about the inhabitants of No. 110. The man had said, 'I think they've gone away for the weekend. Just this morning I saw the children playing in the courtyard.' Reassured, Ferri rang me.

I told Maria that everything seemed to be alright, but she was not satisfied. 'Please ask Dr Ferri to go back again; we know something is wrong.' I phoned Ferri again, and he agreed to go back to the flat. There was still no reply, so he went again on Sunday.

On Monday morning, on his way to court for the continuation of the trial, Ferri decided to go to the flat one last time. He left a note with his name and telephone numbers under the door.

Later that day Ferri emerged from the courtroom to find a group of journalists waiting for him. To his amazement, one of them was clutching the note he had left under the door of the apartment. They told him that Luiz Claudio Cunha, head of *Veja* magazine's office in Porto Alegre, had also received a phone call from São Paulo on Friday, this time from someone with a strong Spanish accent, saying that some Uruguayan exiles who were living in Porto Alegre had disappeared, and asking him to go to the flat.

Intrigued, Cunha, taking with him photographer João Batista Scalco, had gone to Rua Botafogo. This was several hours before Ferri made his visit. Later, in a statement to the Federal Police Department, he described what had happened when he rang the bell of No. 110.

The door had been opened by a young woman, about 30 years old, with straight black hair. She had looked terrified, but confirmed her name was Lilián. As Cunha had tried to explain why he was there, the door had been thrown wide open and a gun had been pointed at him. He and Scalco had been taken into the flat, placed with their hands against the wall, and thoroughly searched. There had been five men inside the flat. Cunha and Scalco had been questioned about the reason for their visit, and their identity documents had been taken from them.

The man who had appeared to be the head of the group had then left the flat for five minutes. When he'd come back, his tone had changed. Now he had been friendly. Now everything had been all right and they had been allowed to lower their arms. But he had told Cunha that he must say nothing about what he had seen. He had said the people in the flat were foreigners who were living illegally in Brazil, and that they were waiting for another person to arrive. If Cunha received another call from São Paulo, he must say nothing about the presence of the group in the flat.

Cunha said that the five men in the flat were all Brazilians and had local accents. He said they did not seem like bandits, but more like policemen from the way they behaved and the way they spoke.

The next day, the newspapers published the story: 'Uruguayan exiles kidnapped by armed men'. It was a bombshell.

In the book he later wrote about those events, Ferri described his feelings at that moment: 'I asked myself: Who is Lilián? Who is Universindo? What were they doing in Porto Alegre? What has really happened to them?' He could have washed his hands of the affair and concentrated on his legal career, but his curiosity got the better of him. He decided that he must find out what was going on.

So he went back to the flat. This time, the door was ajar. Inside, a woman was cleaning. Ferri introduced himself and asked if she knew where the inhabitants of the flat were. She told him they had gone away without saying where to, but had left the keys and a note for her husband, the owner of the flat. Ferri noticed that everything was turned upside down, and there were cigarette ends and spent matches. The carpet was covered with marks left by dirty shoes.

The keys had been left the day before, Monday. So where had Lilián, Universindo, and the children been between Friday night and Monday?

In São Paulo, the Uruguayans had been busy. Maria had called Lilián's sister, Mirtha Celiberti, who lived in Italy, and told her that Lilián had disappeared. Mirtha had rung her mother, Lilia, who lived in Montevideo. Lilia did not hesitate for a moment – the next day, she caught the first bus to Porto Alegre. It was a 14-hour, 800-kilometre journey. When the bus stopped at the frontier town of Chuí, another passenger bought a Brazilian newspaper, and Lilia caught sight of the headline 'Kidnapping Accusation Investigated'.

She borrowed the paper, *Zero Hora*, and read the story. There was a photograph of the note that Lilián had left for her landlord, explaining that she had gone away for a few days. Lilia did not recognize the handwriting as her daughter's.

When she arrived at the bus station in Porto Alegre, Lilia took a taxi and showed the paper to the driver. She asked him to take her to *Zero Hora's* offices. There, when she told reporter Milton Galdino that she was Lilián's mother, he immediately phoned Ferri. Ferri rushed over to the newspaper. He told Lilia everything he knew. Lilia told Ferri she was sure that the signature on the note left for the landlord was not Lilián's. There and then Lilia gave Ferri power of attorney to act for her.

The news of Lilia's arrival spread like wildfire, and a press conference was called for 4 p.m. The journalists smelled a good story, and they were not going to let it rest. Lilia told the reporters how over 100 Uruguayan exiles living in Argentina had been kidnapped and disappeared, and she felt that this was what had happened in Porto Alegre. Her voice shaking with emotion, she appealed, 'At least give me back my grandchildren.' Her plea was transmitted by every radio station in Rio Grande do Sul and became the next day's headline.

The repercussions were enormous. The press in São Paulo, Rio, and Brasília took up the case. The *Folha de S. Paulo* published an editorial demanding an immediate and thorough investigation by the police. Both the federal and state police denied that there had been a kidnapping, insisting that the couple had just disappeared. In Uruguay, the Brazilian papers were banned, but news filtered through.

A couple of days later, a woman called Ferri's house and said: 'I owe Dr Ferri favours. Tell him to act quickly because the children are in danger.' She did not give her name.

A few days later there was another phone call, this time from Montevideo. It was Lilia's husband, Homero, saying that the children had been handed over to him. It was the first piece of good news since the four had disappeared. Lilia cried with relief.

The next day Ferri received another anonymous call, this time from a man who said he was a Federal Police agent but did not agree with the methods being used by his department. He told Ferri that two Uruguayan military officers had been in Brazil, and that when the journalists had 'caused a stir' – referring to Cunha and Scalco's appearance at the flat – the children had been sent to Uruguay. He also said that police inspector Pedro Seelig had travelled to São Paulo.

That same day came the bombshell. In Montevideo, the Uruguayan armed forces issued a communiqué to say that Universindo Díaz, Lilián Celiberti, and Lilián's two children, aged eight and three, had been arrested 'while crossing the frontier from Brazil carrying a large amount of subversive literature'. They were alleged to belong to an international Marxist organization.

Once again, the reporters besieged Ferri. Taken by surprise, he phoned me: 'Jan, what shall I say? The press are all here!' I thought quickly: 'Ferri, say it is most unlikely that anyone would invade a country for subversive purposes with two small children!'

Ferri also pointed out that they were supposed to have 'invaded' Uruguay in two cars, but Lilián did not drive. Later, Lilia said, 'Why would Lilián go back to where she was tortured?'

The question now was, where had they been since disappearing from their flat and entering Uruguay days later? This was the chaotic beginning to an event which for the first time exposed the clandestine cooperation between the security forces of the Southern Cone countries.

In *Clamor Bulletin* No. 4, published just a few days later, we ran an editorial headed 'Solidarity Has No Frontiers'. It read: 'In November four Uruguayans were kidnapped in Porto Alegre. A few days later they re-appeared in the hands of the Uruguayan authorities, in Montevideo. This is clear proof that the agencies of repression in the Southern Cone do not respect the frontiers. So why should solidarity respect them?'

From then on, 'Solidarity has no frontiers' became Clamor's motto. The Porto Alegre kidnapping drew attention to the reality of cross-border cooperation between security forces, which had begun several years earlier but had passed largely unnoticed in Brazil. Later we came to know it as Operation Condor.

Clamor also issued a press bulletin saying that the kidnappings were a flagrant violation of human rights and of Brazilian sovereignty.

If the Brazilian and Uruguayan authorities hoped that the armed forces communiqué would put a stop to the interest of the press in the fate of the four exiles, they were badly mistaken. The press, especially the local reporters in Porto Alegre, and of course the journalist who had unwittingly become a protagonist in the story, Luiz Claudio Cunha of *Veja*, refused to abandon it.

And lawyer Omar Ferri, as tenacious as Sherlock Holmes, was determined to find out what had happened, who had done it, and why.

Clamor remained in close contact with Ferri, publishing stories about the kidnapping and the latest developments in all of its following bulletins. Through our contacts with Amnesty International and the WCC, we ensured that the story of the kidnapping became known outside Brazil and reached a worldwide audience. Clamor was also able to offer financial support for Lilia's travel.

In São Paulo, after that first hurried contact with Maria, a regular link was established, through her, with the Uruguayan exiles, in particular the members of the party to which she, Lilián, and Universindo belonged, the Party for the Victory of the People (Partido por la Victoria del Pueblo, PVP) – the organization that had been most active in resisting the Uruguayan dictatorship.

There was little doubt in Lilia's mind that without the strong reactions in the press and in political circles, Lilián, Universindo, and the children would have suffered the same fate as the Uruguayans, many of them members of the PVP, who had disappeared in Argentina. Several of those Uruguayans' small children had disappeared with them.

From the point of view of Operation Condor, the success of whose operations depended on a climate of terror and fear and a censored press, the kidnapping in Porto Alegre turned into a major disaster. The Uruguayan security forces, used to doing what they wanted in their own small country after the dictatorship installed in 1973 had transformed the former Switzerland of South America into a gigantic prison with a muzzled press, a closed congress, an intimidated legal profession, and a cowed church, had failed to reckon with the very different situation in Brazil, where after 14 years of dictatorship, opposition defiantly flourished.

In addition, choosing Porto Alegre, a relatively small city where everyone knew, or was in some way related to, everyone else, was a fatal mistake, because it meant that sooner or later, details of the kidnapping would emerge. And just as importantly, Porto Alegre and Rio Grande do Sul in general were highly politicized and proud of their relative political independence from the centre. The press, the Brazilian Bar Association (Ordem dos Advogados do Brasil, OAB), and local opposition politicians all refused to allow themselves to be deceived and lied to.

So neither the reporters, nor Ferri, were going to let up. After all, the Uruguayans were not illegal immigrants or wanted criminals. They had entered Brazil legally, and they had committed no crimes there.

When the commander of the Third Army decided to join in, saying that in his opinion there had been no kidnapping and the subject was over, nobody took any notice of him. Instead, members of the only permitted opposition party, the Brazilian Democratic Movement (Movimento Democratico Brasileiro, MDB), made speeches in the Rio Grande do Sul state assembly, repudiating the kidnapping and remembering the case of Flavia Schilling, a young Brazilian imprisoned for six years in a Montevideo jail.

The repercussions spread abroad

Amnesty International's Patricia Feeney phoned to say that Amnesty was beginning a campaign aimed at governments, especially those of Italy and Switzerland, where Lilián had lived before coming to Brazil, asking them to make statements about the case. In London, Liberal peer Lord Avebury wrote to the Brazilian ambassador saying that what he called 'this extremely disturbing case'[1] should be investigated.

On 1 December, the OAB decided to enter the fray. At a packed meeting in Porto Alegre, the lawyers offered their solidarity to Ferri and declared that they could not remain silent before an act of such violence against citizens who were residing in Brazilian territory. Brazil's sovereignty had been affronted, and the truth of what had happened needed to be established.

The OAB then set up two commissions, one to investigate the kidnapping, and the other to travel to Uruguay to interview the Celiberti family and contact lawyers there for Lilián and Universindo's defence. Christmas intervened, so the commission travelled to Uruguay at the beginning of the new year, January 1979. Ferri was one of the four lawyers. Several journalists went with them.

In Montevideo, they found themselves under constant police vigilance. When Lilia went to their hotel, the Victoria Plaza, to meet them, she told them that she had had a visit from 'government people' warning her not to talk to the Brazilian lawyers who were about to arrive.

She told Ferri and the other three lawyers that her grandson Camilo was traumatized by what had happened and was convinced that the Brazilian police were their enemies, whereas the Uruguayans had freed them. She was afraid of losing guardianship of the children if Camilo made any sort of inconvenient revelation.

At night they went to the Celiberti family's flat and showed Camilo photographs, including one of Pedro Seelig, the inspector at Brazil's Department for Political and Social Order (Departamento de Ordem Política e Social, DOPS) who was believed to have led the kidnapping. The boy recognized Seelig. He said there were also people at the police HQ who spoke Spanish.

The OAB commission also attempted to see members of the Uruguayan government, without success.

Back in Porto Alegre, the police continued to deny there had ever been a kidnapping. Instead, they produced several witnesses in a town near the frontier with Uruguay called Bagé to say that the four Uruguayans had caught a bus there to travel to Montevideo, using false names. But the witnesses contradicted each other, and the farce was exposed when a frontier guard said that the bus they had allegedly travelled on had passed border control with only one passenger on board.

The first definitive proof that Brazilian police had been involved in the kidnapping came from nine-year-old Camilo, when a Brazilian newspaper reporter spoke to him at Lilia and Homero's flat and with the directness of a child, he described exactly what had happened. He, his little sister Francesca, and Universindo had been arrested as they left the flat in Rua Botafogo to go and watch a football match. They were taken to a big building full of policemen without ties. There they saw their mother. That night they were all put in cars and driven to the frontier, where they changed cars. After that

Camilo had not seen his mother again. The men who had arrested them had been Brazilians, but there had been two Uruguayans with them.

The police denied Camilo's version of events. The police chief declared that 'this Uruguayan child has never been here' and made threats against the journalists, including Cunha.

National newspapers ran editorials demanding explanations of how foreign agents had entered Brazil and kidnapped a family with total impunity. On whose orders had it been done?

In March 1979, a new organization, the Movement for Justice and Human Rights (Movimento de Justiça e Direitos Humanos, MJDH), was set up in Porto Alegre. Its creation was largely due to the kidnapping, which had brought home the lack of an active local human rights organization like Clamor or the Justice and Peace Commission in São Paulo. The MJDH, led from the beginning by lawyer Jair Krischke, made the situation of refugees and exiles from the neighbouring countries its priority. Over the next few years it was to play an invaluable role in many cases.

Ferri began receiving death threats from anonymous callers, and his wife and four children became fearful of answering the phone. But among the anonymous calls was one that proved significant. It led him to the name of the woman who had looked after the children while they were being held at DOPS, before being taken to Uruguay. Faustina Elenira Severino, a former nun, turned out to be the sister of the man being defended by Ferri on the day the news of the kidnapping first exploded. She felt she owed him a favour for defending her brother. It was she who had called Ferri telling him to act quickly because the children were in danger.

Ferri told the journalists who were regularly covering the case, and they managed to get a photograph of her, take it to Montevideo, and show it to Camilo, who confirmed that she was one of the two women who had looked after them at DOPS.

Another anonymous call brought another tip-off, this time to Cunha. 'You know the football player Didi Pedalada? He was in Lilián's flat on the day of the kidnapping.' Pedalada had left the world of soccer to join the ranks of the police, and Cunha had no problem finding a photo of him and recognizing him as one of the men in the flat.

Two more pieces of the jigsaw had fallen into place. The police, under intense pressure from public opinion, set up an internal inquiry.

In March 1979, in the face of strong opposition from the government party Arena, a Parliamentary Commission of Inquiry (Comissão Parlamentar de Inquérito, CPI) was installed in the Legislative Assembly.

Among those called to give evidence was Faustina Lenira Severino. She appeared with a black eye. Five days after giving evidence to the police inquiry, on 7 May 1979, she died, apparently from a stroke.

Ferri also gave evidence to the CPI. Government party deputies threatened and insulted him and questioned him about irrelevant facts, like a trip he had made to Cuba. He was accused of lying and of inventing the kidnapping.

Triumphantly, Arena leader Cicero Viana produced a document signed by Lilia in Montevideo, denying the kidnapping story. Within a few days this document was revealed to be worthless. Lilia told a reporter, who visited her to ask about it, that she had been coerced into signing it to prevent Lilián from being further tortured in prison.

This revelation deflated the CPI's attempts to demoralize Ferri. Instead, the threats and menaces against the lawyer and the journalists, which had stopped when the CPI began, started again. The Anti-Communist Command, a right-wing terrorist group, sent a letter threatening Ferri's family unless he suspended his activities. Another letter with death threats to Ferri was sent to the OAB.

The police then produced a new piece of evidence: the answers to an interrogation of Lilián and Universindo conducted in the presence of six military officers – a general, four colonels, and a captain – but without a lawyer.

The CPI's conclusions were revealed on 17 September 1979, in a 700-page report contained in three thick volumes. 'There is no proof whatsoever of a kidnapping', it concluded, and therefore, without the crime, nobody was responsible. Instead, the report condemned the witnesses, beginning with Ferri. But the report was rejected by the majority of the CPI members, and on 1 October they chose a new rapporteur, this time from the opposition MDB, who came to radically different conclusions.

The internal police inquiry had also decided that there was no case to answer. Instead, DOPS inspector Pedro Seelig and the lawyer who had defended him were awarded the Order of Military Merit.

Meanwhile, the Federal Police had concluded that the signature on the note allegedly left by Lilián for her landlord was false, after comparing it with her signature on the rent contract and in her passport. But the questions of who had written it and who had delivered it remained unanswered. The police announced that they would charge Lilián and Universindo for using false documents.

When Lilia was eventually allowed, months after her imprisonment, to visit her daughter, she discovered that Lilián had no idea what had happened to the children after she was separated from them at the frontier. She was also completely unaware of the huge story that her disappearance had become in Brazil and abroad, the press coverage, the speeches in congress, the denunciations, the many twists and turns.

Later Lilián managed to send out notes to her mother from prison via a sympathetic guard. Lilia sent them to Mirtha in Italy, who sent them to Ferri. Mirtha said that Lilián was allowed one visit of one hour every two weeks, and fresh air for half an hour three times a week. 'She is allowed to read one book every ten days but is not allowed to write or receive letters. Her state of incommunicado is almost complete, while Universindo, one supposes, remains totally incommunicado.'

Then, two months later, came another bombshell. Ferri had a call from the journalist Paulo Maciel at *Zero Hora*. 'Come here quickly', was all he said.

Once Ferri had arrived, Maciel told him that waiting in a nearby bar was a Uruguayan who said he knew the real story of the kidnapping. Maciel wanted to be sure the man wasn't bluffing.

'I told him to send for the man, and after about two hours of talking to him I decided that he was speaking the truth',[2] Ferri later recalled. The man's name was Hugo García Rivas; he was a soldier in the Uruguayan army, and he had deserted in order to reveal the true story of the kidnapping.

In June, as soon as Rivas was safely out of the country, the OAB brought charges against the police and Ferri launched a campaign for the return of the kidnapped two to Brazil, saying that Rivas' declarations had proved everything he had denounced – namely, that the Federal Police knew about the operation from the beginning and had provided cover for it.

In November 1980, two years after the kidnapping, Lilia went to Brasília to ask the Brazilian authorities to demand that Lilián and Universindo be returned to Brazil. There was a precedent: English train robber Ronnie Biggs, living in Brazil, had been kidnapped and taken to Bermuda by mercenaries, and the Brazilian government had demanded, and obtained, his return. Foreign Minister Saraiva Guerreiro refused to see her, saying he could do nothing to help her because it would imply 'interfering in the internal affairs of Uruguay' even though he recognized that she had been kidnapped on Brazilian soil.

In December that year, *Clamor Bulletin* No. 12 reported:

> Now, after being held two years without trial Lilián and Universindo are to be tried for illegally entering Uruguay carrying arms and subversive material. ... [A]s the kidnapping was proved in a court of law, seen by eyewitnesses, and confirmed by a Uruguayan solder, Hugo García Rivas, who took part in the operation and later defected abroad, this trial will be pure farce. Lilián's mother is appealing for international pressure to prevent her daughter being sentenced for a crime she did not commit.

The same month, by two votes to one, the Criminal Appeals Court in Porto Alegre decided to acquit the three police agents accused of the kidnapping for lack of proof. They also reduced the sentence of Didi Pedalada – the only one found guilty, and, not by coincidence, the lowest-ranking agent – from six to three months. One of the judges felt obliged to point out that there was no way a subordinate officer could carry out such an operation on his own without superior orders.

In January 1981, two years after they were illegally kidnapped in Porto Alegre, Lilián and Universindo were sentenced to five years imprisonment for allegedly 'invading Uruguay'.

In November 1983, after serving five years in prison for a crime she did not commit, Lilián was freed. A month later, Universindo was also released. Interviewed in Montevideo, Lilia said, 'I know that it is thanks to the Brazilians that my daughter and my grandchildren are alive.'

There is no doubt that it was thanks to the courageous activity of lawyer Omar Ferri, the investigative work of a number of reporters, the willingness of some politicians to speak out, and the network of support from human rights organizations that the kidnapping was revealed in all its details, and the cover-up attempted by the authorities was exposed. The revelations of Hugo Rivas (see Chapter 12) only served to confirm their accusations.

Notes

1. Letter from Lord Avebury, 1 December 1978, held in the Clamor archive at the Centro de Documentação e Informação in São Paulo.
2. Ferri, O. (1981) *Seqüestro no Cone Sul: O Caso Lilian e Universindo*, Porto Alegre: Mercado Aberto.

CHAPTER 8
Disappeared children found in Chile

Two days before Christmas in 1976, a big black car drew up beside the playground in Bernardo O'Higgins Square in the Pacific port of Valparaíso, 50 miles from the Chilean capital, Santiago. A small boy and girl were deposited on the pavement, and the car drove off.

Hours passed; then, somebody who noticed the abandoned children called the police and the children were taken to a children's home. They were well dressed, which was unusual for abandoned children, and the little boy's accent revealed that he was not Chilean. He recited his name, Anatole; his sister's name, Victoria Eva; and his parents' names. He gave his address, complete with the house number, the street, the district, and the city, Buenos Aires. When the social workers asked him where his parents were, Anatole said that armed men had invaded the house with a big staircase where the children lived with *mamucha* and *papucho*. He saw his mother lying on the floor in a pool of blood. He was four years old. His sister was 18 months old.

After hearing Anatole's story, the director of the children's home called *El Mercurio*, one of Chile's main daily papers. A reporter and a photographer came to take pictures of the children. On 29 December the paper ran the story on the front page under the headline 'Small Brother and Sister Abandoned in O' Higgins Square'.

Who were they? Noting that Anatole had a strong *porteño* (Buenos Aires) accent, the paper speculated that they were 'possibly the children of Tupamaros, brought to Chile and abandoned to save them from being murdered by the Triple A or in battles with the Argentine security forces'. In the following days, other theories appeared in attempts to explain what became known as 'the mystery of the abandoned children'. Perhaps they had been abandoned by a group of child traffickers from Argentina; perhaps they were the children of Chilean exiles who had joined the guerrillas fighting the Argentine regime.

Anatole gave details about their journey to Chile. He said they had come by car all the way from Argentina and slept on the way. He remembered the name of two Chilean border crossings high in the Andes and seeing snow on the mountains. He said they had travelled in a big car with 'Tia Monica' (Auntie Monica) and another little girl, the same age as his sister. Tia Monica left them to play in the square, saying that she was going to buy some sweets and that she would come back to get them – but she never did. Tia Monica was never seen again.

The children's foreignness was definitively confirmed when they failed to recognize the actors in Chilean children's TV programmes.

Anatole had supplied more than enough information for his family to be located, but the Chilean authorities made no such attempt; neither did they try to discover how two small children had entered the country without passports or any sort of documentation. Neither Interpol, the Red Cross, or any other international agency was asked to help trace the children's family.

The embassies of Argentina and Uruguay in Santiago offered no help. The Argentine ambassador went to see the children and told *El Mercurio* that Anatole was Uruguayan-born, although he spoke with a strong *porteño* accent, and his sister was Argentine. Although these details revealed that the ambassador knew far more about them than he was letting on, he said no more. The Uruguayan ambassador denied any knowledge of missing families, either in Argentina or Uruguay.

After the immediate scandal, the children were forgotten. Nobody came to claim them. They stayed in the children's home until a childless Chilean couple, Jesús Larrabeiti and Sylvia Yáñez, came looking for a baby to adopt. They wanted to take only the younger child, but Anatole was very protective of his sister and clung to her, so they ended up taking both children home with them.

The story would have ended there if one of the social workers from the children's home had not gone on holiday to Venezuela just over two years later, in April 1979. In Caracas, she happened to look at the daily paper, *El Nacional*, and saw photographs of children reported to have gone missing in Argentina, taken from a *Clamor Bulletin*. They were grainy black-and-white pictures, but she thought she recognized the children who had been found in the square in Valparaíso.

A few days later, my phone rang. When I answered it, I heard Maria's excited voice, 'Jan! I have incredible news! I am coming over right now!'

Half an hour later Maria was in my home, her eyes shining with joy.

'We've found Anatole and Vicky!'

'Maria – what? Where? How?'

Maria showed me a small piece of paper with the words 'Valparaíso', 'dentist', 'mamucha', and 'papucho' on it, which she had just received in a letter sent from Paris by Tota Quinteros, a Uruguayan exile. Days before, Tota had been in Caracas to meet her friend Óscar Maggiolo, ex-rector of the University of Montevideo. He told her that he had been sought out by a Chilean social worker with an unbelievable story – the two children who had been abandoned in a square in Valparaíso, her hometown, were the same children whose photos she had seen in a Venezuelan newspaper in a story about disappeared children in Argentina. It was incredible – but could it be true?

The story had really begun on 26 September 1976, when Argentine security forces attacked the house where the Uruguayan couple Roger Julien and Victoria Grissonas, members of the PVP, lived with their two small children, Anatole and Victoria Eva, after escaping over the River Plate from the repression in Montevideo. Under Perón, left-wing exiles from other Southern Cone countries had flocked to Argentina, but after the 1976 coup, the net had been tightening on these political refugees.

They lived at 555 Calle Mitre, in San Martín, a Buenos Aires suburb. Joaquin Castro, a neighbour who witnessed the events that day, later made a statement:

> [A]fter hearing the noise of loud explosions, which at first I thought could be coming from the church because when they have a festival there they let off fireworks, I went to the door of my house and saw a large number of vehicles in the street and heavily armed men in civilian clothes, then when I went to the corner I saw an armoured car arriving with military personnel. ... [S]o I went back to my house which is about 40 metres from the corner and watched with my wife what was happening, the firing and bombs continued. ... After some time I saw them dragging a woman along, once round the corner they shot her. At this exact moment I saw they were leading two small children by their hands, this made me step forward and I heard the children crying inconsolably, and when one of the children asked for his mother, one of the 'beasts' said 'that cow your mother is no more'. I could not see any more because the ones in civilian clothes gesticulated and threatened me to go inside.
>
> ... [T]he next day there was a rumour they must have spread, that the house had been used as a 'people's prison', which I know was not true, it did not exist.
>
> Soon afterwards, the house was emptied of its contents, with lorries parked outside, and then police repaired it, filling in the bullet holes from the shootout, which in fact did not happen, because there were no bullet holes in the houses across the road, which means they did not fire from inside the house. The house was then occupied by police, but soon they moved out and a card appeared: 'Owner selling'. As can be seen they seized everything, they are bastards, they are murderers.

The neighbour was so terrified by the experience that it took him seven years to tell what he had witnessed.

Nobody knew what had become of the children. When their grandmother, Angélica Julien, who lived in Montevideo, went to Buenos Aires in search of them, she found no trace. Like so many others, they had simply disappeared.

Back in Chile, the press had decided that Anatole and Victoria Eva were the children of Tupamaros, abandoned by their heartless parents. After several months in a children's home, they had been adopted by a dentist and his wife. That was all the social worker knew.

And there was Maria, bursting with excitement, overjoyed by the amazing news. Roger Julien and Victoria Grissonas were her comrades, fellow members of the PVP; Roger was one of its leaders. They had disappeared during the second joint operation by Argentine and Uruguayan security forces to round up members of the PVP. Over 50 had disappeared since the March coup.

I called up the other members of Clamor for an emergency meeting. Could this be true?

When we met that night at my house, there was a considerable amount of scepticism. Luiz Eduardo Greenhalgh thought the story just too incredible to be true. Found in Chile? How could they have got there? Why would they take two small children kidnapped in Buenos Aires and abandon them in Chile? Maybe the social worker had got it wrong – after all, she was looking at small, grainy pictures over two years after she had seen the children. Or maybe this was a trap, set to demoralize those searching for the children?

But what if she was right? What should we do? Chile was still under the harsh yoke of Pinochet, so any attempt to trace the children would have to be done with extreme care. We talked long into the night, debating our next move. We knew that the paternal grandmother, Angélica Julien, had never stopped searching for the family ever since they disappeared, filing writs of habeas corpus, appealing to the French government because Roger Julien's father, her husband, had French citizenship, writing to everyone she could think of. UNHCR had also filed a habeas corpus writ, as the family had refugee status in Argentina. For three years all these efforts had met with a deafening silence.

We decided that the first step must be to confirm that the children really were Anatole and Vicky – otherwise we would be engaged in a wild goose chase. So we drew up a plan of action, calling it 'Operation Anatole'.

We set out what we knew: the children were found in the street in Valparaíso, Chile, in December 1976, and taken to the children's home at Cerro Playa Ancha. They were there until September 1978. The juvenile court judge in Valparaíso authorized their adoption by a childless couple, the husband a dentist, the wife a teacher, who were thought to live in the district of Cerro Barón.

Our detailed plan went as follows:

1. Secretly locate and identify the children (take photos), if possible with the help of the Vicariate of Solidarity (Vicaria de Solidariedade).
2. In case of positive identification, inform the grandmother and collect all documents, photos, and means of identification.
3. Inform UNHCR and other international organizations.
4. Get power of attorney signed by the grandparents.
5. Identification: basic hair colour, eyes, age.
6. Other: scars, marks, dental work, blood group, left-handed or not, any special likes or games.

7. Documents: birth certificate, marriage certificate of parents, habeas corpus writs presented in Argentina and Uruguay.
8. Letters: copies of letters from authorities (e.g. French president Valéry Giscard d'Estaing) and organizations.
9. Photos: of the children, grandparents, and parents.

Maria immediately volunteered to go to Chile. She would be travelling on her French rather than her Uruguayan passport, but even so, it would be risky. For Maria, though, this was much more than a political task. The children's parents had been her friends, her *compañeros*, and she owed it to them to leave no stone unturned. They would have done the same for her.

Some members of Clamor felt that it would be too dangerous, because if those who had kidnapped the children had gone to such extreme lengths to hide them, they would also do anything to stop them being found – but Maria was absolutely determined to go. Jaime Wright was worried about something else, however. He asked her, 'If you met the children, could you control yourself? Would you be able to resist hugging them?' Maria said she wouldn't risk everything because of an impulse.

When it was finally decided that Maria should go, Jaime and Luiz Eduardo took her to the airport to get the flight to Chile. Before she left, Maria gave me copies of her documents and a photograph of her small daughter, Sofia, 'in case anything happens to me'. She was only to phone if it was absolutely necessary.

Later, Maria said that even before the plane touched down at Santiago Airport, she was feeling scared. She had heard that computers had recently been installed at the airport and she was afraid that, although she was travelling on her French passport, they would discover that she was really a Uruguayan – and worse, a member of the PVP. But she went through passport control without a problem.

Maria checked into a small hotel and immediately set out to find the UNHCR office, because she knew that Belela Herrera, the coordinator, was a fellow Uruguayan. She wanted to waste no time in beginning the search. When she explained the reason for her visit, Belela called Óscar Maggiolo in Caracas to confirm her story. Then she suggested that Maria contact the Social Aid Foundation of Christian Churches (Fundación de Ayuda Social de las Iglesias Cristianas, FASIC), an ecumenical human rights organization. FASIC coordinator Claudio González listened attentively to her story and agreed to drive her to Valparaíso in his Kombi van that very moment.

The old port town was about an hour south from the capital. Maria had no address for the children's home or for the couple who had adopted them, but she clung to the idea that if she drove around the streets she might see them, somehow recognize them. So they drove slowly round the streets while she stared at any small child she saw. After a couple of hours, Claudio, who was getting more and more nervous, insisted that it was too dangerous to continue, and by 5 p.m. they were heading back to Santiago.

As they drove back up the winding road from the coast, Maria began to despair as she realized the daunting task that she had so enthusiastically embraced. How on earth could she find the children when nearly three years on, they might look very different from their small black-and-white photos? Even if she located the children's home, would they reveal the name and address of the couple who had adopted them? The social worker who had set the ball rolling in Caracas had been too scared to identify herself. Why would the director of the home believe her story? As she turned over the problems in her mind on the slow drive back to Santiago, Maria decided that her only hope was to go back to the UNHCR office and talk to Belela again, hoping that she was not a bureaucrat who hid behind red tape.

As it happened, Belela was a humane, pragmatic person who was not only aware that Uruguayan children had disappeared in Argentina but was acutely interested in helping to find them. She suggested contacting a well-known psychologist who not only lived in Valparaíso, but more importantly also came from Uruguay. As soon as Belela mentioned his name, Maria realized that they had been at school together. Aware that the UNHCR telephones were bugged, Belela did not dare to phone him, but she gave Maria his address.

When Maria left Belela's office, she felt hopeful again, but also hungry and exhausted. It had been a long day. She found a restaurant where they served barbecued meat, but fearful of being identified as a Uruguayan, she decided not to risk asking for *parrillada*, the Uruguayan term, and asked instead for *carne*, the general Spanish word for meat. While she ate, a large TV began showing the day's news, beginning with the big pro-Pinochet demonstration that had been held earlier that day. The dictator himself was there in uniform, receiving the adulation of the crowd, who sang and shouted slogans with a fervour that made Maria think of the Nazis and Hitler. The fanaticism of the crowd appalled her. She thought: 'This is real fascism; you don't see this in Brazil or Uruguay.' Terrified, she paid the bill, went to her hotel, hid the photos of the children at the bottom of her suitcase, and climbed into bed, too scared to sleep.

The next day she left the hotel early and got a bus to Valparaíso. She found the address that Belela had given her and soon was face to face with the psychologist she had shared lessons with long ago at school. He showed no sign of recognition but gave her the name and address of another psychologist, Sol, who worked with the children of political prisoners, and quickly showed her out.

When Maria located Sol, she showed her the photos of Anatole and Vicky and carefully explained her mission. Sol said she had never heard of them, but asked Maria to return the next day. Maria felt sure Sol was suspicious of her and feared she might even inform on her. She found a cheap boarding house for the night, to avoid having to return to Santiago. It was an old wooden house that dated from Valparaíso's beginnings as a port. The wind whistled through it, making the shutters bang and the walls creak. That night, terrified in case Sol had betrayed her, she piled all the furniture against the door to stop the police crashing in.

Next day, overcoming her fear, she went back to the psychologist's clinic. Sol was waiting for her. Without saying a word, she led Maria back into the street and then to an empty soccer stadium, where a woman was waiting for them. The woman had worked in the children's home during the time when the children were found, and when Maria showed her their photos, she recognized them.

From the stadium, still without saying a word, Sol led Maria to a dental surgery. The waiting room was full of patients, but the dentist beckoned them through into his consulting room. Maria sat in the only empty seat, the dentist's chair, and realized that he already knew exactly why they had come. When Maria showed him the photographs, he recognized the children immediately. He said they had been adopted by one of his colleagues – Valparaíso was a small town, all the dentists knew each other, and everyone had talked about it at the time. He told Maria the names of the adoptive parents, Jesús Larrabeiti and Sylvia Yáñez. He knew the school the children went to and suggested that Maria should go there to get the family's address. Maria thanked him profusely and walked out smiling, past the waiting room full of worried patients, confident that now she was on the trail.

Sol went with her to the school, Sacre Coeur College, run by a French order. The director, a priest, agreed to see them, looked at the photos, and listened carefully to Maria's story. Then he showed them the school register with the children's names, dates of birth, and address. Anatole was still called Anatole (he had been given the name in honour of his Lithuanian grandfather), a name completely unknown in Chile. He was registered as Anatole Patricio Larrabeiti Yáñez and his listed date of birth was only seven days later than his real one, 22 November 1972. His sister had been registered as Claudia Victoria Larrabeiti Yáñez, with a listed date of birth 2 August 1975, three months later than her real one, 7 May. Now there was absolutely no doubt in Maria's mind: she had found the children.

Maria was euphoric, and as soon as they had left the college, she hugged Sol. The woman she had feared might betray her had instead led her to the children! Sol, equally emotional, said: 'Have we finished? Let's go back to my house.' When they caught a bus, Sol asked Maria not to look where the bus was going, so she would not be able to reveal Sol's address if questioned. Sol's home was in a very poor district. When they got off the bus, Maria bought a bottle of pisco at a little store, and when they got to Sol's house, they drank it all and talked non-stop till 1 a.m. in the morning.

The next day, Maria found a public phone box and got through to Paris and then to me in São Paulo. Speaking cautiously, she said that she had confirmed everything. I told her to come back immediately, but Maria could not resist the temptation of trying to catch a glimpse of the children.

She found the block of flats where the Larrabeitis lived. Her heart thumping, she rang the bell of the flat. A man opened the door. She said quickly, 'I'm looking for the Ramirez family. Do they live here?' He said 'No' and shut the door. There was no sign or sound of the children.

Back in Santiago, Maria checked out of her hotel and hurried to the airport to get the first plane back to Brazil. At immigration, soldiers searched her luggage and confiscated the bottle of pisco she was taking back, but it was a small price to pay. When Maria emerged from arrivals at Congonhas Airport in São Paulo a few hours later, she found the entire Clamor team waiting for her. In the car, we bombarded her with questions.

An urgent meeting was called to debate the next step. We decided that now we were sure that we really had found Anatole and Vicky, it was time to contact their paternal grandmother, Angélica Julien, who just two months before had sent a letter to Clamor, appealing for help in her search. We needed Angélica to provide the documents and photographs that would help to prove the real identity of the children. Angélica's husband, Luis Alberto, was an invalid, unable to take an active part in the search. We knew from Maria that the maternal grandparents, who had emigrated to Uruguay from Lithuania after the Second World War, had never been involved in the search for their missing grandchildren. Anatolius Grissonas had been *chargé d'affaires* for Lithuania before it was annexed by the Soviet Union, and had died two years earlier, in 1977. A fervent anti-communist who supported Uruguay's right-wing dictatorship, he did not approve of his daughter's political views. And his widow was afraid of doing anything that might displease the authorities. So that left Angélica.

Somebody would have to go to Uruguay – this was one trip that Maria could not make. Nobody from Clamor was available, but Dom Paulo suggested journalist Ricardo Carvalho, who had been sacked from his newspaper after taking part in a strike.

Always ready for an adventure, Ricardo accepted immediately. We booked his return ticket to Montevideo. The night before, we met at his flat to run through the operation. Beforehand, I hurriedly read through *The House on Garibaldi Street*, a book written by a member of Mossad which described the meticulous undercover operation put in place to capture the Nazi war criminal Adolf Eichmann in Buenos Aires in 1960, with the slightly absurd idea of looking for ideas for our own operation. Ricardo began to worry about what would happen if he were arrested and tortured and began to bleed, because he was taking an anti-coagulant drug for a medical condition. We debated whether he should stop taking the drug once he arrived in Montevideo. Ricardo might have been scared, but he did not back down.

We gave him a letter from Bishop Angélico Sândalo Bernardino to the archbishop of Montevideo, Monsignor Carlos Partelli, explaining that Ricardo was a reporter who wanted to write about the Church in Uruguay. Dom Paulo also wrote a letter asking the Church authorities in Uruguay to give Ricardo every assistance.

The next day we were back at the airport, waving Ricardo off on the flight to Montevideo.

Ricardo later recounted the odyssey in his own book, *The Cardinal and the Reporter*. He described how he made his way to Angélica's house, where she lived with her ailing 75-year-old husband and two younger children, and how her sadness turned to tearful emotion when he told her who had sent him and why.

'You are from Clamor?' she asked. 'We knew that you would come one day. Thank God!' Once Ricardo had recounted the amazing news, Angélica set about getting together the various documents needed. There and then she wrote out a letter authorizing Clamor to search for her disappeared family, and the next day she got it authenticated at a nearby notary's office, fortunately run by a friend who did not ask awkward questions and who covered it with the stamps and seals so beloved of Latin American bureaucracy.

That night, as he walked around the centre of Montevideo to kill time before returning to his hotel, Ricardo became convinced he was being followed. The full weight of what he was doing hit him. All the stories he had read of torture, political prisoners, and disappearances suddenly overwhelmed him. Panicking, he made his way to the cathedral, and entering the sacristy, thrust Dom Angélico's letter at a surprised young priest.

As Ricardo recalls in his book, 'Dom Partelli's secretary came to talk to me, very simpático, smiling, asking me how they could help.' Ricardo then decided to tell him about his real mission in Montevideo. 'As the story advanced, his smile disappeared. When I said that I had gone into the cathedral because I was afraid I was being followed by the police, there were two of us panicking.' Ricardo was told that the cardinal would not be able to see him, and that he must leave the cathedral because it was about to close. But he refused, saying, 'The Church must protect those who are afraid, and I am afraid. I am only leaving here to go straight to the airport tomorrow morning.'

The Uruguayans came up with a solution: the cardinal's own driver would take Ricardo to the airport. The next morning Ricardo was collected at his hotel and driven to Carrasco Airport. When his flight was called he ran up the steps onto the plane, a Varig Brazilian Airlines flight, remembering to turn and wave to the driver, who was faithfully waiting on the terrace until he saw Ricardo actually enter the plane.

Once they had taken off, Ricardo felt so euphoric that he asked for a double whisky and then made his way to the cockpit and poured out his story to the bemused pilot. The pilot joined him in celebrating, and several double whiskies were downed before the plane, luckily in the hands of the co-pilot, landed at Congonhas Airport.

With the documents brought back by Ricardo, the third stage of 'Operation Anatole' could now begin. Angélica, accompanied by Ricardo and Luiz Eduardo, who hid all the documents among the clothes in his case, flew to Santiago. On arrival they discovered that the Larrabeitis, unaware of the flurry of activity that now stretched over three countries, were in the process of completing the formal adoption of the children. Under Chilean law, this would put an end to the rights of the biological family. A Brazilian lawyer could not intervene, but at Belela's suggestion they contacted Chilean lawyers Guillermo Cowley and Horacio Varela, who presented an injunction to the Valparaíso court to interrupt the adoption proceedings.

Then they went to see the Larrabeitis. For them, it was a terrible shock – suddenly their house was full of Brazilians and a desperate grandmother, demanding the return of her grandchildren. It was Angélica's first meeting with her grandchildren after almost three years, and neither Anatole nor Vicky remembered their grandmother. She was overcome with emotion and immediately declared that she wanted to take them back to Montevideo.

For the dentist and his wife, who had adopted the children in good faith after years of unsuccessful infertility treatment, their world was suddenly turned upside down. The documents and photos they were shown were irrefutable. They had been on the verge of concluding the adoption proceedings, but now everything was up in the air.

But the Larrabeitis were not going to give the children up now, after two years of caring for them, bonding, seeing them adapt and settle down and become part of their family. Angélica was equally adamant, however. She had lost her son and her daughter-in-law, and now that she had miraculously found her grandchildren, how could she leave them again?

With the question of the children's future undecided, the Clamor team flew back to São Paulo to report to Dom Paulo and make arrangements for revealing to the world the unbelievable news. It was decided that an international press conference would be called, but four days before it was due, a new problem arose. Cardinal Raúl Silva Henríquez, archbishop of Santiago and head of the Vicariate of Solidarity, phoned Dom Paulo asking him to suspend the press conference until he could personally transmit the concerns he had, including fears for the safety of the children.

Someone had to go and hear what the Chilean cardinal had to say, so Jaime made a flying visit to Santiago as Dom Paulo's special envoy. As it turned out, Cardinal Silva Henríquez was fearful that if the Chilean government were to be accused of connivance in the kidnapping of the children, this would increase the already existing tensions between church and state caused by the Vicariate's work with political prisoners.

Jaime promised the cardinal that there would be no specific accusations against the Chilean government, nor were there any plans to promote a legal battle between the grandparents and the adoptive parents for custody of the children, another concern of the archbishop. He suggested instead that Dom Paulo could appeal to the Chilean government to collaborate in solving similar cases. He also promised that there would be no mention of FASIC or of the Vicariate during the press conference.

Chile was still a repressive dictatorship, and care had to be taken not to do anything that might provoke reprisals against the organizations that worked for human rights. Clamor's members could drop in and out, but they were there always.

The news conference to announce the spectacular discovery of two children who had disappeared in Argentina, hundreds of miles away on the other side of the Andes, drew a large crowd of reporters, both Brazilian and foreign, who packed the room. The correspondents of *Le Monde*, the BBC, and the Associated Press were there. Angélica sat next to Dom Paulo as he announced the amazing news. She spoke of her happiness and also of her determination to bring the children back to Uruguay. Jaime and Luiz Eduardo gave details of the operation to find the children. The identity of the original source of the news and Maria's role in the discovery were kept secret.

The news made headlines around the world. It was sensational because it was the first time any of the disappeared had been found. The news agencies and the European, American, and Brazilian press all gave it huge play, but in Argentina it was tucked away on inside pages, while in Uruguay it was completely censored.

The discovery of the children gave an enormous boost to the families of other missing children because everyone concluded that if these two children had been taken all the way to Chile, others could have been taken too.

In Buenos Aires, the news prompted the group Grandmothers of Plaza de Mayo to apply to the courts for a habeas corpus in favour of 5 other disappeared children and 27 babies believed to have been born to disappeared mothers.

In Chile, the destiny of Anatole and Vicky became a topic of intense debate in the Chilean press. On the one hand, there were the adoptive parents who had taken in and given a home to two small, abandoned children; on the other, there was the biological grandmother who had spent three years looking for them. Each side made emotional appeals. The Larrabeitis, 32-year-old dentist Jesús and 29-year-old kindergarten teacher Sylvia, said the children had already lost their parents once, and if it happened again, they would be traumatized. 'We fell in love with them at first sight, and now they are our children and our reason for living.'

Angélica fought back by showing all the letters she had received in reply from military, ecclesiastical, and political authorities as proof that she had never stopped searching for the children. She recognized that the children were being looked after with affection but argued: 'I should have them with me because my son might appear one day and ask where his children are.'

In Santiago, lawyers, churchmen, social workers, diplomats, and UN officials all joined in the debate about the children's fate. The Uruguayan ambassador, Dante Paladini, declared that his government had never heard of the children and had never received any complaint from their families. He claimed the whole story, the appearance of the children as well as the story of their disappeared parents, was an exaggeration and had a political agenda, trying to create problems between the two countries. The 'so-called' disappeared always turned up somewhere else. He said the embassy would deal with the case at the level that it deserved – consular.

The Chilean newspaper *El Mercurio*, which had run the first story, said that when Anatole was taken to the children's home after being found abandoned in the street, he told social workers that his home had been invaded by uniformed men. He said that he had seen his mother fall down, bleeding, after being hit by shots, and that his father had hidden the children in a bathtub. The paper commented: 'Although the Valparaíso dailies reported the existence of the two abandoned children with their photos a few days later, speculating on their origin, it seems that nobody connected them with the disappeared in Argentina, in spite of an international campaign to find them.'

A right-wing Chilean paper ran a story entitled 'What's Behind this Case?' The author, José Mayorga Martínez, said a young professional couple, who only wanted to give a happy home to two children, had found themselves involved in an international intrigue. He accused Angélica of wanting to revive the problem of human rights in Chile, a problem 'which for many months had been forgotten'.

A declaration by the Families of Disappeared Prisoners group reminded Chileans of some of the larger issues behind the case: 'How do you explain that a whole family of Uruguayans is seized by Argentine and Uruguayan agents in Buenos Aires and then the children are abandoned in a public square in Chile? How and with whom did such young children enter the country? These doubts must be resolved; public opinion must be told the truth.'

Guillermo Cowley and Horacio Varela, the two Chilean lawyers who had been hired by Clamor to represent Angélica and interrupt the adoption process, had asked the judge to postpone any decision until Angélica could obtain all the necessary documents. They also hoped to reach a formal agreement on access.

Later they said[1] that the police had not allowed them to have a copy of the original file on the children even though this is normal practice in custody cases. Varela said the director of the children's home in 1976 was a man very closely linked to the Chilean government and was someone who was able to manipulate the judge, Eugenia Márquez Wahl. Varela said that she had only ordered a routine investigation into the case in 1976 and that no contact was made with Interpol. 'This would suggest there was some complicity in the kidnapping and concealment of the Uruguayan children on the part of local authorities in Valparaíso at least.'

In Uruguay, the heavily censored Uruguayan press had still not reported a word about the case.

Angélica remained adamant that she wanted to take the children back to Uruguay. She had lost four members of her immediate family – this was a chance to recover two of them. She wanted to go back to Chile immediately and start a legal battle to win custody.

There were anguished discussions. The Uruguayans wanted the children to be returned to their grandparents – it would be an important political victory. But the children had found a stable environment with the Larrabeitis, who obviously loved and cared for them and apparently knew nothing, or had not tried to find out, where they really came from. To uproot them again, to take them away from their adoptive parents and bring them back to Uruguay, would be another violent trauma in two very young lives.

All agreed, however, that their real identities must be established, and regular links with their biological family should begin. Dom Paulo persuaded Angélica that to uproot them yet again would not be good for them. In the end she agreed, for the sake of the children, and for the time being, that they should remain in the care of the Larrabeitis, but that regular visits to Montevideo would begin as soon as possible.

For Angélica, this was a tough decision. She had devoted all her energies to searching for the children since they disappeared, she had appealed to everyone from the pope to the president of France, she had scoured courts and children's homes in Argentina, she had written countless letters. Now she had found them, how could she give them up?

In September 1979, an agreement was drawn up by Angélica and the Larrabeitis stating that the children would keep their natural and biological surname and would stay in Chile under the tutelage and care of the Chilean couple. If the real parents appeared, the situation would be reviewed. The Uruguayan family would have unlimited, permanent visiting rights and the children would visit Uruguay whenever possible.

The discovery of the small brother and sister in Chile, three years after they had disappeared in Argentina, aroused worldwide interest. It confirmed the existence of collusion between the Southern Cone dictatorships. Otherwise, how could two small children, without any sort of documentation, travel from Argentina to Chile, passing border controls?

But was theirs the only case? Might other disappeared children have been transferred to Chile from Argentina? Had adults been transferred? The discovery of Anatole and Vicky solved one family's quest but threw up a whole raft of new questions.

Note

1. *El Mercurio*. (1979) 'Ninos Uruguayos Secuestrados en Argentina Hallados en Chile', 1 August.

CHAPTER 9
The grandmothers

The discovery of the two children in Chile was a huge boost for all the Argentine grandmothers who had also been searching for their missing grandchildren, fearful that they would not find them alive. Soon after the discovery of Anatole and Vicky, Clamor received a visit that would determine its priorities from then on. Two of the Argentine grandmothers who had set up the organization known as the Grandmothers of Plaza de Mayo (Abuelas de Plaza de Mayo) came to see us.

For them, the discovery of Anatole and Vicky was incredibly important. It was the first indication that children who had disappeared or been born in captivity to their imprisoned mothers could still be alive. Up until then, nobody had dared to imagine what might have happened to them. The idea that the military junta had put in place a systematic plan to steal them and hand them over to military families, some of them the torturers and murderers of their parents, to be brought up in those families' image, had not occurred to anyone. Later one of the dictatorship's generals, Ramón Camps, admitted in an interview to the Spanish magazine *Tiempo*: 'Personally I did not eliminate any child, what I did was to give some of them to charities so they could be found new parents. The subversives educate their children to be subversive. That's what we have to prevent, to stop.'

The grandmothers got to know each other during the weekly protest of the Madres, the Mothers, as they walked in silent circles around the grounds in front of the presidential palace, the Casa Rosada, a practice that began in 1977. When they realized how many of them not only had sons and daughters who had disappeared but grandchildren too, they decided to form a separate group.

From November 1977, they began meeting in some of the tea shops that abounded in Buenos Aires. They pretended to be just a group of middle-aged ladies with time on their hands, but as they sipped their tea and nibbled their cakes, they were planning their activities. Their number grew rapidly from the initial dozen into a much larger group. As soon as they heard about the discovery of the two children in Chile, they wanted to know more about Clamor, a group they had never heard of before.

Their first president was María Isabel Chorobik de Mariani, known as Chicha, whose three-month-old granddaughter, Clara Anahí, disappeared after the house where she lived with her parents in La Plata was attacked with mortars, killing her mother and several others. Chicha's son, the baby's father, was not there, but was tracked down and killed soon after. The grandmothers decided that Chicha and the group's vice president, Alicia Zubasnabar

De la Quadra, known as Licha, should travel to São Paulo to find out more about the organization that had discovered Anatole and Vicky. They had no address or telephone number, just a contact given to them by Adolfo Esquivel of the human rights group the Service for Peace and Justice.

Unaware that São Paulo was a huge metropolis, they arrived at night, bringing with them, like good grandmothers, boxes of *alfajores*, the famous Argentine *dulce de leche* biscuit. They did not have a hotel reservation.

In the book she later wrote, Chicha described what happened.

At the airport they took a taxi and asked the driver to take them to a hotel, but every one he tried was full. They began to get desperate, so when the taxi stopped at traffic lights and Chicha saw a hotel sign, she ordered the driver to pull up. At first he refused, but the grandmothers were tired after their journey and insisted. Later on they would understand why he was so reluctant to leave them there.

Inside the hotel, the man at the reception desk at first refused their request for a room, but not speaking Portuguese, they did not understand why. They insisted, too tired to go on looking, and an argument began, with neither side understanding the other, until the man at the desk gave up and took them upstairs to a room. 'It had a deep red carpet, there was a mirror which covered an entire wall, a huge round bed and a small camp bed', wrote Chicha. When she inadvertently touched a switch, coloured lights flashed and loud music began to play.

The next morning they sought out Brother Alamiro, the contact that Esquivel had given them. When they gave him a card with the hotel name on it, he blushed red and asked his secretary to hurry to the hotel, pay the bill, and bring their suitcases. Then he explained to the grandmothers that the hotel they had stayed at was in fact a *motel* in the red-light district.

Alamiro contacted Clamor and we arranged to meet that same day. Besides the *alfajores*, the grandmothers had brought with them dozens of dossiers with details and photographs of the children who had gone missing. They were thrilled to find a sympathetic audience.

The visit of the grandmothers, with the photographs of so many young couples and small children who had disappeared, besides the large number of pregnant women who had vanished into the unknown, prompted Clamor to make the search for these children their priority. We had already published a special *Bulletin* listing the pregnant women who had disappeared, with their expected delivery dates. Now Clamor decided to launch a worldwide campaign to draw attention to the large number of disappeared children in Argentina. In the following years, we also published two calendars containing photos of the missing children.

In turn, we opened up our growing files of documents to the Abuelas, including many handwritten testimonies from the refugees and exiles who were arriving in São Paulo. During the next few years the Abuelas returned many times to read through the testimonies that continued to arrive, looking for clues, for names, for any mention of a pregnant woman seen in one of the clandestine detention camps, or any scrap of information that might lead them to their stolen grandchildren. When they found something of interest, they copied it in tiny letters onto rice paper. They bought boxes of Garoto chocolates (a well-known Brazilian brand), ate some of the chocolates but kept the wrappers, then put the rolled-up rice papers inside them, and returned them to the boxes. The grandmothers were smart. They put the boxes in the middle of their cases, under shoes and tights, and even under plants with roots and earth, to put off anyone who might search their cases. It always worked, and in this way the Abuelas smuggled a lot of information back into Argentina.

The Abuelas' visits always included an audience with Dom Paulo, who offered them the spiritual support they had failed to find in the Argentine religious hierarchy.

A long and fruitful partnership developed between the Abuelas and Clamor. On their way to denounce the situation to organizations and politicians in the US or Europe, they would stop off in São Paulo to bring news and information, get contacts, plan publications. From New York, Geneva, or Rome, Chicha sent letters and cards to us telling of her meetings, her successes, and her disappointments. Chuck Harper at the WCC became a good friend and an important source of support.

In Rome, however, the grandmothers had less luck. They made at least 18 trips to the Vatican, leaving files full of documents about their disappeared grandchildren for the pope. Chicha thought that Pope John Paul II, formerly Karol Wojtyla, would speak to her because of her Polish ancestry. Once, they were instructed to wait in St Peter's Square for the pope to pass by, when he would stop and speak to them – but just before he reached the place where they stood, somebody whispered into his ear and he turned to face the other side, ignoring them. They never managed to speak to him.

They wanted to ask him to intercede on behalf of the children who had disappeared in Argentina for political reasons, as he had done for children who had been kidnapped and held for ransom in Italy.

While they sought help overseas, the Abuelas never gave up trying to get replies from the military junta. In August 1981 they sent a courageous letter demanding answers, saying: 'We have presented every sort of appeal to judges, to civil and religious authorities. We have visited hospitals, children's homes, juvenile homes, religious orders. We have requested the revision of every adoption process carried out since 1976, and of late birth registrations.' They said they had concluded, based on the evidence of witnesses and on the four children who by then had been recovered, that 'the highest authorities in the land have access to information on the present whereabouts of each one of our grandchildren. … Many years of searching, of official silence, of evasive and senseless replies, have not weakened our integrity as women, as mothers and grandmothers. We will continue demanding the return of our grandchildren, as long as we live.'

Following the discovery of Anatole and Vicky in Chile, children began to be discovered in Argentina. The first was Paula Logares, who in 1978, aged two, had disappeared with her parents from their house in Montevideo.

The first news of the Logares' disappearance had come with a ring at my doorbell early one morning. On the doorstep stood a nervous young man who told me that a Uruguayan couple and their small daughter had been kidnapped in Montevideo a few days before. He gave me a photo of the family and a piece of paper with their names. Claudio Logares and Mónica Grinspon were Argentine militants who had fled across the River Plate to Uruguay to escape persecution but had been tracked down by the Argentine security forces.

Once again, fortuitous coincidences and solidarity played a role. Two years later in Buenos Aires, a young Uruguayan woman who worked in the home of a police agent overheard a noisy quarrel. 'You killed this child's parents and now you want me to look after her', shouted the policeman's wife. The child in question was four-year-old Paula.

Alarmed at what she had heard, the woman managed to steal a photo of the child and took it with her the next time she went to visit her family in Montevideo. There she showed it to the group of families of the disappeared. One of them was Angélica Julien, who took it with her the next time she travelled to São Paulo, and showed it to Jaime Wright. When Chicha arrived on her next visit, Jaime gave it to her to take back and show to the other grandmothers. One of them was Elsa Pavón, Paula's grandmother, who at first didn't think it was her granddaughter, but when she showed it to other family members, they decided it was.

On the back of the photo was the name and address of the police agent, Rubén Lavallen. Later the Abuelas discovered that he had worked at the clandestine detention camp located inside the San Justo Investigations Brigade, where Paula's parents had been taken.

Elsa lived in the suburb of Banfield, but she began travelling into the centre of Buenos Aires every day to stand watch outside the apartment building where the policeman lived, in the hope of seeing Paula.

One day she saw a little girl getting off a school bus. The girl had her back to Elsa, but Elsa thought that she walked in exactly the same way as Paula's mother, Mónica.

'I heard her saying "Mummy" to the woman who waited for her. That was painful', said Elsa.

Soon after that the family moved, and for two years Elsa did not know where to look for her granddaughter. Then the Abuelas received an anonymous tip-off, one of many they had begun to receive as the junta got more and more unpopular. The new address was a two-hour journey by train and bus from Elsa's home but she went there every day, to keep watch, pretending to buy fruit at the market in front of the building. Her family joined her in the vigils.

Eventually the Abuelas discovered that Paula had been registered with a birth date two years younger than the real one, which held her back at school, and that she was much smaller than she should have been for her real age. Although they were convinced that they had found Paula, the family and the Abuelas decided to wait until the military had left power before going to court to reclaim her.

In December 1983 President Raúl Alfonsín took office, putting an end to seven nightmare years. Now it was possible to go to court, although the Abuelas soon discovered that many judges were reluctant to order restitutions even when the evidence was clear. Lavallen and his wife insisted that Paula was their biological daughter and had been born at home, to explain the lack of hospital records.

But by now the Abuelas had a powerful weapon on their side, and Paula's was the first case in which it was used. This was the recently discovered Grandparenthood Index (Indice de Abuelismo), which offered a solution to the problem that had become more urgent as more children were discovered: how to identify children born in captivity or seized when they were very small. DNA testing had yet to be invented.

The question of how to conclusively identify their stolen grandchildren had begun to torment the grandmothers. Blood tests could prove that a child was not the biological child of the parents who claimed it as theirs, but how to prove that it belonged to those who were claiming it? The grandmothers went to see scientists in Sweden, France, and the US, meeting blank looks until they appealed to the director of the New York Blood Bank, who became interested in the problem. In May 1984, the American Society for the Advancement of Science held a symposium in New York to discuss the matter, bringing together geneticists and haematologists. They identified four components that provided genetic markers: blood groups, HLA or histocompatibility, serac proteins, and blood cell enzymes. Now, even without the parents, blood samples from the closest relatives, grandparents and uncles and aunts, were enough to prove a child's identity with 99.9 per cent certainty.

Lavallen and his wife refused to provide the blood samples that would show beyond any shadow of a doubt that Paula was not their daughter, but tests done with the Abuelismo Index showed that she was Elsa's granddaughter.

Even so, the judge hesitated to order the restitution, and Paula continued to live with her appropriators for another year. Only when the Abuelas appealed to a higher court was she finally handed back to her real family, a year after they had begun their case.

When Elsa took Paula back to the house where she had lived before she disappeared with her parents, she was eight years old, and six years had passed since she had been in the house. Even so, Elsa recounted, she instinctively climbed the stairs to her old room.

CHAPTER 10
The UN goes to Argentina

Three years after the coup in Argentina, when it was no longer possible to ignore the avalanche of denunciations about disappearances, the Organization of American States (OAS) sent a mission to investigate the situation.

When the seven members of the mission arrived in Buenos Aires in September 1979 for a two-week visit, they found themselves the target of a campaign secretly orchestrated by the junta to create a hostile atmosphere towards them. The day of their arrival was declared by the pro-government magazine *Cabildo* to be 'The National Day of Shame'. Cars circulated with stickers reading 'Los argentinos somos derechos y humanos' (We Argentines are correct and humane), a play on the words *derechos humanos*, or human rights. Some 250,000 of these stickers had been specially ordered and then distributed by the government, at a cost of over US$11,000.

The slogan had been thought up by American public relations company Burson-Marsteller, hired by the Argentine junta in 1978 to improve the government's image as the denunciations of forcible disappearances, clandestine detention camps, and mass executions piled up. By labelling the denunciations an 'anti-Argentina campaign' and printing the stickers on a background of the Argentine flag, they sought to cast the families and the human rights groups as traitors.

The junta had resisted the visit, authorized by an OAS motion the year before, for as long as it could. It should have happened in May, but this would have meant that the mission's report would be presented to the OAS annual general meeting in July 1979. By delaying the visit until September, the junta ensured that the report would only be examined and voted on a year later.

The aim of this manoeuvre was to prevent a negative report affecting the re-election chances of OAS secretary general Alejandro Orfila. An Argentine diplomat who came from the pro-junta oligarchy, Orfila was a key element in the government's diplomatic offensive to hide the truth of what was going on.

The junta took elaborate steps to prevent the mission members receiving information from the public. A month before they arrived, the police raided the offices of four human rights organizations that were preparing lists of the disappeared and of kidnappings, and copies of the testimonies of camp survivors, for the mission. Fortunately, the organizations were prepared and had kept copies of their documents in safe places.

A few days before the mission arrived, the military junta suddenly announced its solution to the problem of the disappeared. Anyone who had been declared missing within the last five years would be declared dead if they did not appear within the next three months, and even if the family opposed this. Once a disappeared person was officially declared dead, their families could no longer bring any legal action or habeas corpus petition to court.

The decree aroused a storm of criticism. Amnesty International pointed out that the decree 'failed to deal with the fundamental question of whether these people are still alive or have died. If they are alive, it is necessary to know where they are: if they have died, it is necessary to know where, when and in what circumstances they lost their lives and where their remains are buried.' Clamor said, 'The law not only justifies all the arbitrary acts committed by military governments but could also serve as a pretext for the assassination of those prisoners who have not yet been killed or of people who may still be detained.'

Two days before the OAS mission arrived, Clamor and other organizations held a special ecumenical service in Brazil to draw attention to the potential genocide of the estimated 12,000 disappeared, following the Argentine junta's cynical decree. The Church of the Consolation, in the centre of São Paulo, was packed with refugees, exiles, and those who wanted to show their solidarity. Dom Paulo preached a forceful sermon, comparing the tortures practised by the Argentine junta with the tortures of the Middle Ages. He said 'Tonight we want to proclaim our hope and our solidarity with the Argentine people. May this ecumenical mass be an opportunity for each one of us to promise to continue the fight for the respect of human rights.' A few days later, he received a letter from Cardinal Raúl Primatesta, head of the Argentina Episcopal Conference, criticizing his 'interference' in Argentine affairs.

The junta had obviously hoped that the new law declaring the disappeared to be dead, which came into effect on 12 September, would demobilize the families. But wherever the members of the OAS mission went, in Buenos Aires, Cordoba, or La Plata, thousands queued for hours to present their denunciations to the mission. Queues of sad but determined men and women stretched round the block, in stark contrast to the feel-good stickers on the cars and kiosks. Besides receiving the relatives, the seven members of the mission also interviewed authorities, visited prisons and cemeteries, and talked to members of political parties, unions, and human rights organizations.

Before leaving Argentina, the mission announced that the Argentine government had given guarantees that no reprisals would be taken against the individuals or organizations who had presented denunciations – but the junta did not keep its word. As soon as the mission left on 20 September, many people began receiving threats and either left the country or went into hiding.

In its *Bulletin* No. 9, Clamor told the story of a young Uruguayan who had helped the families of Uruguayans disappeared in Argentina to prepare their documents for the mission, and then himself had disappeared on the border between Brazil and Argentina on 21 October. Sigifredo Arostegui had come to

Brazil to print pamphlets with news of the OAS visit, and then caught a bus back to Buenos Aires, where he never arrived.

As soon as he heard the news of his son's disappearance, Sigifredo's father travelled to São Paulo from Montevideo and appealed to Clamor for help. Clamor decided to send lawyer Plauto Rocha with him to the frontier town, Foz do Iguaçu, where the bus would have crossed the border. There they discovered that Sigifredo's name was on the list of passengers entering Argentina, but as soon as the bus had crossed the border, he had been arrested by the police and taken off the bus.

They got a taxi to Puerto Iguazú, on the Argentine side of the frontier. When they inquired about Sigifredo at the border post, they were detained, put in a jeep, and driven to a naval barracks, surrounded by soldiers armed with machine guns. Questioned by an officer, Plauto produced the letter that Dom Paulo had given him, authorizing him to act on the archbishop's behalf. He also said that Sigifredo was a refugee under the protection of UNHCR. They were then told that Sigifredo was being detained in the town of Pousadas. Clamor asked the Swiss ambassador to grant him asylum, and after several months detention he was allowed to travel to Switzerland. Without Clamor's speedy intervention, it is very likely that Sigifredo would have become just another member of the disappeared.

In 1980, the OAS published its report on the mission to Argentina, concluding that between 1975 and 1979, 'numerous and grave violations of fundamental human rights' had been committed. The report made it clear that the Argentine junta's attempts to pull the wool over the mission's eyes and to harass and intimidate the human rights organizations had failed. The members of the mission had listened to hundreds of people and had read thousands of testimonies. The evidence about what had happened in Argentina was so detailed, so widespread, so huge, that they had no alternative but to issue a damning report.

Even so, they stopped short of placing the blame for the violations where it really belonged: on the shoulders of the highest authorities, the generals who had seized power and ruled by means of state terrorism. Secretary General Alejandro Orfila saw to that.

CHAPTER 11
The role of the Catholic Church

The year when Clamor began its work, 1978, was a time of turbulence in the Catholic Church. It became known as 'the year of the three popes'. Pope Paul VI, a sick man, died in August. Albino Luciano, the patriarch of Venice, was chosen to succeed him, and took the name John Paul I, although he also became known as the smiling pope. Thirty-three days later, he died unexpectedly, ending the shortest ever papacy. He was then succeeded in October by Karol Wojtyla, John Paul II, who died in 2005, after the longest papacy.

In *Clamor Bulletin* No. 4, published in December that year, the editorial 'Solidarity Has No Frontiers' asked: 'Will the church convert itself into the voice of all these families shouting their despair before governments, before the world?'

In Argentina, the answer was 'no'. When the Mothers and Grandmothers of Plaza de Mayo turned to the Catholic Church to help them find their missing children and grandchildren, they met a wall of silence, with a few notable exceptions. In some cases, there was obvious complicity with the regime. Grandmother Chicha appealed to Monsignor José Maria Montes, who had married her son, for help in finding her missing three-month-old granddaughter, Clara Anahí. Instead, he told her that the child was in good hands. 'Go and pray', he said.

Only a very small number of bishops and religious were prepared to defy the military and help the families. Without the support and protection of the Church hierarchy, some of them paid with their lives, including the two French nuns, Léonie Duquet and Alice Domon, of the Soeurs des Missions Etrangères, who had begun to work with the Madres. In December 1977 they were helping to prepare a full-page newspaper ad appealing to the government to reveal the whereabouts of the disappeared – but there was a spy in their midst. Pretending to be the brother of a disappeared woman, and using the false name of Gustavo Nino, naval officer Alfredo Astiz had infiltrated the group of mothers, gaining their trust in order to betray them. (Astiz later became famous during the Falklands War, when he surrendered the South Georgia Islands without a fight. The British government refused requests by human rights groups to put him on trial and handed him back). That same month the nuns were among 12 people, including several of the Madres, who were identified by Astiz and kidnapped, most of them from the Santa Cruz Church in Buenos Aires.

A few days later, on 15 December 1977, *La Nación* quoted the mother superior of the sisters' congregation in France, saying that the papal nuncio in Argentina had told her that the sisters had been detained but remained alive and in good health. Argentine TV showed what the government claimed was a video made by the Montoneros, who the authorities accused of the kidnapping. In early 1978 the mother superior, Marie Jo Catteau, went to Argentina in the hope of finding the sisters.

She said she met a 'wall of silence'. After three months she wrote, 'I have experienced what thousands of families have during their efforts to find news of their disappeared ones: "nothing is known". The families ask the government just one thing: to tell them where their disappeared ones are.'

While Catteau was in Argentina, a Swedish newspaper published a story about two mutilated bodies found on a beach that had been identified as those of the two nuns. But no confirmation of their identity had been sought from those who knew them, either families or colleagues, and the bodies were said to be wearing crosses and rosaries, which the two women never did.

Years later, survivors from the clandestine detention camp at ESMA described how the nuns had been taken there and savagely tortured. They were made to sign statements and write a letter to the head of their mission saying they had been kidnapped by the Montoneros. Days later they and the other members of the Madres group were put aboard a navy plane and thrown into the sea off the coast of Santa Teresita, on one of the regular death flights operated by the military.

As soon as the military took power, all the religious who belonged to the progressive Movement of Priests for the Third World became targets for elimination. Most of them worked in shanty towns. Three priests and two seminarists of the Pallottine Order from the parish of San Patricio, Buenos Aires, were murdered in the early hours of 4 July 1976, and a month later, on 4 August, Bishop Enrique Angelelli of La Rioja was killed in a faked car accident. A federal policeman, Rodolfo Fernández, who later fled to Brazil, told how all the documents which had been in the bishop's car at the time of the alleged 'accident' appeared almost immediately at the Ministry of the Interior. The minister of the interior, Albano Harguindeguy, took a special interest in the progressive clergy. A year later, another bishop, Ponce de Leon, was also killed in a suspicious car crash as he was on his way to deliver documents on the disappeared to the papal nuncio. Altogether, in the years immediately following the 1976 coup, at least 16 priests were killed or disappeared, besides the two French nuns.

The Church hierarchy looked the other way. Only a handful of bishops spoke out – such as Bishops Jorge Novak, Jaime de Nevares, Miguel Heslayne, and Vicente Zaspe – but at the meetings of CELAM, they were in a minority. Many of the other bishops knew what was going on in their dioceses but voted with the majority to say nothing. The papal nuncio, Pio Laghi, admitted to President Carter's secretary for human rights, Patricia Derian, that 'we know perfectly well everything that is happening all over the country [in terms of repression] because we have 6,000 priests distributed throughout the territory and we have chaplains in every military unit'.

Faced with the refusal of the Church hierarchy to intervene on their behalf, the Mothers and the Grandmothers, most of whom were devout Catholics, decided to appeal directly to Rome. At his inauguration, John Paul II had pointedly ignored General Jorge Videla and the other Latin American dictators who came to demonstrate their Catholic credentials – a promising sign.

Together with the families of the disappeared from all over the continent, who had created the Latin American Federation of Associations of Relatives of the Detained-Disappeared (Federación Latinoamericana de Asociaciones de Familiares de Detenidos-Desaparecidos, FEDEFAM), the Mothers and Grandmothers now saw the ten-yearly CELAM conference, to be held in Mexico, as a chance to get the attention of the new pope. Planned originally for October 1978, the Conference was postponed until January 1979 after the death of John Paul I. For the new pope, it meant making his first international trip to the most Catholic of all continents, a continent now dominated by dictators.

The families wanted the archbishop of São Paulo, Cardinal Arns, to be their spokesman in Puebla because of his reputation as a courageous defender of human rights. They hoped that the bishops would not only debate the situation in the countries where human rights were being so persistently violated, but vigorously condemn the regimes which were bringing death and terror to them in the name of Christianity. Right-wing totalitarian regimes had taken power in 11 countries of Latin America. The entire Southern Cone was under military rule. In most of these countries, the Catholic Church and Protestant churches like the Methodists were the only independent voices left, as every other organization of opposition had been closed down, banned, or eliminated.

Clamor described the situation: 'The Church has discovered, little by little, her true mission on this Latin American continent: to be the voice of those who cannot speak, either because of fear, or because of prison, or because of death.'

But even before the Conference began, Puebla had become a battleground between the progressive wing of the Church, which wanted to confirm the 'option for the poor' of the previous Medellín Conference in 1968, and the conservatives, who instead wanted to roll back what they called the 'ferment begun by Medellín'. Cardinal Agnelo Rossi, Dom Paulo's reactionary predecessor in São Paulo, said, 'The responsibility of Puebla is to put the Church back on the right track.'

Could the bishops, meeting in a continent so dominated by regimes of terror, ignore the reality around them? It seemed they could.

The final document referred to the situation in general terms, but the conservative majority blocked attempts to name specific countries. Dom Paulo failed to get approval for a document on torture. The groups of families of the disappeared who had come from Argentina to lobby the bishops and get a strong condemnation of the junta's activities went home empty-handed. What is more, one of their leaders, Thelma Jara de Cabezas, of the Argentine organization Families of the Detained and Disappeared for Political Reasons, was herself detained and disappeared soon after her return from Puebla to Buenos Aires.

Nine months later, during the papal sermon of the Angelus in St Peter's Square, John Paul II made a reference to the disappeared – and it did not go down well with the Argentine junta. On his return from Rome a few days later, leading churchman Cardinal Raúl Primatesta even tried to downplay the importance of it, saying that the pope's statement had been taken 'one-sidedly'.

Progressive bishops seized on the Papal words, however. The bishop of Viedma, Miguel Esteban Hesayne, proposed at the December meeting of CELAM that the bishops should give clear and definitive support to Pope John Paul II's unequivocal request for a solution to the case of the disappeared. Nothing happened.

A year later, on 30 August 1980, during another sermon in St Peter's Square, John Paul again returned to the theme of the disappeared and the lack of respect for human rights in certain Latin American countries, including Argentina.

Yet the Catholic hierarchy continued to ignore even the exhortations of the pope. In 1983, the Madres published a newspaper ad addressed to the CELAM conference. They had begun denouncing the detention and disappearance of their children in 1977, and they recalled that:

> In 1978, when we asked the Episcopal Assembly to intervene, the reply was silence. In 1979, when we implored their mediation, the reply was a lukewarm document. In 1980, when we demanded the appearance alive of the detained and disappeared, the Church proposed a dialogue. In 1981, when we insisted on all of our previous demands, the Church proposed reconciliation. In 1982, when we asked for the punishment of those responsible, the reply was to pardon. In 1983 we said: Neither silence nor documents nor dialogue nor reconciliation nor pardon.

But while Pope John Paul II acknowledged the existence of the disappeared and appealed for the families, he did not demand explanations for the murder and disappearance of Church members like Bishop Angelelli, the Pallottine priests, or the French nuns.

Emilio Mignone, a lawyer, human rights advocate, and founder member of the human rights organization the Centre for Legal and Social Studies (Centro de Estudios Legales y Sociales, CELS), became one of the most articulate critics of the Church's failure to take an active stand on behalf of the families. His daughter Monica was one of the disappeared, and he was in regular contact with Clamor. A devout Catholic, Mignone described the attempts to get the Church to take a position, especially after both Pope Paul VI and Pope John Paul II had made clear public references to the question of the disappeared. In his book *Witness to the Truth*, Mignone complained that 'instead of using these statements to back up their own efforts to influence the situation, most of the bishops downplayed them, or ignored them. ... In fact, many bishops were in explicit complicity with the terrorist dictatorship as is apparent in their own statements.'

This complicity was evident in some of the declarations of the Church's highest authorities. When interviewed by a foreign reporter, Cardinal Juan Aramburu, primate of the Argentine Catholic Church, denied the existence of mass graves containing the disappeared. He said, 'The disappeared? You mustn't confuse things. You know there are disappeared who are living peacefully in Europe today.'

In 1978, Argentina declared a state of war with Chile over the disputed Beagle Channel in the Antarctic. 'For many observers, the real reason for the dispute is the need to divert attention away from the country's real problems: the worsening economic situation, the divided military junta and the magnitude of the political repression', was the analysis of Clamor in its *Bulletin* No. 4. 'The defence of national sovereignty can be used to try and arouse popular support for an unpopular regime.'

Clamor also noted that war victims already existed – the thousands of Chileans living in Patagonia who were being ruthlessly expelled, allegedly for lack of documents. 'They are detained in midnight roundups and taken in trucks to be dumped on the frontier, with just the clothes they are wearing. All the fruits of their labour – homes, furniture, clothes – and often even their families, are left behind, especially when the wife is Argentinian.'

The fact that from early January 1979 the pope was a mediator in the territorial dispute between Argentina and Chile possibly inhibited him from being more forthright about human rights abuses in both countries. A group of Catholics sent the pope a message criticizing his decision to mediate the dispute, because while the aim of the Vatican intervention was to avoid bloodshed, 'it should be remembered that thousands of citizens in Argentina and Chile have been killed, have disappeared, or been tortured, with the agreement of their governments, during the last two years'. They noted that no Vatican mission comparable to that sent by the pope to try to resolve the Beagle dispute had been sent to address human rights abuses in the two countries. 'This silence, which the ordinary Christians of our countries interpret as support for these regimes that despotically defy God's plan, is a counter witness attributed directly to your Holiness.'

Emilio Mignone came to the conclusion that in spite of his public declarations, Pope John Paul II never really understood, or had not wanted to understand, the peculiar case of the detained and disappeared in Argentina, who were eliminated by state terrorism.

When the pope came to Brazil in July 1980 for a 12-day visit, the Madres and Abuelas saw it as another chance to get the pontiff's ear. In São Paulo, Dom Paulo was unable to arrange a direct meeting for them but conveyed a letter from the Madres. In Porto Alegre they had better luck, and a group of them had a meeting with the pope on 5 July thanks to the good offices of

Cardinal Vicente Scherer, the archbishop. The pope listened to them, held their hands, and told them to have faith, patience, and hope.

When the pope visited Argentina in 1982, there was no meeting with the human rights organizations. In the plane on the way back to Rome, he told reporters, who asked him if the question of the disappeared had been raised, that he understood things had improved, and said, 'Now they try to give answers, whereas previously they didn't.'

While the Argentine Catholic hierarchy avoided the question of the disappeared, the Nobel Committee in Norway recognized it by awarding the 1980 Peace Prize to former political prisoner and human rights campaigner Adolfo Pérez Esquivel, who worked with the families of the disappeared. Esquivel was president of SERPAJ, an ecumenical organization supported by the WCC. He had been arrested in April 1976, tortured, and held for 15 months. Worldwide pressure from those who knew his work with non-violent movements throughout Latin America led to his release on the last day of the World Cup in Argentina, in July 1978.

The decision to award the Nobel Peace Prize to Esquivel was an embarrassment not only for the Argentine military, but also for the Argentine Catholic Church. Instead of celebrating the award, CELAM put out a statement denying that SERPAJ had anything to do with the Conference's own Justice and Peace Commission. What was even more galling for both bishops and generals was the recent decision of the junta to pay a generous pension to any Argentine who won a Nobel Prize, in the expectation that writer Jorge Luis Borges would carry off the Nobel Prize in Literature.

The following year, 1981, Nobel Peace Prize winner Esquivel was arrested when he arrived in São Paulo to take part in a seminar led by Dom Paulo. He was taken to a police station, but was released after the cardinal interceded on his behalf.

This was not the first time Esquivel had been arrested in Brazil. In 1975 he was detained and interrogated by military officers, with a hood over his head, and only released after Dom Paulo's intervention. For Esquivel, it was a vivid illustration of the difference between the Church hierarchies in Argentina and Brazil. 'Dom Paulo saved me twice', he later told the press.

CHAPTER 12
The defectors

In July 1980, a slight young man with fair hair arrived in São Paulo. He looked unremarkable, but in his suitcase he carried documents and photos that would blow wide open the official story about the kidnapping of the Uruguayans in Porto Alegre a year and a half earlier (see Chapter 7). Hugo García Rivas, a military photographer with the Uruguayan army's Coordinating Organization for Anti-Subversive Operations (Organismo Coordinador de Operaciones Antisubversivas, OCOA), had decided to defect and reveal the true story behind the operation to capture Uruguayan dissidents in Brazil and take them over the border by force.

The operation, codenamed Operación Sapato Roto by the Uruguayans, was described in detail in *Clamor Bulletin* No. 10, published in August 1980. It was carried out with full support from the Brazilian security forces, particularly the DOPS of Porto Alegre. Rivas gave the names of the Uruguayan officers who had taken part and revealed that they maintained permanent contact with the Brazilian police by telex, using a code mixing letters and numbers. He said that Lilián Celiberti had been tortured in a place called Santa Teresa, normally used by Brazilian army officers for their summer holidays. He also described in detail his work with OCOA, also known as the Company. He made statements to the MJDH in Porto Alegre and to Clamor and the Association of Latin American Lawyers (Associação de Advogados Latinoamericanos, AALA) in São Paulo.

Rivas served in the Company from 1976 to the end of 1979. He worked as a photographer but also carried out surveillance in the street, following those believed to be conspiring against the government or those accused of belonging to the Communist Party. He said the Company was set up after a group of officers had begun planning a counter-coup to return the country to civilian rule. The group was discovered and wiped out, and the Company was created to detect any other attempts at rebellion within the armed forces.

In statements given to Clamor and AALA and published in *Clamor Bulletin* No. 10, Rivas explained:

> When detained, a person was interrogated to obtain information, to see if they had links with extremist or left-wing groups.

> They were always interrogated with different types of torture, but the most common type was the *tacho* or *submarino*. The *tacho* is a barrel cut in half and filled with water, the person is tied to

a plank and his head dipped into the water until he makes some sort of a sign that he will answer the questions. Sometimes they are naked, sometimes not. Nobody died during the *submarino* but I know of someone who died during torture. Humberto Pascaletti was a worker at the paper factory in Montevideo, he was accused of sabotaging their machinery with another three people. Pascaletti had an ulcer, he had to take medicine for it, but they refused to let him take his pills, and that, added to the beating they gave him, ended in his death. This was at the beginning of 1977.

Other torture techniques were hanging a person from a hook in the ceiling with their hands tied behind their backs, men and women. They are left there till they talk or [the torturers] are convinced the person has nothing to say. If the person faints, he is revived and then hung up again.

[Another torture is] placing needles under fingernails, it is very painful. [Another is] the *planton*, being made to stand for hours.

Many became ill after torture, they couldn't resist any more, they were allowed to recover a bit, then the torture began again. A couple of military doctors were on call. Some became delirious, said things that made no sense, but I don't know of anyone going mad. When it was realised nothing more could be got out of them, they were transferred to other army centres. If I saw photos of [the prisoners] I could recognise them.

I never took pictures of people being tortured, I don't think anyone did, it would be proof of torture. Children were never ill-treated, Lilián's children were well looked after.

We asked Rivas if he himself had participated in torture. He said:

Yes, I did, I felt good, I wasn't aware of what I was doing, and I had to do it, because if I refused they would arrest me too. I don't know any cases of soldiers who refused to torture, they all knew that if they refused they would be arrested. We tried not to be available when they wanted us to participate. Our superior officer wanted everyone to take part in torture. We had to obey otherwise we were going against the Military Penal Code.

I volunteered for the Army, I didn't know what intelligence involved, what they did in the Company, then I was called to serve in it, by the time I learned, I was in it, I had no idea that people were detained and tortured like this in the Army.

After a while I became convinced I must leave, I couldn't go on doing this. I began to feel sorry for the prisoners. I felt that people didn't deserve this treatment just because they joined a group working against the government, for example members of the Communist Party, generally they hadn't used arms, they hadn't practised crimes. Or people who had just stuck a poster on a wall, who were tortured till they were 'between life and death'.

We were torturing not people who belonged to armed groups but people who had different ideas – even people who had just been seen picking up a pamphlet with anti-government propaganda.

Plainclothes police in the street listened in to what people were saying, in any place where there were a lot of people, they followed people who they had heard saying something, then watched them to see if they had contact with others.

Rivas said his wife had a cousin who was arrested and tortured, and when he later died an agent was sent to the wake to listen in to what the family said. 'Many of my companions feel the same way, but they are afraid to leave.'

Rivas recalled an intelligence course at the Army School of Intelligence, located in a building on the same street as the Company, where operatives were taught torture techniques. It was a three-month course on surveillance techniques, disguises, how to invade homes – always in the early hours, because people are more likely to be at home and there are less likely to be witnesses, and always dressed in civilian clothes, not identifiable as members of the army. 'The military teach them that any group not in agreement with the government is subversive, that Amnesty International is just a bunch of foreign left-wingers who criticize Uruguay because it is anti-communist. The campaign against torture is just to undermine Uruguay.'

During the course, Rivas said, they were given lessons in torture, using instruments and prisoners, usually somebody who had already confessed or had nothing to confess, both men and women. The students had to practise as well.

Rivas continued: 'There were ten or eleven in the class, when it was officers there were twenty to twenty-five. They came from all the armed forces and the police force. Some were foreigners, Chileans, Paraguayans, Salvadoreans, Guatemalans, Venezuelans. Mostly they were Paraguayans and Salvadoreans.' Rivas said that he never saw Brazilians.

'The instructors were usually Uruguayans but when I did the course one session was conducted by a foreigner, we reckoned he was an American, because of his accent, but we never knew his name so I don't know if that is true.'

Rivas' work was taking photographs, sometimes for making false documents for a prisoner who had been arrested, in order to justify his arrest for possessing false documents. He also took photographs to make false identity papers for officers, and they were kept in a safe in the Technical Section.

The Russian embassy was watched, and this surveillance was financed by the Americans.

> Foreign journalists, including Brazilian journalists, and the visit by the [OAB] lawyers, they were followed right from their arrival. There was no time to tap their phones because their visit was very sudden. But Lilián's mother's phone was tapped, and her house watched. [The Company was] always warned by someone in Porto Alegre, I suppose DOPS. They had close relationships after the kidnapping.

Rivas provided the names of all those who had taken part in the kidnapping of Lilián Celiberti and Universindo Díaz. His defection was arranged by the PVP after lengthy negotiations. He arrived in Porto Alegre in May 1980, and was questioned by Jair Krischke of the MJDH, to check that he was genuine – but he was a very hot potato and Krischke was worried about his safety in Porto Alegre, where the Uruguayans had already demonstrated that they had close connections with the Brazilian secret police, DOPS.

As soon as possible, the MJDH sent Rivas up to São Paulo so that we could arrange to get him out of Brazil. He was not alone; he had brought his wife and their small daughter with him. When they arrived in early May I booked them into a discreet hotel in Rua Timbiras, called the Lord Hotel, near the rather run-down city centre.

We began debriefing Rivas at the office of the AALA president, lawyer Belisário dos Santos Junior. There were long question and answer sessions, counting on the expert knowledge of the PVP's Maria. At the same time, we worried about how we were going to get Rivas out of the country. As a self-confessed torturer, he was not eligible for UNHCR status as a political refugee. In addition, he and his wife had fled Uruguay carrying only their identity cards, without passports, and the little girl had no documentation, just a note on their marriage certificate.

By now May had turned into June, and the fear of the security services catching up with Rivas grew greater every day. We decided to approach the Norwegians, who up until then had taken only a handful of Latin American refugees, while their Scandinavian neighbour, Sweden, had accepted thousands.

Belisário and I flew up to Brasília for an interview with the Norwegian ambassador. He listened to us sympathetically and promised to help.

He was as good as his word, and soon we were told that Rivas would be given a visa and asylum in Norway. We called a press conference for 12 June, calculating that by the time the story was published, he would be safely on his way to Europe with his family, aboard a Scandinavian Airlines flight.

That left just two problems – somebody had to go to the Norwegian consulate in Rio to pick up the temporary passports with the visas, and then obtain an exit visa from the Federal Police, timing it for the day before the flight so as to give no time for suspicions to be aroused or deductions to be made.

I volunteered to go to Rio. I got a shuttle flight, arriving at the consulate in Glória at 3.30 p.m. The consul had been briefed and had everything ready. I jumped into a taxi and we sped to the Federal Police HQ just behind Praça Maua, arriving just as the large iron and glass door was being firmly closed by a burly policeman who said, 'It's 4 o'clock, we are closing.' I cannot remember what I said, but I gave him my best smile, and I was in. Inside, a crowd of people were standing in front of a counter, anxious, impatient, gesticulating. I found a space, thrust out the passports, and mumbled some story, and a harassed official stamped the exit visas. Exultant, I hurried to Santos Dumont Airport, not far away, and flew back to São Paulo. Now it was plain sailing. The next day, we would drive Rivas and his wife and child to Viracopos, put them on the plane, and that would be that.

Instead, it turned into a nightmare. In the morning I rang Rivas at the Lord Hotel to tell him what time we would pick him up. There was no answer. I rang several times, getting more and more nervous. No answer. Where was he? Had he been tracked down? I didn't dare to go to the hotel in case it was being watched. I went to a fruit juice bar for a calming drink of maracuja, but I was so nervous I couldn't remember how to say it. 'Marucaju ... mm ... marucuja', I stuttered.

I rang the hotel again. This time Rivas answered, but now he was the one who was nervous. His wife had gone out shopping hours ago and had not returned.

To get to the airport at Viracopos, over an hour's drive away, in time to catch the plane, we would have to leave immediately. I rang Belisário and we decided that we would go ahead with Rivas, by taxi, and his colleague Iberê Bandeira de Mello would follow as soon as the wife turned up at the hotel. The taxi raced along the motorway to the airport. Rivas checked in and we sat down to wait for the others, who would be bringing his luggage. All he had with him was a plastic bag full of what I assumed were clean shirts.

The last call came and there was no sign of them. Rivas was in a state, understandably reluctant to travel without his wife and child. But we knew he had to get the flight because next day the newspapers would be full of his story, revealed at a press conference the day before. We practically frogmarched him to the departure gate, insisting that he took the plastic bag with him (later I learned that it contained disposable nappies, not shirts).

No sooner had the flight taken off with Rivas on board than a Kombi drew up outside the airport with a screech of brakes. A dishevelled Iberê, followed by Rivas' frantic wife and crying child, tumbled out. The Kombi had got a flat tyre, and it had taken ages to change it.

We booked them another flight for the next day. No shopping trips were allowed, they arrived at the airport on time, and she flew to Norway to join her husband.

The papers gave ample coverage to Rivas' story. He said that the Uruguayan military had expected that DOPS would prevent the case from being reported by the Brazilian press. He said this coverage had saved the lives of Lilián and Universindo, who had begun to be tortured when still in Brazil.

The *Folha de São Paulo* published an editorial saying, 'The participation of DOPS of Porto Alegre and members of the Brazilian Federal Police in the operation to kidnap the Uruguayan couple Lilián Celiberti and Universindo Díaz in Porto Alegre and remove them to Montevideo is irrefutable.'

Rivas' confessions were not reported in the Uruguayan press, but people learned about them from Brazilian papers, from the international press, and from foreign radio stations like the BBC. Coming just before the plebiscite in October, they probably had some effect on the vote which overwhelmingly rejected the military's constitution.

In September that year, Rivas' father and nine members of his family also fled to Brazil and asked UNHCR for asylum. The father claimed he was under pressure in Uruguay to reveal his son's address in Norway.

Five months after Hugo Rivas had arrived in Brazil, another Uruguayan defector appeared in São Paulo. Daniel Rey Piuma was a 22-year-old ex-naval recruit who brought with him horrifying photographs of bodies that had been washed up along the Uruguayan coast. They were bloated after days or weeks in the sea, which gave them a faintly oriental look, and the newspapers speculated that they were Chinese seamen, the victims of violence on board a ship. The testimony from Rey Piuma that they were the victims of violence, thrown into the sea from planes by the Argentine security forces, was hidden from the press.

Piuma obtained UNHCR protection as a political refugee soon after his arrival in October. Unlike Rivas, he never took part in torture, although he witnessed it. In a preliminary statement to the International Secretariat of Jurists for Amnesty in Uruguay (Secretariado Internacional de Juristas por la Amnistía en Uruguay, SIJAU), AALA, and Clamor, he said he had tried to help the political prisoners who were detained by the Port Authority's Intelligence Division. He fled Uruguay after his contact with the prisoners was discovered, and he was threatened with and submitted to a disciplinary tribunal. He asked to be dismissed from the navy. His request was refused, and his movements were then controlled. His parents' house was being watched.

Piuma said that bodies had begun to appear in the River Plate in 1976. 'About 50 bodies appeared floating in the waters of the River Plate, near the coast at Rocha and Maldonaldo. The armed forces immediately burnt the bodies which showed their haste to hide them as soon as possible and a communiqué was issued saying they had Asiatic features.'

Piuma recalled that he went to work for the Port Authority in 1977, and had access to confidential archives because he had done courses in classified intelligence. The Intelligence Archives documented the bodies that had appeared over a period of nearly four years between 1976 and 1979; most had appeared in 1976 and 1977. All shared similar injuries except those of 1979, whose heads had been burnt with a blowtorch. There was also a girl of about 20 whose left breast had been burnt with a blowtorch. Others had hands and feet tied, signs of violence, open fractures. In some there were bullet holes, in others cuts in muscles and caved-in skulls; some showed signs of rape.

At the end of 1979, and in 1980, remains of bones also appeared, churned up by dredges. 'The quantity of bodies buried in the waters of the River Plate is probably greater', Piuma said. The bodies appeared always in April, May, and June, carried down the Uruguayan coast by a tidal phenomenon that brings the waters from upstream.

Piuma said there had been several clues to the origin of the bodies. An Argentine ID was found on one, in the name of María Cristina Cámpora. Another had an Argentine coin in its pocket, while on others there were remnants of clothes with labels reading 'Industria Argentina'. They had no rings or watches.

Fingerprints were taken where possible, but some bodies had been in the sea for a long time, which made it very difficult.

The cases of the unclaimed bodies in the water were submitted to a judge as cases of murder. Information available was hidden or falsified, the photographs held by the intelligence services were withheld, and the data about the tides was never submitted. The bodies never received proper autopsies. Afterwards, they were cremated.

'The first bodies had been shown on TV but that was when they didn't know who they were', Piuma explained. 'When they began to suspect that they were tortured Argentine political prisoners they never showed them again.'

The Argentine Port Authority was informed, but denied any knowledge of the bodies. Piuma recalled:

> Once an Argentine army corporal called Victor Peña got drunk during a trip to Uruguay during the 1978 World Cup, and said that they killed people, took them up in helicopters and threw them into the river Paraná, tied up, with weights on their bodies. Victor Peña said that once they were told to suspend the torture because they were killing too many people. They were interrogating them until they died. They had 'exaggerated' like this with over 100 people, who had nothing to do with anything.

Piuma said that the Argentines and Uruguayans had exchanged lists of wanted people: 'The Uruguayans had lists of all the left-wing Argentine groups, like the Peronistas.' He recalled that he had sometimes heard the screams of the tortured, and had seen people being tortured when the room being used for torture was next to the bathrooms used by the service personnel.

In January 1983, a defector from Argentina arrived in São Paulo. Rodolfo Peregrino Fernández was 32 years old and had served in his country's Federal Police between 1969 and 1977. From 1976 he was a member of the security detail for the minister of the interior, General Albano Harguindeguy. This unit also coordinated contacts between the Ministry of the Interior and the armed forces and security agencies charged with the fight against subversion.

Fernández said that he began to have problems with his fellow officers, fundamentally for reasons of professional ethics and differences over the reach of the police function. As a result, he asked to be transferred, and in revenge, he claimed, he was accused of fraud. Fearing for his life, he went into hiding. When his case came to court, he was acquitted. He then fled to Brazil.

When Fernández was questioned in January 1983 by members of Clamor, AALA, and the PVP in Brazil, he asked that his statement not be given to the press but be sent only to Amnesty International, for that organization's confidential use.

Fernández described the power structure and the organization of the fight against subversion in Argentina. Members of the abduction task forces, known as *patotas*, or 'gangs', carried out their illegal detentions, wearing plain clothes, and often wigs and false moustaches. They acted with a certain amount of autonomy, but all the details of the previous day's operations – the kidnappings, the interrogations, the information given by the prisoners – were included in top secret confidential briefings prepared by the Secretariat of State Intelligence (Secretaría de Inteligencia del Estado, SIDE), for the eyes of the high command, including General Videla and other members of the junta, alone. After reading, they had to be destroyed immediately.

The order was to leave no one who had taken part in urban guerrilla movements alive. In the factories, orthodox Peronistas were not troubled; the target was those workers who belonged to the 'combative' sections of the trade unions.

Fernández said that General Harguindeguy was especially interested in the Catholic Church. The Ministry of the Interior had an archive with the names of 300 priests who belonged to the progressive Third World movement. When Bishop Angelelli was killed in an alleged car accident in 1976, Fernández said: 'What attracted my attention was that all the documents which the bishop was carrying when he died arrived at the Ministry, including a series of letters which he exchanged with Monsignor Zaspe, the Archbishop of Santá Fé.' Documents which had belonged to two Pallottine priests, who were killed in 1976, also arrived at the Ministry, including a notebook with telephone contacts of one of them. 'The division which exists in the Argentine Church between the so-called progressive and conservative Church is well-known, and surveillance is kept on the so-called Third World priests. Relations between the military government and the leaders of the conservative Church have always been extremely cordial.'

When asked about the destination of the disappeared, Fernández said he knew of the death flights organized by the navy, when prisoners were thrown into the sea. He said he had heard that once a prisoner who was about to be thrown to his death clutched at the naval officer who was pushing him out of the plane and pulled the officer with him. He said that the dead who were cremated in cemeteries were described as killed in combat. Collaborators might be kept alive for two or three years, but then they were also killed.

Asked about the fate of the children who had disappeared or were born in captivity, Fernández said that the Federal Police had a special place for these children, run by Sub-commissioner Acosta of the Provincial Federal Police. Children who were too young to talk were handed back to their grandparents. Some children were placed in orphanages.

Fernández believed that only 10 per cent of the federal police and even less of the army took part in the 'dirty war'. Cars and houses were stolen from the disappeared, who were made to sign documents transferring their ownership.

As a former member of the forces of repression, Fernández was not eligible for UNHCR refugee status. Jaime Wright contacted one of the Dutch Protestant church organizations that supported Clamor, and they agreed to help. We saw him off at Congonhas airport on a flight to Amsterdam, where he would be met and immediately ask for asylum.

A few weeks later, Fernandez gave evidence to CADHU, an NGO based in Geneva. In this statement he also described the preparations for the 1976 coup, the links between the army and the Triple A (the Argentine Anti-Communist Alliance), the methods used to prevent the judicial system from being effective, and corruption in the armed forces.

Although the number of former members of the armed forces who felt the need to defect and tell what they knew was relatively small, they provided invaluable corroboration of the information supplied by refugees, exiles, and the families of the disappeared and political prisoners in Argentina and Uruguay.

CHAPTER 13
A bloody coup in Bolivia

With so much going on elsewhere, Clamor had hardly registered what was happening in Bolivia, a country not normally considered part of the Southern Cone. That changed on 17 July 1980, when the Bolivian armed forces, aided and abetted by the Argentine junta, staged a well-planned coup to prevent Hernán Siles Zuazo, who had just won the presidential elections running for an alliance of centre and left-wing parties, from taking power. Interim president Lidia Gueiler was ousted and a wave of terror was unleashed, with mass arrests, killings, and censorship. Besides the left-wing parties, trade unions, and popular movements, the media and the churches were targeted. Catholic radio stations were closed down, and priests and Protestant ministers were arrested.

A few days after the coup, the WCC's Chuck Harper called Clamor and asked if we could send somebody to find out what was happening and to convey solidarity from the outside world to the beleaguered Churches, both Catholic and Protestant. As the only person available, it was decided that I should go.

Just six days after the coup had taken place, I boarded the daily Lloyd Aéreo Boliviana flight from São Paulo to La Paz. It took off seven hours late, which meant that we had to land and spend the night in the city of Santa Cruz, because an all-night curfew was in place in La Paz. At Santa Cruz Airport, there were soldiers everywhere. We were searched and our names checked against a list before we were taken to a hotel. The next morning, we flew up and over the mountains to La Paz, which sits on the Andean plateau and is one of the highest cities in the world.

I lost no time in going to the office of Archbishop Jorge Manrique Hurtado to convey the messages of solidarity from the WCC and from Dom Paulo. The archbishop was deeply appreciative and immediately wrote out a communiqué to all parish priests, religious communities, and Catholic institutions, advising them of the visit of an envoy sent by Dom Paulo Evaristo Arns and the WCC. In their beleaguered situation, the knowledge that the outside world was concerned about their plight and wanted to help was an important ray of hope.

While I was in La Paz, I had three meetings with the archbishop. He supplied me with lists of people who had been detained, killed, or disappeared, with details of the raids on religious radio stations, and with general information about the repression. A committee of four priests had been set up to visit prisoners.

Both the Catholic and Methodist Churches denounced the violent repression unleashed by the military. Although Bolivia was no stranger to coups – over 180 in its 160 years of independence – and had recently lived for seven years under the dictatorship of General Hugo Banzer (1971–78), this one was different in several ways. Not only was the violence much more extreme, but the Church was one of the main targets. Churches, priests' houses, and schools were invaded, radio stations were closed down and sometimes physically smashed up, and around 30 priests, ministers, and religious workers were detained. A campaign of slander and lies was launched against churchmen and churchwomen, calling them 'reds', 'communists', and 'extremists'.

The coup had its origins in the events of the previous November, when Colonel Alberto Natusch Busch had seized power but was quickly forced out after widespread popular resistance, including a general strike led by the powerful trade union organization the Bolivian Workers' Federation (Central Obrero Boliviano, COB). After 16 days, Busch handed over power to an interim president, the Chamber of Deputies leader Lidia Gueiler, who called general elections.

What made this coup different from previous ones was the participation of military advisers from Argentina, and the use of paramilitaries to carry out repression. The popular movements, unions, and left-wing political parties had formed an alliance to protect democracy, called the National Committee for the Defence of Democracy (Comité Nacional de Defensa de la Democracia, CONADE), and as soon as the coup was announced on 17 July, they gathered to discuss resistance at the COB union building, located in the centre of La Paz. The building was surrounded by paramilitary gangs who burst in and shot dead Marcelo Quiroga, leader of the Socialist Party, although he was unarmed and had his hands up. The others, including COB leader Juan Lechin, were arrested.

The coup was not unexpected. It came not, as the military claimed, in reaction to electoral fraud, which was non-existent, but as the final act in a plan to retake power. It was preceded by months of violent acts by right-wing forces, aimed at disrupting the democratic process.

These began on 22 March with the assassination of Jesuit priest Luís Espinal, the well-known editor of the weekly newsletter *Aquí*, after he was kidnapped and savagely tortured. The paper's offices were destroyed by a bomb.

The Democratic and Popular Union, the moderate centre-left alliance that had won the election, was targeted with assassination attempts. A plane crash killed three leading members of the party, leaving the vice-presidential candidate, Jaime Paz Zamora, with serious burns. Hernán Siles Zuazo, the presidential candidate, survived a bomb attack that killed four people. The offices of unions and peasant organizations in different regions of Bolivia were attacked with bombs and dynamite.

It was in reply to these attempts to sabotage the elections, and the growing threat of another right-wing army coup, that unions, political parties, and social movements had set up CONADE. They planned to resist any coup attempts with the same methods that had foiled Natusch Busch – that is, a general strike and road blockades.

The day after the coup, the archbishop of La Paz issued an exhortation condemning it in the strongest terms. He said that many citizens had been detained and were incommunicado, including several religious and priests, and the whereabouts of some of them were unknown. He wrote:

> The church radio stations Fides and San Gabriel have been attacked and the equipment and installations at Fides were brutally destroyed and their directors and journalists have been detained. The Catholic newspaper *Presencia* has been occupied by armed men. A convent was invaded by military forces, who then withdrew. The lack of freedom of the media keeps the country in a fearful silence, and we lack full information about events.

The archbishop demanded the release of those detained without charge, the payment of reparations for the damage to Church radio stations, freedom to broadcast, and an end to the occupation of the *Presencia* newspaper. He also protested at the use of ambulances by armed military forces for repression instead of humanitarian missions.

The military concocted a fake version of the archbishop's exhortation, which they printed and distributed, inserting phrases to make it seem as though the Catholic Church not only supported the coup, but admitted that Marxism had corrupted the Church.

La Paz, deprived of news by military censorship, seethed with rumours. Many had gone into hiding or fled the country. Nobody knew what was happening in the big tin mines to the south, where thousands of men belonged to highly organized unions. In the capital, the COB building was now occupied by the military, who claimed that the miners had stopped their resistance and were supporting the coup. It seemed unlikely – but there was no way of knowing.

With other journalists, I decided that the only way to find out was to go to the mining zone, several hours' journey across the Altiplano. The foyer of the Hotel La Paz, where most of the foreign press was staying, had become our HQ. About a dozen reporters decided to set off the next morning in a hired van, but at the appointed hour, only three of us turned up: myself, Ray Bonner of the *New York Times*, and Tim Ross of CBS. The others had been warned by their embassies not to go because it was too dangerous.

Instead of a van, we hired a taxi and set off. By the time we got to Oruro, it was dark and the curfew was about to begin, so we found a cheap hotel, had dinner, and went to bed early, as there was nothing else to do. It was bitterly cold. The next day we drove in the direction of Siglo XX, Bolivia's biggest tin mine. We were stopped at a military blockade, manned by Army Rangers, who told us that we were entering a military zone and could not continue.

We turned back to Oruro. Our taxi driver said, 'Why don't you visit the San José mine? It's right here in Oruro.'

The mine was on the outskirts of the town. A lot of miners were hanging around, and when we said we wanted to speak to the union leaders, they took us inside the mine entrance. We thought they were taking us to a room, but suddenly we found ourselves standing on a tiny open platform that was hurtling 1,000 feet down into the depths of the mine. We were too surprised to panic. When we reached the bottom and staggered out, we found ourselves in an underground tunnel. A small shrine to 'El Tio', the devil god who protects miners, contained offerings of *pinga* and coca leaves. Inside a tiny room, hewn out of the rock face, sat the secretary general of the miners' union, who had narrowly escaped a machine-gun attack by local paramilitaries. After a guarantee of no reprisals if they went back to work, the assassination attempt had brought them out on strike. Sixty miners now occupied the underground galleries, living on coca leaves, cigarettes, and whatever food was sent down from above ground.

The union official told us that the entire mining district had gone on strike against the coup, but there had been fighting and many had been killed at other mines, like Huanuni and Catavi. He gave us a list of dead and wounded, and a rations box which had 'Ejército Argentino' printed on the side – proof of Argentina's support of the coup.

Later we learned that at the big Siglo XX mine, they had decided to resist the coup, organizing strike committees. Housewives had organized food distribution, and Bolivian flags fluttered everywhere. Thousands of peasants from the nearby mountains had joined the miners, bringing with them old weapons – Second World War rifles – and building roadblocks. There was a great atmosphere of solidarity. Radio Pio XII, run by the Oblate fathers, joined a 'democracy chain' with other radio stations from mining towns, in opposition to the 'national chain' imposed by the junta on radio stations in the cities to transmit their propaganda.

The miners and their families made banners reading 'Soldier, don't kill your brothers'. Many soldiers deserted and joined them. Helicopters and planes flew overhead, scattering propaganda pamphlets and sometimes machine-gunning houses.

Campesinos (farmers) decided to attack the army barracks in Catavi, not far from Siglo XX. The battle lasted all night and ended with the peasants occupying and looting the barracks.

Next day a meeting was called between the army authorities, the miners, and the Radio Pio XII priests. The military demanded the surrender of all weapons, the closing of the radio station, and a return to work. When this proposal was put to the miners' assembly, it was refused and the strike continued.

But the miners' old rifles were no match for the machine guns, tanks, planes, and bombs of the armed forces, and the strike was crushed, with the loss of many lives. In the Catavi mining area, 20 were reported killed. In Siglo XX, women and children had been killed, gunned down on the streets or in their homes. An eyewitness reported what happened in Caracoles, one of the mining villages that tried to resist the coup, on 4 August 1980.

> To crush their resistance, the Army surrounded the mining districts and invaded the villages, killing, wounding and taking hundreds of prisoners. In the Caracoles district, at four o'clock in the afternoon about 400 soldiers descended from the mountains onto the village of Villa El Carmen. They looted everything they found. They raped the women. They stole money, kitchen articles, clothes, furniture.
>
> ... [M]any miners and their leaders remained hidden in the mountains for several days. In the mining villages all was desolation and fear. During the night military lorries shone their lights on the houses, shooting at the slightest suspicious sound. A group of young men was forced to dig a big ditch behind the cemetery of Villa El Carmen to bury the dead.

Bolivia Libre, an underground newspaper, later reported that 3000 miners had died fighting or had been killed in the days following the coup.

At the end of our interview in the depths of the mine, the miners who had gathered to listen sang *Viva Bolivia*, a patriotic song, with great emotion.

After an hour underground, we squeezed onto the tiny platform and returned to the surface, clutching our cameras and tape recorders with their precious contents, elated at what we had obtained. As we climbed into our waiting taxi, a small man appeared, identified himself as a police informer, and told the driver to head for the military barracks. We could do nothing – but under the cover of the poncho I was wearing I removed the tape from my recorder and hid it in my boot, replacing it with a blank tape.

At the barracks we were taken to the room of a colonel, who already knew exactly where we had been and shouted at us for talking to 'subversivos'. Obviously there were informers inside the mine as well as outside. All our equipment was confiscated, but we were told we could get it back the next day at the Miraflores military HQ in La Paz. The two men were searched, but because there was no woman to do it, I was not, so my tape was not found.

After a couple of hours, we were released and told to drive straight back to the capital. As our taxi was leaving Oruro, it was stopped by paramilitaries with guns. They squeezed into the taxi with us and ordered the driver to turn round and go to a police station. There, we were shoved into a bare room. Inside was a *chola*, a peasant woman, whose face was bruised. None of us spoke; we were all too scared. After a while, we were told there had been a mistake and that we were cleared to go.

Back in La Paz, we shared our dramatic news with the other reporters. The next morning, I called the British Embassy and asked for someone to go with us to Miraflores.

Accompanied by a diplomat, we presented ourselves at the barracks. Inside, a row of people, old and young, were lined up against a wall with their hands on their heads. I described the scene at the barracks in the special *Clamor Bulletin* on Bolivia:

> Dozens of new ambulances, without number plates, were parked in the internal courtyard. There were over 50 of them with the letters CNSS [Caja Nacional de Seguridad Social, National Social Security Fund] and a green cross painted on their sides. Dozens of paramilitaries in civilian clothes, clutching machine guns, were sprawled around. I saw some men arrive carrying something wrapped in a shroud, it looked like a corpse. At one moment, a soldier shouted out '*Al servicio*' (to work), and a group of armed men appeared pushing two prisoners: an elderly man with white hair, wearing a black coat and hat, who looked like a professor or a politician, and a younger man in a beret. They were put up against the wall with their hands on their heads. Then another group appeared, bringing a young woman in jeans, very pale.

The military returned our equipment, minus the tapes, films and notebooks – but I had my hidden tape.

Before leaving for Brazil, I returned to see Dom Jorge Manrique. He gave me copies of the various documents issued by the Church and the names of priests known to have been detained. He said there were reports that prisoners had been taken to the football stadium at Chonchocolo, six kilometres outside the city. They were forced to lie in horse dung or human excrement, without food or water. Prisoners confined in the dressing rooms had to sleep standing up, because there was no room to lie down. There were reports of systematic torture.

Many leading politicians, including deposed president Lidia Gueiler, had taken refuge in embassies, some, including the wife and daughter of the president-elect, Hernán Siles Zuazo, in the Brazilian embassy. Several Bolivian ambassadors abroad resigned rather than serve the junta. On 6 August, from his secret hideout, Zuazo announced the formation of a government in exile.

In September, Clamor produced a special *Bulletin* on the coup with details of the repression and a list of the military officers linked to the cocaine trade, beginning with coup leader General Luis García Meza and Interior Minister Luis Arce Gómez.

A week after the coup, Brazil became only the third country to recognize the new Bolivian government, after Argentina and Paraguay. The countries of the European Economic Community refused to recognize the military junta, while the government of Jimmy Carter in the United States, having acknowledged that control of the cocaine trade was one of the main motives for the coup, kept quiet.

By sending one of its members to obtain first-hand knowledge of the coup and its effects, and publishing the results, Clamor helped to inform the Brazilian and international public about the scope of human rights violations in Bolivia.

CHAPTER 14
Paraguay: The iron fist of General Stroessner

Paraguay, ruled with an iron fist by dictator General Alfredo Stroessner since he seized power in 1954, had become virtually a one-party state. Opposition politicians were harassed, imprisoned, exiled. Every five years the state of siege was lifted for 24 hours to allow the president to be re-elected with 90 per cent of the vote. This enabled Stroessner to maintain that Paraguay was a democracy. A personality cult thrived, with posters and pictures of the great leader everywhere. Airports, roads, and towns were named after him. Official publications extolled the virtues and genius of the president, while in reality, repression, intimidation, and corruption were rife.

In September 1979 Clamor published an entire *Bulletin* dedicated to the shocking repression and lack of freedom in Paraguay, covering the previous two years. It began with a brief article on the history of the landlocked country:

> In the 19th century Paraguay became economically self-sufficient after freeing itself from Spanish colonial repression, but the War of the Triple Alliance (1865–70) waged against it by Brazil and Argentina, defending the commercial interests of the British empire, left it in ruins. With most of the male population slaughtered during the war, it became South America's poorest and most backward country.
>
> Indigenous resistance against the Spanish invaders had taken extreme forms, with women preferring to abort rather than bear children who would become slaves. Paraguay was the only Latin American country where the indigenous language, Guarani, became one of the official languages, alongside Spanish.

Looking to the present, the *Bulletin* noted that almost 1.5 million Paraguayans had left their country, reducing the population to 2.8 million. Most had emigrated for economic reasons, a million of them to Argentina.

The *Bulletin* carried information on arrests, torture, deaths, and disappearances. While most of the opposition leaders lived in exile in Buenos Aires, small groups of guerrillas made several failed attempts to spark revolution. But Stroessner's grip on power, aided by a network of informers, was too strong.

By the mid-1970s, the *campesinos*, inspired by popular movements elsewhere in Latin America, like Salvador Allende's Popular Unity front in Chile, had organized Christian Agrarian Leagues, living in communities, producing collectively, and running their own schools where lessons were taught in Guarani, the children's mother tongue, not in Spanish, as was the norm in Paraguayan schools. Encouragement came from both the Communist Party and the more progressive sector of the Catholic Church.

The Catholic Church had played a key role in Paraguay since the beginning of Spanish colonization, providing loyalty and collaboration with the ruling power in exchange for protection and support for its work. But the findings of Vatican II and the option for the poor celebrated at the 1968 CELAM conference in Medellín led it to question its mission in Paraguay. It began to distance itself from the dictatorial regime of Stroessner and identify more with the needs of the people. Progressive priests went to live close to the people, helping to arouse political awareness, inspired by the teachings of liberation theology. But this self-sufficiency and independence was in direct defiance of the Stroessner regime, which encouraged the concentration of land and the maintenance of an illiterate, ignorant peasantry.

In 1976 the Stroessner regime moved against the Agrarian Leagues and members of the progressive Church. Over 2,000 people were detained and tortured, and others were killed or disappeared. Catholic social programmes were banned, and Church institutions were raided. Ten Jesuits were placed on a 'wanted' list, and the foreign ones, most of them Spanish, were expelled.

Hundreds of prisoners, including many women with babies, were crammed into the cells of the 24 police stations in Asunción. Most of them were badly tortured. In September 1976, about 300 of them were transferred to Emboscada, a former penal agricultural colony converted into a prison, 50 kilometres from the capital.

In response to the arrests, an ecumenical committee, called the Churches' Committee for Emergency Aid, was set up under the auspices of the Roman Catholic archbishop of Asunción, Dom Ismael Rolón, following the example of the Vicariate of Solidarity in Chile. The first coordinator was Padre Blanch, who had been one of the ten Jesuits detained in the government's crackdown. It became known as the Churches Committee (Comité de Iglesias).

Committee members began visiting the prisoners, taking food and medicines. They received financial aid from German and Dutch churches for the large number of women being held with children, and for the babies born in prison.

One of those arrested was Basilica Espinola Nuñez, a young militant in the organization Young Christian Workers (Juventude Operária Católica, JOC). In an interview many years later, the softly spoken Basilica told me what she had been through:

> We were 40 women held in a cell above the room where they
> tortured prisoners. When somebody was being tortured,
> they always played the same music, *La Virgen Morenita*, sung

by an Argentinian singer. When we heard the music, we would ask ourselves – who is being tortured now? Some prisoners disappeared, including four brothers[1] who left behind ten children. As their mothers were also detained, the orphaned children were handed out to other families.

Once they brought in a woman who only spoken Guarani, with her baby. She was barefoot; she had never been in a car before. Her first ride was to the police station. They brought her in because they could not find her husband. She left 12 other children behind at home. She was held for a year, like everyone else, without trial. They tried to make her reveal her codename, but she had no idea what they were talking about. She never spoke to the other prisoners, until the day some of them suggested it would be better for the baby to be cared for out of prison. Then she spoke, passionately, saying, 'I am not here because I don't know how to care for my baby.'

Five months later, on September 5, we were told we had five minutes to get ready, because we were going to be moved – but they didn't tell us where to. They put us in trucks and pickups and took us to Emboscada, a former prison colony. About 500 prisoners who had been held in the police stations were moved there on the same day.

We were given an hour's 'freedom' together. Many had no idea if their wives or husbands were dead or alive; they hadn't seen each other since the day they were arrested. It was a moment of despair for some and relief for others, everyone asking, 'Have you seen my husband, my wife?' I discovered that Miguel, my husband, was alive, but he had been very badly tortured.

In November Basilica and many others were released, and in January 1977 she began working as secretary for the Churches Committee. She and Miguel joined others who were trying to reorganize the Political Military Organization (Organización Politico Militar, OPM), an armed guerrilla movement.

Later that year, she and Miguel fled to Brazil to escape arrest. In São Paulo they contacted Jaime Wright, and after Clamor was created Basilica began to help, organizing the correspondence that was arriving.

Before the Churches Committee came into existence in 1976, the only human rights organization in Paraguay was the National Commission for Human Rights, founded in 1967. Carmen de Lara Castro, its first president, came from the social and political elite. Her son, Jorge Lara Castro, told me how his mother took food to prisoners. 'She held "tea parties" for other society ladies as a cover for collecting money for prisoners', he explained. 'She was very courageous. When she took food to prison, sometimes the guards would deliberately spill the rice on the floor, so she would have to go down on her knees to pick it up, to be able to give it to the prisoners.'

The Commission campaigned for the release of all political prisoners, whether communists, militants of guerrilla movements, or any of the many others held for criticizing or opposing the Stroessner regime. They campaigned to have prison conditions improved. Many of the detained were held in cells without beds or mattresses, or toilets, and with little food.

In December 1979, Clamor sent the journalist Fernando Morais to Asunción to press for the release of two leading Paraguayans who were being held incommunicado. He was also São Paulo state deputy for the opposition party, the MDB, which gave him a certain immunity.

When Morais got to Asunción he was not allowed to see the prisoners, opposition leader Domingo Laíno and journalist Alcibiades González Delvalle, general secretary of the recently created Journalists Union and main columnist of a leading newspaper, *ABC Color*, who was arrested after writing a series of articles about corruption, political arbitrariness, and human rights violations. What had apparently earned him the particular displeasure of the Stroessner government was his article referring to a French minister who had committed suicide when he was accused of corruption. It was headed: 'Let's Hope This Example Is Not Followed Here in Paraguay Because There Won't Be Enough Room in the Cemeteries.'

A few months later, in March 1980, Clamor asked another São Paulo MDB state deputy, Marco Aurélio Ribeiro, a militant Catholic, to go to Paraguay and investigate reports that many peasants had been killed during an army operation in Caaguazu a few days before. Ribeiro's mission was to collect information and transmit the support of the Brazilian Church to the Paraguayan Church.

In Paraguay he managed to get into the conflict area, near the border with Brazil, despite military controls, and talk to local people there. Several priests were too afraid to talk to him. Churches had been invaded; meetings could not be held in them. In his report, he wrote: 'On 8 March, 21 people, led by Vitoriano Centurion, left Acaray-mi, a peasant settlement near the frontier with Brazil, ... boarded a bus and forced the driver to take them to Asunción, where they intended to complain to the President about their poor conditions, and the seizure of their land by a landowner called Olga Ramos Gimenez.'

After driving for about 100 kilometres they were intercepted by an anti-smuggling patrol, leading to a confrontation. The peasants were armed with two revolvers and a rifle. They fled from the scene but were hunted down, killed, and buried in a mass grave. Some reports said that four, including the leader Vitoriano Centurion, had managed to escape. The army was aided by militia of the official Colorado Party.

The massacre was followed by violent repression, 'with the invasion and looting of peasants' homes, and mass detentions, principally of all the men, fathers and sons of Acaray-mi, and relatives and friends of Centurion in the Caaguazu region, and of ex-members of the Agrarian Leagues'. An estimated 40 were arrested in Acaray-mi and 200 in Caaguazu. Ribeiro's report continued:

> Some of the wives of the arrested say that their families, including the children, are going hungry, there are sick people, and the harvest is being lost because their husbands are not there to reap it.

> The government banned the press from reporting the facts, accusing the peasants. Only the government's official declarations, speaking of bandits and robbers, have been published. The peasants consider Centurion their friend and do not believe he is a bandit or robber.

At the end of March, 13 peasants, including 3 minors, one of them only 13 years old, were charged with crimes related to the bus hijack. Some of them had been tortured, and another man, Marcelino Casco, died in custody.

Ribeiro obtained an interview with the minister of the interior, Sabino Montanaro, who received him courteously, until he explained the aim of his visit. Then the minister became furious, shouting that Paraguay was a sovereign, independent country, and that Dom Paulo was meddling, and so was Ribeiro. He said the Brazilians should worry about their own human rights and put an end to the death squads. After this rant he expelled the Brazilian deputy from the Ministry.

Over the next few years, Clamor relied on several courageous Paraguayans who travelled to São Paulo to bring news of arrests, disappearances, hunger strikes, and acts of resistance. One of them was Regina Viuda de Rodas, whose husband had been murdered soon after the Caaguazu attack. Regina was coordinator of the Permanent Commission of Families of the Disappeared, which she had founded with other widows and relatives in March 1983. They demanded that the government hand over the bodies of the people who disappeared during the Caaguazu attack in 1980. She was also a member of the Paraguayan Peasant Movement, and on her trips to São Paulo, she brought us information about detentions of peasants.

Another frequent visitor was Luiz Ocampo Alonso, a student leader who brought news of the activities of the Paraguayans in Europe Accord, a united front formed by groups of Paraguayan exiles in Europe.

On 17 September 1980, Paraguay was stunned by the assassination of the ex-dictator of Nicaragua, General Anastacio Somoza, who, following his overthrow by Sandinista rebels, had been offered asylum by fellow dictator General Stroessner. Somoza lived in a luxurious mansion in Asunción, surrounded by members of his family, friends, bodyguards, and 36 Paraguayan soldiers, on guard day and night.

Somoza's armoured car was hit by a bazooka, fired by members of an Argentine guerrilla organization, the ERP. He died instantly. On 9 October, Clamor released a special press bulletin about the aftermath of the assassination, based on information received from Paraguay. It said that hundreds had been arrested, many summarily expelled, and the press had been censored.

> Several hundred people have been detained for weeks or days in subhuman conditions in the Police Investigations Department and local police stations in Asunción. According to one man, freed after five days, '74 of us were locked into a room five metres by six, among us there were men, women and a two-year-old child.' Another man said he was held in a small cell with 50 people of different nationalities, all standing, without any room to sleep. Now and again a policeman in plain clothes came and said to the prisoners, 'Do you know why you are here? Because you came here to disturb our peace.'

The bulletin said that at least 160 foreigners, mostly Argentines, had been expelled. Among them were many Argentine men married to Paraguayan women, with Paraguayan children, some of them arrested when they tried to cross the border.

The Stroessner regime naturally saw things differently. An English-language publication of the Ministry for Industry and Commerce painted a rosy picture of a country making great economic and social advances, due to the peace and harmony which reigned: 'Paraguay has the rare distinction of being a country in which the convulsions of massive public disorders, strikes, organised violence and other demonstrations of popular discontent and dissent do not occur. This harmony is clearly evident even in the sensitive field of labour management relations.'

Note

1.   Adolfo, Elixto, Francisco, and Policarpo López, who were detained on 14 May. See Clamor. (1980) 'Repression after the Death of Somoza', special press bulletin, 9 October.

CHAPTER 15
The nightmare of Remigio Giménez

One day in March 1980, a distraught woman appeared at the Curia in São Paulo. She was tall, with grey hair, and her name was Dirce Mecchi. When we sat down to talk to her, her story came spilling out.

Dirce's husband, Remigio Giménez, was Paraguayan, but he had lived in Brazil since 1959. The couple lived in São Mateus, a working-class district in São Paulo. He worked as a shoemaker; she was a seamstress. They had no children.

Fifteen months before Dirce found her way to the Curia, having been referred there by a student law centre where she had sought help, Remigio had travelled to Foz do Iguaçu, on Brazil's border with Paraguay, to visit his daughter by an earlier marriage. It was December 1978, and he should have been back in São Paulo for Christmas, but he never came back.

A month after he disappeared, Dirce received a letter from the wife of a friend of Remigio's telling her that on 19 December, Remigio had been arrested by Brazilian police in Foz do Iguaçu. He had been handed over to the Paraguayan police just a short distance away, across the Ponte de Amizade, the Friendship Bridge, which links the two countries.

She heard nothing more for another nine months, until a note arrived, smuggled out of prison, to say that Remigio was alive. She did not know what to do, so she waited for more news. Six months passed before another letter came, telling her that Remigio had been transferred to the army's Guardia de Seguridad, where many of Paraguay's political prisoners were held.

Clamor asked MDB deputy Marco Aurélio Ribeiro, who was about to visit Paraguay to investigate the massacre of peasants at Caaguazu, to try to visit Remigio. He did so, and Remigio told him that he had been tortured for two months, held incommunicado and forced to sign documents whose content he was unaware of. He was accused of participating in the anti-government guerrilla movement 14 de Mayo in 1958.

Unlike most other political prisoners, Remigio had no ready-made support network from a political party, trade union, church, or social organization. He had not been involved in politics since leaving Paraguay in 1959. He and his wife were working people on low incomes; they had difficulty writing letters, and no experience in campaigning.

Over the next nine years, Remigio continued to be held prisoner in spite of a lack of evidence for the various crimes of which he was accused, in spite of appeals and hunger strikes and campaigns. Clamor became a vital source of support, both practical and emotional. Clamor members accompanied Dirce on several of her visits to Paraguay to visit Remigio and talk to his defence lawyers. We campaigned continuously for his release, liaising with the other human rights organizations like the Churches Committee in Asunción, which provided defence lawyers for him, and Amnesty International in London, which adopted him as a political prisoner.

The Brazilian press showed considerable interest in the case, reporting any new developments. In March 1981, reporter José Meirelles Passos of the magazine *Isto É* went to Paraguay and interviewed Remigio in prison. Remigio told him that his arrest in Foz do Iguaçu had been caused by an unfortunate coincidence. He had bumped into a Paraguayan to whom he had lent money eight years before. The man, Ramón Rodriguez, said he could pay Remigio back, and they arranged to meet the next day, just 200 metres from the Friendship Bridge. It was a trap. Rodriguez had tipped off the Paraguayan police, who arranged Remigio's capture with the Brazilian police.

Meirelles quoted an unnamed diplomatic source saying, 'It was routine; on the frontier this happens all the time. Giménez ended up becoming an object of exchange, which happened all the time, prisoners or favours, between the police forces.'

Remigio told Meirelles that he was counting on Brazilian solidarity, because he had been kidnapped by Brazilian police.

Clamor issued a press release comparing the Brazilian government's treatment of train robber Ronnie Biggs, who fled to Brazil after escaping from prison in the UK, with that of Remigio Giménez. It was headed 'Dois Pesos e Duas Medidas' (literally, two weights and two measures) or 'Double Standards':

> We remember that when a British citizen – condemned by a court and on the run from his country and living illegally in Brazil – was kidnapped some months ago, the Brazilian government announced that 'for humanitarian reasons' it would ask for his return. The Brazilian government acted with speed and efficiency. The criminal had a Brazilian underage child.

'Remigio Giménez is not a criminal', continued the press release, which went on to list his documents, with their dates and numbers. He had been admitted to Brazil as a permanent resident on 10 March 1961. He had married a Brazilian, Dirce Mecchi on 23 June 1962. He had been employed since 1962, he paid income tax, he paid council tax. 'Summing up, he is an exemplary citizen, fully identified with Brazil, against whom there is no police complaint. The Brazilian Government has asked for the English robber to be returned from Barbados to Brazil, guaranteeing him the protection of our laws. But it leaves the Paraguayan citizen, a humble and honest shoemaker, legally resident in Brazil, totally unprotected.'

In 1982, I accompanied Dirce on the 24-hour bus trip to Asunción. We arrived on a Saturday, and on Sunday morning caught a local bus to the Guardia De Seguridad. As only family members were allowed to visit, I said I was Remigio's niece. The guards, their ears pressed to transistor radios that were broadcasting a World Cup football match, only glanced at our documents in a cursory fashion, and opened the barrier. Inside, prisoners were sitting at tables under the trees. It seemed an idyllic scene, but Sunday morning was the only time they were allowed out of their cells._

In 1984 Remigio was transferred to the big central prison of Tacumbú, where hundreds of prisoners, from murderers to petty thieves, were locked up, and very often forgotten. After being held for six years without trial, he was suddenly accused of a whole range of crimes, including terrorism and drug smuggling.

A few months later, in September 1985, the Paraguayan prosecutor asked for the death sentence, rejecting the defence argument that the crime, allegedly committed in 1958, had proscribed. Now Remigio was accused of murder, car theft, and other crimes. The judge rejected the death sentence and instead sentenced him to 30 years' imprisonment.

Faced with the prospect of a further 23 years in prison for crimes he did not commit, Remigio got desperate. In mid-December 1985 he began a hunger strike, the third since his detention in 1978.

Transferred in a delicate state of health to the Police Polyclinic, he called off the hunger strike on 10 February 1986 after receiving promises that his case would be reviewed. He was then returned to Tacumbú. The promises were forgotten.

On 2 January 1986, Amnesty International released an urgent action appeal for Remigio, expressing concern for his health as a result of the hunger strike, and legal concerns about his situation. 'He has been in detention now for 7 years (3 years without charge) and is still awaiting sentence', the organization wrote. Amnesty said that under the statute of limitations, the charges for some of his alleged crimes should have expired in 1982.

The accusations against him had changed, without any proof to back them up. He was variously charged with terrorism, subversion, murder, drug trafficking, car theft, and armed robbery, most of them allegedly committed when he was living in São Paulo. His lawyers found 28 irregularities in the case against him, but nevertheless, he had been given a 30-year sentence. In December 1987, Paraguay's Supreme Court confirmed the sentence.

A month later, on 30 January 1986, Dirce appealed to Brazil's foreign minister, Olavo Setubal, for help, asking him to take action over Remigio's case. Democracy had been restored in Brazil the year before; all the political prisoners had been released, and exiles had returned from abroad. Remigio had been kidnapped on Brazilian soil, so surely the government could do something.

In 1986 I accompanied Dirce on yet another trip to Paraguay, this time to visit Remigio in Tacumbú. There had just been a riot at the prison, and the guards were saying that visits would not be allowed. I wrote about the scene at the prison for the *Guardian*:

> Tacumbu holds 1,500 men from all over Paraguay. Hardened criminals, murderers and drug traffickers mix with illiterate

peasants accused of minor offences, young first offenders and political prisoners.

Outside the prison more and more women arrived on the rickety No. 10 bus, carrying bags and babies. A Mercedes Benz drew up – white collar criminals are also held here. Twelve of the directors of Paraguay's Central Bank are awaiting trial for their part in a gigantic swindle involving the sale of a good part of the country's hard earned dollar reserves. Of the two men whose signature appears on Paraguayan banknotes, one, the manager of the Central Bank, is on the run, and the other, accused of complicity, remains in his post. ... At eleven o'clock the prison director came out to tell the huge crowd of tense, waiting women who had refused to budge, that one short visit would be allowed. ... Long queues formed to be let in to the visiting room for a hurried ten minute conversation through a thick wire mesh screen, fifteen at a time.

Prison rules dictate that women visitors have to wear skirts, but for those like me who have come wearing trousers, the solution lay in a dirty hovel near the prison walls. For 300 guaranies (approx. 30 pence) I was offered a box of assorted skirts to choose from.

I chose the least grimy and was allowed in to see Remigio, together with Dirce, for a few brief minutes.

It was only after the fall of Stroessner, in February 1989, over ten long years after his illegal detention in Foz do Iguaçu, that Remigio was finally released. A court decided that his sentence of 30 years had been unconstitutional.

He was freed on 29 August 1989, aged 65, and within a few days he was on a bus to São Paulo to be reunited with Dirce. I waited with her at the bus station to see him arrive. After almost 11 years of suffering, separation, frustration, despair, and injustice, at last there was happy ending.

CHAPTER 16
The suffering of Uruguay

While the more numerous Madres and Abuelas in Argentina could count on the active support of other human rights groups, those in Uruguay were isolated and intimidated. Many struggled alone for years to find their missing loved ones, unaware that others, maybe living just a few streets away, were in the same situation.

The Uruguayan press was heavily censored. The 'disappeared' were never mentioned, even in funeral notices, as María Ester Islas Gatti found when she went to place the notice of her husband Ramón's death in the newspaper *El País* in July 1980. Depressed by the lack of news about his only daughter, Emilia, his son-in-law Jorge, and his grandchild Mariana after they disappeared in Buenos Aires four years earlier, Ramón suffered a fatal heart attack.

Ester wrote out a death notice and took it to the classifieds department of the newspaper. After her own name, she added those of Emilia, Jorge, and Mariana, along with the word 'disappeared' and the sentence 'Wherever they are, they received the news with grief but with dignity.' But when the man at *El País* read it, he looked at her and shook his head.

'What about putting "absent" instead of disappeared?', he suggested. Ester refused, so the funeral notice was never published.

Constantly looking for news of her family, Ester's search took her to the office of the Council of State. This body had been created by the military to replace the Congress that they had dissolved. Made up of very conservative jurists, its role was to rubber-stamp the decisions taken by the ruling junta of generals.

Ester hoped to see the council secretary and beg him to find out what had happened in Buenos Aires. Another woman was already sitting in the waiting room. She was tall and elegantly dressed. They sat in silence for a long time until an assistant came out and curtly told them that they would have to go on waiting – the council secretary was busy. Ester protested: 'We've been waiting long enough!' The other woman said quietly, 'You're right.' In the climate of fear that pervaded Uruguay, strangers did not talk to each other, but Ester intuitively guessed that this woman was there for the same reason she was.

When they were finally turned away without being seen, the two women began talking and discovered that they shared the same sorrow. Luz Ibarburu's son, Juan Pablo Recagno, had also disappeared in Buenos Aires in 1976, like Ester's family. They exchanged telephone numbers and addresses and decided to join forces. Luz had the advantage of owning a car and a typewriter.

Soon they discovered others in the same situation, and after a while they formed the group Families of the Disappeared in Argentina. Over 120 Uruguayans had disappeared on the other side of the River Plate, almost all in the months following the March 1976 coup. About 50 relatives, mostly mothers, but also a few fathers, brothers, and sisters, joined the group.

As with the Argentine Abuelas, the discovery in Chile of a small brother and sister, the children of a Uruguayan couple who like so many others had fled to what they thought was the safety of Argentina but disappeared in Buenos Aires in September 1976, was a huge encouragement to the Uruguayan group. The government did its best to hide the story, forbidding any mention of it in the press. On 31 July 1979, Dom Paulo held a press conference in São Paulo to announce the news; the next day, Brazilian and Argentine newspapers were banned from entering the country. Even the conservative Chilean newspaper *El Mercurio* was banned because it carried full coverage of the amazing story. But news filtered through, not least because Anatole and Vicky were the children of Uruguayan exiles, and Angélica Julien, their grandmother, became an active member of the group. As Clamor became known to them, groups of mothers from Montevideo began to travel to São Paulo, to hand over to us reports, letters, and information about their missing sons, daughters, and grandchildren, and tell us of their activities.

By contrast, in sad, fearful Montevideo, the Catholic Church was afraid to show open support for the families. Very reluctantly, in answer to a request from Luz's husband, a devout Roman Catholic, Church authorities agreed to act as a poste restante for letters from international organizations that had been contacted by the group.

The most the families could do was to stage silent protests in front of Montevideo Metropolitan Cathedral – protests that were sometimes misunderstood. When the Chilean cardinal Raúl Silva Henriquez, who had founded the Vicariate of Solidarity to defend human rights in Santiago, came to Montevideo and conducted a mass at the cathedral, the mothers stood outside and held up pictures of their disappeared sons and daughters. But many people who saw the photographs of young people thought they were the victims of the terrible plane crash in the Andes a few years before, when a handful had survived for weeks in the mountains before being rescued.

So dense was the climate of fear and so thorough was the censorship that most Uruguayans not directly affected had no idea what was being done in their name.

In August 1980, Clamor published a special *Bulletin* on the human rights situation in Uruguay. It noted: 'The degree of repression is so high that it remains impossible to form even a small ecumenical committee to discuss the human tragedy that has befallen Uruguayan society.'

Becoming an organized group brought new problems for the families. The police began to harass them. Even though their public protests were silent, police agents would demand to see their identity documents. Some of the mothers were detained and questioned. Plain-clothes policemen sat in at their meetings, openly taping the testimonies they gave about their disappeared relatives.

It was not until 1981, when a branch of SERPAJ, a group led by Nobel Peace Prize winner Adolfo Esquivel in Buenos Aires, was set up in Montevideo, that the families began to get regular support from another organization in Uruguay. The branch was led by a courageous Jesuit priest called Luis Pérez Aguirre.

In 1982, a group from Uruguayan Mothers and Families of the Disappeared in Argentina began to cross the River Plate every Thursday to join the Madres in their weekly vigil in the Plaza de Mayo in front of the Casa Rosada. The Uruguayan mothers decided to copy the tactics of the Argentine Madres, and in May 1983, wearing white scarves with the names of their disappeared sons and daughters written on them and carrying their photos, they gathered each day in a different square to walk in silent protest. The week of protests culminated on 13 May with the delivery of a letter to the government, calling on it to protest against the Argentine government's new law declaring that all the disappeared were to be considered dead. But while the Madres in Buenos Aires now numbered hundreds, the Uruguayan women were few in number and their protest passed largely unnoticed.

Clamor became more and more aware of the terrible conditions in which thousands of political prisoners were being held in Uruguay, as we received reports and personal visits from the relatives of the detained. Besides the main prisons – the ironically named Libertad, for men, and Punta Rieles, for women – many prisoners were also kept in clandestine detention centres and military barracks.

In *Bulletin* No. 3, published in October 1978, we included the testimony of journalist Enrique Rodríguez Larreta, now exiled in Europe, who had gone to Argentina to look for his son, also a journalist, who had been forcibly disappeared on 1 July 1976. Two weeks later, he himself, together with his daughter-in-law, was also seized when armed men broke down the door of his son's apartment. 'Hooded and handcuffed, he and his son's wife were taken to a clandestine prison where there were many other people. He recognised his son's voice among them.'

The torturers were both Argentine and Uruguayan army officers from OCOA. 'Two of them were busy packing up all the articles they had robbed during the kidnappings – they called it "battlefield booty" – for taking back to Uruguay. The booty included dismantled cars, freezers, TV sets, typewriters and calculators, domestic appliances, bicycles and books.'

On 26 July, Larreta and the other prisoners were secretly flown back to Montevideo, where they were again tortured and interrogated. A month later, OCOA leader Major Gavazzo offered them a 'deal', reminding them that they were entirely in his hands because nobody knew their whereabouts. In exchange for 'saving' them from being murdered in Argentina – the usual fate of the disappeared – they would confess to plotting an armed invasion of Uruguay. They would then be tried and sentenced to between 15 and 30 years.

The prisoners refused the deal. Indignantly, Larreta told Major Gavazzo that he did not belong to any political organization, and there was no proof linking him to any such organization.

> Nevertheless, for two months, I had been ill-treated, tortured, kept blind-folded and bound, eating badly, sleeping on the floor with a dirty blanket, without news of my family, who must have taken me for dead ... all without any accusation. ... I had no criminal past, but I had been abducted, taken by force to Uruguay for the sole reason that I was in Buenos Aires searching for my missing son, with all my documents in order and taking the steps that the Constitution and the law permitted me.

Larreta was finally released without charge and immediately went into exile. The other prisoners were given long sentences and sent to Libertad and Punta Rieles. One of them was Sara Méndez, the mother of a newborn baby who was torn from her arms when she was detained in Buenos Aires.

In *Bulletin* No. 4, Clamor published photographs of Sara's baby, Simón Riquelo, and the three other children of Uruguayan exiles who had disappeared in Buenos Aires in 1976, under the title 'Where Are They?' In reality, no photograph existed of baby Simón, but rather than publish a blank space, the resourceful Maria came up with the photograph of another newborn baby, which, from then on, became Simón.

Sara was sentenced to eight years for her part in the faked 'invasion' of Uruguay, allegedly carried out by the exiles. Frantically trying to discover what had happened to her 20-day-old son, she had clung to the hope that somehow her family had managed to find the baby, once they realized she had gone missing.

It was a bitter blow when she discovered that for the first year of their detention, political prisoners were not allowed any visitors at all, even their families. It was one of the cruellest features of the inhumane prison regime. Eventually she managed to smuggle out a message to her parents asking if they had found Simón; when the answer eventually came back, 'No', she was devastated.

The following year, 1977, a new British ambassador, Bill Peters, took up his post in Uruguay. A humane man, he decided that he ought to find out more about the human rights situation, although it meant swimming against the tide of feeling within the diplomatic service. Many British diplomats were sympathetic to the strong measures of the Uruguayan government, especially after an earlier ambassador, Geoffrey Jackson, taken hostage in 1971 by the Tupamaros, had been held in solitary confinement for eight months in a 'people's prison', emerging from his captivity with a long white beard.

At the Foreign Office, Peters was told that previous ambassadors had reported nothing about human rights violations, but when he visited Amnesty

International's HQ in London, he heard a very different story. They told him Uruguay had the highest number of political prisoners per capita in the world, and that torture was regularly used.

Soon after arriving in Montevideo, Peters took the unusual step of requesting permission from the Uruguayan government to visit the prisons. No other ambassador had done so. Only the Dutch took practical steps to help prisoners, offering asylum when they were released and meeting them at the prison gates to make sure no 'accident' befell them.

Permission was reluctantly granted, and Peters chose the women's prison for his first visit. Among the several hundred inmates at Punta Rieles, he saw women with atrophied limbs, which he attributed to the physical after-effects of torture. The prisoners had been forbidden from speaking to the ambassador, on pain of severe punishment. There was total silence as he walked along the corridors, past the women who stood to attention outside their cell doors. But as he passed Sara she fell on her knees before him, imploring him to help her find her baby son. The astonished ambassador could do nothing when guards rushed up and pulled her roughly away.

After the visit, the ambassador contacted Sara's family and made discreet inquiries about the fate of her baby; he did not discover anything. His long report to the Foreign Office, concluding that prisoners were being tortured, was ignored. There were no protests to the Uruguayan government. He was told later by the papal nuncio, the senior diplomat in Montevideo, that Sara had been severely beaten for speaking to him.

By mid-1980, the amount of information about human rights violations in Uruguay had become so overwhelming that we decided to publish a special *Bulletin*, No. 10, which appeared in August of that year. Entitled 'Human Rights in Uruguay', it described in detail the brutal conditions in the prisons where thousands were being held. After the peak of repression that followed the 1973 coup, the number of political prisoners had reached almost 6,000 out of a population of 2.8 million; by March 1980, it had dropped to 3,800.

Libertad, the men's prison, was located 50 kilometres from Montevideo, while the women's prison, Punta Rieles, which had been converted from a former Jesuit seminary, was only 14 kilometres from the city centre. Prisoners' relatives and friends were convinced that the harsh and inhuman conditions were specifically designed to cause the maximum psychological and physical suffering, even death, in a country that had no capital punishment.

The slightest transgression was severely punished with weeks or months in solitary confinement, and strict rules controlled every moment of the prisoners' day. Fortnightly visits from family members were allowed for only one hour, but relatives, including children, were submitted to humiliating searches. 'When a prisoner gave his daughter two flowers to put in her hair ..., the policeman who searched the child as she left the prison tore them out and threw them away, leaving the child in tears.'

Prisoners were denied access to newspapers, magazines, and most books. The prison library, which once contained almost 10,000 books, was deliberately destroyed in 1974 by order of the then prison governor, Major Arquímedes Maciel. Handcrafts were allowed, but there was a long list of forbidden themes – doves, linked hands, clenched fists, workers. During cell inspections, guards would destroy pieces of handwork that were almost finished, or mix tobacco with tea, talcum with sugar.

Many prisoners developed mental health problems but were denied treatment. Even when they became sick with serious physical problems, treatment was denied or inadequate. As a result, many who could have survived died. The *Bulletin* lists the names of 11 men and 5 women who died, untreated, from cancer, heart problems, rheumatoid fever, and peritonitis. Three committed suicide. At the Military Hospital, another four deaths were listed, including Hilda de la Croix, who died from untreated ovarian cancer which spread to her other organs. On the last day of August 1976, Hilda, near death, asked to be allowed to see her children. Permission was refused, and the next day she died.

When prisoners were due for release, their families were presented with a bill for the junta's 'hospitality' which had to be paid before they could walk free. Even when the prisoner had died because of the inhuman conditions or lack of medical care, families still received a bill.

The nine top Tupamaro leaders were held at military bases in subhuman conditions, denied all contact with the outside world. 'They have been turned into hostages of the military regime. Raul Sendic, Jorge Pedro Zabala Waksmann, Julio Marenales Sanez, Henry Engler Golovchenko, Jorge Amilcar Manera Lluvera, Jose Mujica Cordano (later to become President of Uruguay), Adolfo Wassen Alaniz, Eleuterio Huidobro and Mauricio Rosencoff.'

Reading in groups, an activity that prisoners had found helped them psychologically, was banned by the authorities, who only allowed them to read alone. One former prisoner of Punta Rieles recounted:

> Group reading is something that helps many of the comrades who are going through a particularly difficult period, so even though it was banned, we continued to do it, with two colleagues on lookout, while another read aloud. The fact of being discovered became of secondary importance, the important thing was to continue. In this way we imposed our will.'

> Our contact with the family is minimal and has a bitter taste. The visits last half an hour every two weeks, and are conducted by telephone, separated by a thick painted glass, leaving just a space to see the face. They are recorded. The children are searched and manhandled and they hear their mothers being shouted at. The children fear and hate it. The older children find it difficult to talk to their mothers, because of the presence of soldiers. After the

visit by the Red Cross in 1980, armed guards were withdrawn from the place where the children were.

It should be remembered that the prisons are in the hands of the most Fascist sector of the Uruguayan army. All those in charge (officers with the rank of captain or major) are men of torture.

On 30 November 1980, the military held a plebiscite, confident that the cowed population would vote to approve reforms which would effectively legitimize military rule for the foreseeable future. They included presidential elections with a single candidate, and the creation of a new 'fourth power' called the Constitutional Tribune, composed of 'nine personalities aged over 50 and under 75, chosen by the generals, to exercise political control'.[1] Only the two traditional parties, the Blancos and Colorados, would be allowed to exist. All other parties were banned.

To the surprise of the military, almost 60 per cent of voters rejected their project. The regime reacted with fury, arresting more and more people, including the relatives of political prisoners. Over the next few months, thousands were detained by the police during raids in working-class districts.

While the military regimes in Brazil and Argentina were reluctantly bowing to the pressure to return their countries to democracy, the Uruguayan military continued to row against the rising tide of civilian discontent. It intensified the repression in an attempt to impose the changes to the Constitution which had been rejected by a majority in the 1980 plebiscite.

Note

1.   'The Institutional Picture', *Clamor Bulletin* 10, August 1980, p. 3.

CHAPTER 17
Chile in the grip of Pinochet

The discovery of the disappeared children Anatole and Vicky in Valparaíso in 1979 led to Clamor establishing close relations with the two most important human rights organizations in Chile – the Catholic Vicariate of Solidarity of the Archdiocese of Santiago, and the ecumenical group FASIC.

Clamor's bulletins carried articles about the discoveries of clandestine cemeteries in Chile, where people shot in the days following the coup had been buried. The first mass grave was found in an abandoned mine called Lonquén, 50 kilometres south of Santiago. The existence of the clandestine cemetery was revealed to a priest. A committee of Catholic religious, including the auxiliary bishop of Santiago, two lawyers, and two well-known journalists, visited the mine to investigate and found the remains inside a lime kiln.

About 30 bodies were found, including those of two women. As Clamor noted in its *Bulletin* No. 4: 'The discovery caused understandable alarm amongst the families of the detained and disappeared, whose efforts to find them always met a wall of silence.'

In November 1979, following the discovery of Anatole and Vicky, *Bulletin* No. 8 reported that other children and their mothers had disappeared in Chile.

> These facts confirm the denunciation that we – the families of disappeared prisoners – have been making all these years: the connection and complicity existing between the security services of the military dictatorships of the Southern Cone, and the scorn for the lives not only of adults detained and disappeared but also of innocent children. How many other children have the security organisms of these dictatorships trafficked?

In *Bulletin* No. 9, of March 1980, Clamor reported on the UN Human Rights Commission's motion condemning human rights violations in Chile, which had been approved by 96 votes to 6, with 33 abstentions. It referred to the discovery in Santiago's main cemetery of hundreds of unidentified graves believed to contain the remains of victims of political executions.

In a special *Bulletin* dedicated to Chile in March 1981, Clamor published details of the discovery of another 18 bodies in a clandestine grave in the cemetery of Yumbel, in the province of Concepción in central Chile. They were believed to be the bodies of 18 of the 19 men who had been detained by the police in the nearby towns of Laja and San Rosendo, soon after the coup in September 1973. Eight were employees of the local paper factory, two were train drivers, two were primary school teachers, and one was a student. Between them they left over 40 orphaned children.

The bodies were exhumed in October and their families were called to recognize them from their clothes because there was little left of the bodies, which had apparently been covered in a chemical solution.

At first the Chilean authorities tried to claim that the men had been killed in armed confrontations. A strongly worded note from the archbishop's office in Concepción pointed out that:

> All of them had been taken into custody by the Carabineros, after presenting themselves voluntarily, some accompanied by a priest. They were kept there for between 1 and 4 days and seen there by their families who brought them food and clothing.
>
> Later, handcuffed and guarded, they were taken from the Carabineros unit to be transferred, so it was said, to the political prisoners' camp in the barracks of the Army regiment in Los Angeles, but their destination was, in reality, definitive disappearance.

The bodies were exhumed and reburied in Laja after a memorial service. In his sermon, the parish priest said their deaths were the result of an 'irrational act of hatred and revenge', but a Jesuit priest who was also present, Father José Aldunarte, later wrote:

> I began thinking while I celebrated the mass with him, that perhaps it had not been so irrational. Wasn't there operating here an implicit and diabolical cleverness, the same we had seen operating in so many different places? These 19 sacrificed Chileans, weren't they part of the 'social cost' necessary to guarantee the 'system' so that for many years the Laja Paper Company would not have any more problems, nor would the railways; so that the countryside would be pacified, and foreign capital could enter? And might not whoever identified himself with these aims logically maintain that the 'cost' had not been excessive? The present economic policy which leads to unemployment and low wages, isn't it at heart the application of the same murderous logic? If you opt for money, you have to offer up your victims to this god. Therefore, rather than a mere local revenge directed against 19 citizens, the sin that ought to be denounced was the blow struck against the heart of a people, their reduction to a fearful mass of ghosts, the emptiness of their existences. And all this planned from the highest levels of political and economic power.

The murdered men of Yumbel and Lonquén were just some of the defenceless prisoners who were assassinated soon after the coup. Others were executed by a flying death squad known as the Caravan of Death. Commanded by General Sergio Arellano Stark and Colonel Sergio Arredondo González, this group used a helicopter to fly to small towns in the north of Chile where they shot dead a total of 73 prisoners who were being held in police custody, after summary trials. The Clamor archive contains the identical death certificates of a group of 21 men executed by a firing squad in Calama. The youngest was only 18, the oldest 42.

Several years later, in 1986, Arredondo was discovered to be living in São Paulo and working for Codelco, the Chilean National Copper Corporation. In collaboration with AALA, Clamor sent a letter to the Ministry of Justice asking for his immediate expulsion. This was refused, but he soon left Brazil after intense press coverage of the story and the publication of his photograph.

In 1979, five survivors appeared after spending years in hiding, fearing for their lives after they had miraculously escaped execution attempts. One of them was Blanca Ester Valderas Garrido, who a week after the coup was taken by the Carabineros to a bridge over the Bueno River. With her husband Joel Fierro Inostroza and another four people, they were lined up on the bridge and shot – but none of the bullets hit Blanca, who fell into the river and was carried downstream by the current. Eventually she managed to struggle ashore and find shelter. She had left five children at home when she was detained, but she did not dare to go back to them, for fear of being killed.

A week later, a peasant leader was shot beside a river; he was hit by two bullets but survived. He secretly returned to his home, where he lived hidden in an outhouse for another six years while his wife struggled to bring up their several small children alone.

The excuse of armed confrontations, used to explain the discovery of bodies in clandestine graves, was also used to justify the disappearance of political prisoners, as in the case investigated and reported by Clamor in a press release of 21 July 1980. This was the fifth anniversary of a complex operation involving the collaboration of three countries – Chile, Brazil, and Argentina – to create a fictitious story and so hide the truth about the real fate of 119 Chilean political prisoners. Clamor decided to investigate the story after receiving innumerable appeals from Chilean mothers.

In July 1975, two small, virtually unknown publications, the newspaper *O Dia* of Curitiba, in Brazil, and *Lea*, a weekly magazine in Buenos Aires, published two exclusive stories. The headline in the Curitiba paper was 'Chilean Terrorists Die in the Interior of Argentina', and the story listed the names of 59 people who were supposed to have been killed or had fled during an anti-guerrilla operation in Salta, in the north of Argentina. *Lea*'s story was headlined 'MIR Assassinates 60 Comrades', and it told of how 60 Chileans had been eliminated in the three previous months by their comrades in the Chilean left-wing guerrilla organization the Revolutionary Left Movement (Movimiento de Izquierda

Revolucionaria, MIR), in half a dozen different countries, namely Argentina, Colombia, Venezuela, Panama, Mexico, and France.

The United Press International news agency picked up the *Lea* story in Buenos Aires, and its dispatch was reproduced by Chilean newspapers under the headline 'MIR Members Assassinate 60 of Their Comrades'. *O Dia's* story, meanwhile, was reprinted by the Chilean dailies: *La Segunda* under the headline 'MIR Members Exterminated Like Rats', and *Últimas Noticias* with the title 'Argentine Security Forces Kill Chilean Extremists'.

Patricia Lorca, who later wrote a book about the coup, was in a queue of women waiting to visit imprisoned family members when someone arrived carrying a copy of *La Segunda* with the story. The women pored over the list, looking for the names of relatives who had disappeared. Several found them, and there were shouts and cries of 'It's my son, my son'; 'They've killed my husband, they've killed him'; 'My God, it can't be – it's a lie, it's a lie!' Some of the women fainted, while others banged on the doors of the prison.

When Clamor, at the request of the Chilean mothers, decided to investigate, Jaime Wright wrote to the Paraná Public Library, and discovered that *O Dia* had ceased publication on 30 June 1961. Fourteen years later, in June 1975, the paper suddenly reappeared for just four days, publishing the story about the Chileans. In Argentina, *Lea* magazine had an even shorter life, appearing only on 21 July 1975 with the story of the 60 Chileans. Clamor also discovered that the address given for the paper did not exist.

Clamor concluded that 'the disappearance of 119 Chileans confirms the collaboration among the organs of repression in Southern Cone nations'.

Throughout the 1970s and into the 1980s, the Vicariate of Solidarity and its predecessor, the Committee of Cooperation for Peace in Chile (Comité de Cooperación para la Paz en Chile, COPACHI), set up just a month after the coup to protect persecuted Chileans, suffered constant pressure, threats, and intimidation. They deliberately avoided direct opposition to the government, but their work with political prisoners and their denunciations of human rights violations brought them into conflict with the authorities. Lawyers and doctors who worked for the Vicariate were threatened and sometimes arrested.

In his book on the WCC's work in Latin America, Chuck Harper recounted an incident in May 1975 involving COPACHI, which offered support especially to people from working-class areas who had been subject to raids, searches, detention, torture, and other forms of repression. The building where COPACHI had its offices was surrounded by soldiers and National Intelligence Directorate (Dirección de Inteligencia Nacional, DINA) agents, after a young leader of the Socialist Party, Sergio Jaime Zamora Herrera, escaped from a DINA vehicle and dashed through the front door, with two DINA agents in hot pursuit, guns drawn. When they tried to grab him, the staff surrounded him, shouting, 'This is the house of the archbishop, the cardinal!'

The cardinal was alerted to what was going on. Phone calls asking for urgent support went out to the US ambassador and the Supreme Court, and to scores of churches. Harper described what happened next:

> From all over the city, Protestant pastors and Catholic priests rushed to put on clerical collars (some, unused to wearing them in a modern society, scrambled into backroom trunks and boxes to find them). Crosses of venerable or less venerable origin, in impressive or discreet shapes and sizes, draped the necks of lay people and clergy alike. By the time this battalion of 'clergy' arrived from both ends of *Calle Santa Monica*, DINA agents and police were everywhere, waiting for orders to go in and take Zamora by force. Their astonishment and irritation was palpable as dozens of men of the cloth walked calmly through their midst. It was an electric moment. Slowly, the members of COPACHI emerged from the building to go home. As they did, each man or woman was surrounded and accompanied by four or five members of the religious community for protection. ... Finally, all had departed and the lights were turned off. The 'Cardinal' had won this one.[1]

A few months later, COPACHI was closed down on General Pinochet's orders and its directors were arrested or expelled from Chile. Cardinal Henríquez immediately replaced it with the Vicariate of Solidarity, whose staff also came under attack, but whose institutional position within the Church, and physical position literally next to Santiago Cathedral, saved it from closure. The Vicariate offered shelter to the families of the disappeared, provided legal assistance to victims, and ran soup kitchens and child nutrition programmes. It also became one of the main sources of reliable, organized information, secreted out of Santiago by visitors, especially members of religious orders, past the heavy security at Pudahuel Airport.

In *Clamor Bulletin* No. 12, of December 1980, we reported on the 'New Escalation of Terror in Chile' with details of kidnappings, assassination, and the use of secret prisons. The notorious DINA, implicated in the murder of Orlando Letelier in 1976, had been succeeded by the National Intelligence Centre (Central Nacional de Informaciones, CNI), but the methods were the same.

On 11 September 1980, exactly seven years after the coup, the Pinochet government organized a plebiscite to gain approval for a new constitution, the ironically named Constitution of Liberty, which would keep the dictator in power as president of the republic, with increased personal powers, for another eight years. The aim was to preserve Chile's free market economy from any political challenge.

When the 'yes' vote won easily, the opposition parties denounced fraud. The new constitution took effect on 11 March 1981, legitimizing the dictator who had overthrown a democratically elected president, Salvador Allende, and introduced a reign of terror, with assassinations, torture, and disappearances. Over 3,000 had been killed or had disappeared after arrest, while at least

10,000 people had asked for political asylum in other countries, and hundreds of thousands had emigrated for economic reasons.

Pinochet had won the plebiscite, but resistance was growing as economic conditions worsened. Since the coup, the regime had done everything it could to destroy Chile's powerful trade union movement. Clamor's *Bulletin* No. 14 listed 65 union officials who had been killed or disappeared between 1973 and 1976.

In 1978 a new Labour Plan disbanded national federations and confederations, both industrial and peasant. Instead, worker representation was fragmented into thousands of tiny organizations without representation, deprived of any real bargaining power. The peasant union structure was destroyed.

Among many other measures aimed at weakening the workers' power, in mid-1981 employers were allowed to hire people under 18 or over 60 for less than the minimum wage. While mass unemployment followed the closing of hundreds of small firms, those who had jobs had to work more for lower pay. Four hours were added to the working week, under the pretext of 'national reconstruction', while wages were cut by up to 50 per cent.

In 1979, there were said to be over 600,000 unemployed people out of a population of 10 million. For the Unemployed Workers National Coordination Committee, the economic model introduced by the Pinochet government depended on a 'large army of unemployed labour'.[2]

In 1983, a National Day of Protest was organized by labour unions on 11 May. It had begun as a strike by the workers in the copper mines, the backbone of the Chilean economy. To avoid a bloodbath after troops surrounded the mines, it was transformed into a national non-violent protest, terminating in a *panelaço* – banging of pots and pans at night. Over a thousand people were arrested, but non-violent resistance, organized at the grassroots, was gaining support, creating new methods of protest. Some were inspired by the film *Gandhi* and the Solidarity movement in Poland. Sit-ins with people chanting 'We have clean hands', while holding up their hands, were held outside places known to be used as torture centres. Priests and nuns were often present.

Not everyone believed in non-violent resistance, however. By the end of 1983, a hard-line leftist alliance of the People's Democratic Movement (Movimiento Democrático Popular, MDP) and the MIR had begun a campaign of attacks against the Pinochet regime, with over 700 bombings around the country, including attacks on subways and power pylons. The response was increased repression.

Notes

1. Harper, C. R. (2006) *O Acompanhamento: Ecumenical Action for Human Rights in Latin America 1970–1990*, Geneva: WCC Publications.
2. *Clamor Bulletin* 14, December 1981.

CHAPTER 18
The list

As more and more lists of disappeared people arrived at the Clamor office, and the numbers rose into the thousands, we began to realize that there was a danger of forgetting that every number represented a real person, an individual. To talk about 10,000, 15,000, or 30,000 disappeared people showed the scale of the repression in Argentina, but it did not convey the human drama behind each disappearance.

We decided that we needed to show who each and every one of the disappeared was, to show that they were not just names on lists, but also fathers, sons, mothers, wives – people with identities, with trades and professions, with families. Later we discovered that in the secret detention camps, the aim was the opposite: the prisoners were known by numbers, their identities erased.

The idea of making our own list, with as much detail as possible about the people on it, took shape. In the days before computers, it would be no simple task. We would have to compare all the different lists, denunciations, testimonies, and reports, and extract the information we needed to show who each person was. Ideally, to make sure the information was correct, we needed to have more than one source. It would be a gigantic task. Who would do it?

The members of Clamor all had regular jobs besides the hours they spent on human rights work, so none of us had the time needed. Jaime Wright worked full-time for Clamor, but administration tasks, correspondence, writing articles, and getting the bulletins printed and posted took up all his time. We decided that we would have to find a person (or persons) to take on the task, preferably an Argentine who was already involved with human rights.

I contacted several refugees and exiles. They were all keen to help, but gave up when they realized what a mammoth task it would be. Then I was approached by a young couple, Gustavo Pierola and Marisa Magni. At first, they seemed unlikely candidates for a task that would require intense dedication and meticulous research – they were physical education teachers, aged 22 and 23, with two small children. Gustavo had a job as a basketball instructor at the São Paulo Tennis Club. They had arrived in São Paulo in 1978 seeking a safe place to have their first child after Gustavo's brother disappeared and they were in danger of arrest. They did not belong to any political organization, but they wanted to stay close to Argentina and to do something useful for the victims of repression there.

Even after learning more about the huge challenge we were proposing, they were keen to take it on. Their only equipment was a small Olivetti 33 typewriter.

We decided that the best way to organize the information would be with index cards. Each card would have a series of numbers, and each number would correspond to an item of information like name, age, civil status, occupation, nationality, or identity document number. Then there were the place and date of detention, the name of any disappeared family members, and observations such as 'seen in such and such camp' or 'born in captivity'.

Gustavo and Marisa began work on the Clamor List in 1981. Jaime suggested they move to Embu, a city suburb, for security reasons. With funding from the WCC, via the ever-helpful Chuck Harper, he rented a large empty house. Having little furniture was an advantage, because in the empty rooms they could spread out the documents, papers, and index cards, and work without fear of being disturbed.

Jaime was a frequent visitor to the house in Embu, bringing new information, checking on their progress, and sometimes bringing visitors like the Abuelas. The Abuelas began to visit on a more regular basis, to consult the growing body of organized data for any scrap of information, any name, place, or detail that might lead them to their grandchildren. They also brought with them information from Argentina.

One of the main sources of information for the List was the detailed testimonies provided by many of the refugees who arrived in São Paulo after surviving detention in prisons and clandestine camps. Then there were all the lists drawn up by human rights organizations, both Argentine and international, by exiles' organizations and by professional bodies. All these had to be compared, collated, checked, and rechecked.

At the end of 1982, the laborious work was concluded, and the List was printed as a chunky 416-page book entitled *Desaparecidos en la Argentina* (Disappeared in Argentina). The book contained 7,291 names in alphabetical order, and included an appendix containing information received after the main List was finished, with the names of 494 persons who had been freed or were known to have been killed.

Although the great majority of the disappeared were Argentines, 26 other nationalities were represented on the List. There were people from ten European countries (Germany, Austria, Spain, France, Italy, Poland, Sweden, Switzerland, Ireland, and England), from three Middle Eastern countries (Israel, Syria, and Lebanon), and from the Far East (Japan). The disappeared also came from most of the countries of South America (Bolivia, Brazil, Chile, Colombia, Ecuador, Paraguay, Peru, Uruguay, and Venezuela), and from the US, Cuba, and Guatemala.

The disappeared came from 54 different trades and professions, ranging from musician to meteorologist, from diplomat to dentist, from prison guard to housewife. There were lawyers, architects, artisans, social workers, artists, carpenters, accountants, peasant farmers, vets, bank clerks, teachers, nurses, writers, secondary schoolchildren, university students, pensioners, doctors, parliamentarians, journalists, psychologists, priests and nuns, church lay workers, academics, chemists, radiologists, weavers, and factory workers in many different industries. There were policemen, sailors, and army recruits. Some 50 per cent of the total were manual workers or employees, while 23 per cent were students, and 20 per cent were from the professions.

Of the people on Clamor's List, almost three quarters (72 per cent) were men, and just over a quarter (28 per cent) were women. Two thirds (67 per cent) were young people aged between 19 and 30, and 4.3 per cent were teenagers aged between 13 and 18. A further quarter (24.5 per cent) were aged between 31 and 50. Just over 3 per cent (3.2 per cent) were over 50 years old, while 1 per cent were children aged under 12.

Almost half (46.6 per cent) had disappeared in 1976, the first year of the coup. Another 36 per cent had disappeared in 1977, and a further 11.5 per cent in 1978. Almost three quarters (72.8 per cent) had been abducted in Buenos Aires, 8.7 per cent in Córdoba, 7.7 per cent in Tucumán, 3 per cent in Santa Fé, and 2.2 per cent in Mendoza.

The book also contained the names of 61 clandestine detention centres known to exist, with maps to show their locations. Most of them were in Buenos Aires and La Plata. Many were hidden inside military installations, police stations, or prisons, but some were in civilian properties, like Automotores Orletti, a car repair workshop near the centre of the capital, or La Cacha, located in a former radio transmitter near La Plata, or the camp in an old weapons factory in Rosário. Much of the information on the camps was collected personally by Gustavo during a risky trip to Argentina in 1982.

Dom Paulo's preface to the book recalled all the international conventions and treaties on human rights signed by Argentina which had been so flagrantly disrespected. In January he went to Rome and presented a copy to Pope John Paul II, who examined it with interest and said, 'The Church cannot remain silent before criminal actions that involve the disappearance of people, without trial, leaving behind, in addition, their families in cruel uncertainty.'

Letters began to arrive from families. Graciela and Agostin Colombo wrote asking for their son's name to be removed from the List because his body had been returned to them. The mother of Dardo Marcelo Cristino Benavides wrote asking to be put in touch with the person who had supplied his name for the List; she added, 'My husband died of sadness.' Raul Luis Perriere from Entre Ríos wrote to say that the List had provided him with the first news of his daughter and son-in-law.

In 1983, Gustavo hid a copy of the book at the bottom of his rucksack and took the bus to Argentina. The end of the military regime was now in sight and disappearances had almost completely stopped, but even so, the Argentine border guards searched the passengers for subversive literature or incriminating documents. When the guard felt something hard at the bottom of his rucksack and asked what it was, Gustavo said it was a box of chocolates. Once again, chocolates saved the day.

Sister Michael Mary Nolan, the American nun who had joined Clamor in 1978, filled a suitcase with copies of the book for the Abuelas, the Madres, and other human rights groups, and carried it through Ezeiza Airport without a problem, though her knees were shaking, and not from the weight of the case.

For years afterwards, families of the disappeared who still had no idea where their missing relatives had been taken, or where those relatives' remains were, sought out Clamor in their desperate efforts to find out something, anything, about what had happened to them.

In January 1984, the National Commission on the Disappearance of Persons (Comisión Nacional sobre la Desaparición de Personas, CONADEP), set up by Argentina's newly elected civilian president Raúl Alfonsín, asked us to provide the original index cards used to make our List, which Jaime duly packed into boxes and sent off. The Clamor List became one of the bases for the list of over 9,000 disappeared persons prepared by CONADEP.

In 2006, the archbishop of Buenos Aires, Cardinal Jorge Bergoglio, later to become Pope Francis, asked for copies of the Clamor index cards, which, now digitized, were duly sent.

PART 2
Light at the end of the tunnel (1983–1989)

CHAPTER 19
Where are Carla and Maria Eugenia?

The Abuelas de Plaza de Mayo continued to work tirelessly to find their grand-children. As the Argentine military dictatorship, demoralized by defeat in the Falklands war, weakened, they received more tip-offs from people who suspected that a neighbour's child, or a colleague's child, could be one of the disappeared children whose pictures were beginning to appear on posters.

Each case was different, but those that involved getting a court order for blood tests to establish the child's real identity proved the hardest because, for many judges appointed during the dictatorship, their sympathy with the military regime and its practices overrode their obligations to carry out the law under the new democratic government.

After the discovery of Anatole and Vicky in Chile, Clamor played a role in several other cases with international connections, involving searches in Bolivia, Paraguay, and Brazil itself, besides Argentina.

In Bolivia, we became involved in the case of Graciela Rutilo Artés and her baby daughter, nine-month-old Carla Rutilo Artés. They were detained in Oruro in April 1976 and taken to La Paz. Days later, Carla was separated from her mother and placed in a children's home under the false name of Norah Nemtala.

'The little girl was taken several times to see her mother being tortured', read a report from Bolivia's APDH, 'with the aim of softening up Graciela'. They even dangled the baby upside down by her feet, naked, to persuade her mother to talk. Another source later said that Graciela had been tortured by Argentine agents wearing hoods, as well as Bolivians who did not bother to hide their faces.

Later Carla was moved to the Villa Fatima orphanage, where she was registered under her real name, but on 25 August, she was taken from the orphanage against the will of those looking after her. Graciela was forced to sign a paper saying that she had received the child in a perfect state of health. Four days later, the two were said to have been handed over to the Argentine security services at a border post. 'Since this date there has been no news of either mother or daughter', the APDH report noted.

Several years passed without further news. Meanwhile, as strikes and protests grew, the Bolivian dictatorship of General Luis García Meza, enmeshed in cocaine smuggling and corruption, was crumbling. Hernán Siles Zuazo, the man who had been legally elected in 1980 but prevented from taking office by the coup, became president in October 1982.

With the restoration of democracy in Bolivia, Carla's grandmother, actress Matilda Artés Company, known as Sacha, wasted no time in travelling there to find out about the fate of her disappeared daughter and granddaughter. She was living in Spain after death threats forced her to leave Argentina. On her way to La Paz, she broke her journey in São Paulo to talk to Clamor and enlist our help.

Sacha discovered that many people believed Carla might still be in Bolivia, although this was based entirely on circumstantial evidence. The wife of General Juan Pereda Asbún, a former president of Bolivia and the minister of the interior at the time of the disappearance, had visited Carla while she was in the children's home, and then appeared at the family hacienda in Santa Cruz with an adopted child the same age as Carla, called Juanita.

We decided that although there were reports that Carla had been sent to Argentina with her mother Graciela, there were enough indications that she had remained in Bolivia to justify investigating further. I remembered Lupe Cajías, a Bolivian journalist I had met there in the days after the coup. We had maintained contact ever since. In December 1983, she agreed to take on the investigation, with her expenses paid by Clamor.

By now all sorts of conflicting stories, false leads, and deliberate bits of misinformation were swirling around, including that Carla and Graciela had been killed and thrown into a lake or buried on a farm near Cochabamba. People whom Lupe wanted to interview mysteriously disappeared. The reports from the social workers at the orphanage, which Lupe had left with the commission set up to investigate forced disappearances, had got lost during one of their many moves.

As there were many clues pointing to the family of General Pereda Asbún, Lupe decided to beard the general in his den. She travelled down to Santa Cruz, where disconcertingly, they welcomed her and willingly gave her copies of Juanita's footprints, to be matched with Carla's. They authorized the taking of blood samples from the nine-year-old, who, unlike her older sisters, was fair-haired and blue-eyed. But their goodwill made Lupe suspect that Juanita was not Carla.

By now, Enrique Araoz, a journalist working for Spanish TV, who was a personal friend of Sacha's, had arrived in La Paz. He came with the support of the Spanish president, Felipe González, who had become interested in the case. Clamor provided US$300 towards his expenses in Bolivia. Arriving at the end of 1983, he and Lupe worked together for a while, following up the many confusing leads and rumours.

While it seemed more and more likely that Graciela and Carla had been transferred to Argentina, Sacha still held onto the idea that Juanita, the Pereda Asbúns' adopted daughter, could be her granddaughter.

In her last report, covering March and April 1984, Lupe suggested continuing the search in Argentina, with the help of the Abuelas. Democracy had been restored there, and a civilian president now ruled.

And it was the Abuelas who found Carla. Sacha had sent them a photograph of Graciela when she was about the same age that Carla would be now, and they included it on posters with the faces of other missing children.

One day, Chicha, one of the founders of the Abuelas, received a phone call from a woman who told her that the girl on the poster was a schoolmate of her daughter. The daughter had recognized the girl and told her mother, 'That's Gina.'

The woman said the little girl's name was Gina Ruffo, and her father's name was Eduardo Alfredo Ruffo.

Chicha phoned Sacha and told her to come to Argentina immediately, because she had important news. In Buenos Aires, now breathing the fresh air of democracy, Sacha appeared on a TV show holding the photograph – and was seen by eight-year-old Carla herself, who innocently asked the man who had appropriated her why that woman was holding her photo. The answer was a beating; she was told never to ask that question again.

The Abuelas discovered that Eduardo Ruffo had been a member of the right-wing death squad Triple A, which had been given a free hand during the government of Isabel Perón to kill left-wingers and provided many of the torturers at the clandestine camps after the coup. Ruffo had worked at the Automotores Orletti camp, where Graciela was taken after being handed over by the Bolivians in 1976. He had taken Carla from her mother and registered her as his own child, Gina Ruffo, because his wife could not have children.

The Abuelas went to court to denounce Carla's appropriator and get her real identity re-established. It took another year, with one judge declaring himself incompetent and another flatly refusing to hear the case, before Carla Rutilo Artés was restored to her grandmother in August 1985.

By the time the case went to court, Ruffo had gone into hiding with Carla, but he was tracked down and arrested with his wife, Amanda Cordero, at a house on the outskirts of Buenos Aires. At the house the police found not only Carla, but arms, munitions, and false passports. Ruffo was eventually sentenced to six years for falsifying a document, but he was not tried for abducting a minor, and he was pardoned under President Carlos Menem's amnesty.

Many years later, Carla talked about meeting her grandmother and said it was like a fairy tale. She left behind the man who had not only beaten her frequently but who had also sexually abused her, and went to live in Spain with a loving, kind grandmother. In 2010, she came from Spain to give evidence at Ruffo's trial for torture and abuse at the secret detention camp of Automotores Orletti. He was sentenced to 25 years. Tragically, Carla died of cancer in 2017, aged 42.

In Argentina, the children and babies who had disappeared were being sought by their grandparents, or in a few cases, by one of their parents who had survived. But one case was unique: a husband and wife whose children were disappeared had both survived.

The couple, Ana María Caracoche and Oscar Gatica, nicknamed Negro, came to Brazil and sought out Clamor in 1980. They told us their children had disappeared in 1977 on different dates.

In March that year they had left María Eugenia, then aged almost two, at the house of their next-door neighbours and friends, Susana and José Abdala, in La Plata, while they took baby Felipe to the doctor in Buenos Aires. When they returned a few hours later, 'the usually noisy street was deathly quiet'. Worse still, the Abdalas' house stood empty. Frightened neighbours told them that a carload of armed men had arrived, burst into the Abdalas' house, and dragged them all out: two small children, María Eugenia and two-year-old José Sabino, the Abdalas' son, along with his mother, hooded, and his father.

Afraid the men would return, the Gaticas hurriedly moved to the home of another friend, Roberto Amerise, in Berisso, another district of La Plata.

A month later, at 10 p.m., that house was invaded by a group of about 10 armed men in civilian clothes, wearing masks. One of them wore a clown's mask. They smashed in the front window and climbed through it. Negro was in the kitchen at the back of the house, and hearing the noise, he escaped over the fence at the back of the house. Ana María was changing baby Felipe. 'One of them pushed me against the wall, beating me violently on the head and asking me where my husband was', she later recalled when I interviewed her for an article in the *Guardian*.[1] 'When I realized that they were going to take me away and separate me from my little son, I tried to free the arm they had twisted up behind my back and they broke it, so that I lost consciousness for a few moments.' In spite of her broken arm, Ana María was handcuffed and hooded and pushed into the boot of a car with Roberto, then driven off. She was held in the detention camp known as La Cacha for a month and tortured to make her reveal the whereabouts of Negro, a trade union organizer.

Unable to tell her torturers anything because she did not know where he was, she was released after a month, probably in the hope that she would lead them to Negro. She immediately returned to Berisso to find out what had happened to the baby. Neighbours told her that Felipe and Camilo, Roberto's small son, had been left at a neighbour's house, with instructions to give them to whoever came to get them. This neighbour said that the next day, Camilo's grandmother came to collect him. Three days later, a couple who said they were Felipe's grandparents came and took him away. But Ana María and Negro's parents lived in Bahia Blanca, in the far south of Argentina, and had no idea of what had happened.

Eventually Ana María managed to contact Negro, who had gone underground, moving from place to place. It was impossible to begin searching for their children when they themselves were still in danger. Soon Ana María became pregnant, and their third child, María da Paz, was born. They decided that, with a small child, it would be safer to leave Argentina. They got the bus to Brazil, using false documents, and made their way to the town of Vitória, up the coast from Rio de Janeiro. There they were welcomed by members of a church they had met at an ecumenical congress in Argentina.

In Vitória, their fourth child Manolo was born. Now, once again, they had two children. But never for a moment did they forget the two who had disappeared. As soon as María da Paz and Manolo were old enough to understand, they were told about their older brother and sister.

Ana María and Negro heard about Clamor through the church in Vitória, and they came to São Paulo to see us. As soon as it was safe to do so, we paid Negro's fare to return to Argentina, and early in 1984 he travelled to Buenos Aires to consult the Abuelas. In Berisso, Negro found the neighbour with whom Felipe was left on the night that Ana María was seized, and persuaded her to tell him what had happened to the baby.

She admitted that fear had made her lie to Ana María about the grand-parents. She told Negro that she had passed Felipe on to a childless married woman called Nelly, who later separated from her husband and brought him up on her own, as her own child. When Negro tracked Nelly down, she at first refused to believe him. 'But the evidence was too strong', recalled Ana María. 'Felipe is the image of his father.' In September 1984, Nelly finally agreed to restore the small boy, now seven years old, to his rightful parents, but they agreed that she should remain in touch, visiting frequently.

As I wrote in my *Guardian* article: 'Felipe came back into the family he had never known with amazing ease, helped by his younger brother and sister. Now they all wanted their older sister back. At meals, they kept an empty chair for her.'

Ana María, who had travelled from Brazil to join Negro in Buenos Aires, now began the search for María Eugenia, with the active help of the Abuelas. At the Abuelas' office they pored over photos of children suspected of being illegally appropriated, the testimonies of released prisoners, and the information in the anonymous tip-offs which were flooding in now that the military had left power.

They discovered that the chief of police in San Nicolás, Inspector Rodolfo Oscar Silva, who was known to have participated in the repression during the dictatorship and had been stationed in La Plata, had a child who looked very like María Eugenia. The Abuelas began surveillance. They discovered the school she went to, and that she lived with Silva's first wife, Amanda Collard, and spent the weekends with the inspector. She had been registered as Elizabete Silvina Silva, born in July 1977, over a year and a half after her real birth.

When the case went to court, at first Silva admitted that he 'got the child' during a police operation,[2] but he later denied it and refused to allow her to be submitted to the blood tests demanded by the judge, which would prove her real identity. In María Eugenia's case, the Abuelismo Index test (see Chapter 9) was not necessary because her real parents were alive.

Carried out compulsorily, the tests proved her real identity. On 2 September, court officials were sent to Silva's home to carry out her restitution, but minutes before they arrived the inspector and his wife fled with María Eugenia, presumably alerted by a tip-off.

At a press conference organized by the Abuelas, Ana María said her worst torture was not the physical suffering endured during her captivity, but the mental anguish of not knowing what had happened to her children. Speaking of María Eugenia, she said, 'Now, we are awaiting her return. For many years we have saved up our love for her, as have her younger brothers and sister. We are certain that soon we will have her back in the family, either with the help of the state, which would be best, or without it.'

In mid-September Silva gave himself up and María Eugenia was restored to her family by the court. 'Finally, a judge handed María Eugenia, bewildered and crying, back to her parents, eight and a half years after she had disappeared. At first she cried and refused to speak to them.'[3] With the help of a psychologist, she quickly adapted and was soon playing with her brothers and sister.

Ana María and Negro returned to Brazil and went back to live in Vitória with their four children.

Notes

1. Rocha, J. (1986) 'The Agony of Seven Stolen Years', *The Guardian*, 7 May, p. 10.
2. *Clarín*, 4 September 1985.
3. *Ibid.*

CHAPTER 20
The search for Mariana

When they read the news of the discovery of Anatole and Vicky in Chile and Anatole's statement that there had been a third child in the big black car that left them in the Valparaíso square, Marta and Julio Zaffaroni were convinced that this must be their granddaughter, Mariana. She had disappeared in Buenos Aires with her parents just a few days before the others, aged one and a half. Her parents were also militants of the PVP who had fled to Argentina for safety. On 7 August, a week after Dom Paulo's press conference in São Paulo, the grandparents flew to Santiago, sure they would find Mariana.

Belela Herera was waiting for them at the airport. The next day they gave a press conference and handed out photographs of Mariana and a detailed description of the little girl. She had a pale blemish on her arm and a scar on one foot from a burn. The Chilean press covered the story with enthusiasm, and the photos of Mariana appeared in most of the papers.

Marta and Julio hired two lawyers to help them and got an interview with the minister of the interior and the regional military commander in charge of frontier control, who promised that the entry records at every frontier crossing would be checked to try to determine where the children had entered Chile. Both officials were very curious about the identity of the mysterious 'Tia Monica'.

They tracked down the *El Mercurio* journalist who had written the first story about Anatole and Vicky on 29 December 1976. He had one new piece of information. The Argentine ambassador had gone to the children's home after the story was published and then told the journalist that the boy was Uruguayan, the girl Argentine. How did he know this unless he knew their real identity? Although Anatole had been born in Uruguay, he had spent three of his four years in Argentina, and he spoke with a *porteño* accent. Vicky had been born in Buenos Aires.

Marta and Julio then went to the Playa Ancha children's home in Valparaíso, from where Anatole and Vicky had been adopted. The staff were friendly and allowed them to look through the register, searching for children who had been left there between September 1976 and the end of 1977. They drew a blank. They did the same at a large home for abandoned children in Santiago. 'The staff of their own free will spent an entire night checking the register, which is enormous, to see if they could trace Mariana but this too was unsuccessful', Marta reported in a subsequent letter to Ester, Mariana's other grandmother.

Finally they went to see the couple who had adopted Anatole and Vicky, the Larrabeitis. By this time Angélica Julien and the Larrabeitis had come to a mutual agreement under which the children would keep their real names but remain with their adoptive parents. The biological family would have permanent visiting rights and if the real parents appeared, the situation would be reviewed.

Now the Larrabeitis were anxious to help Marta and Julio find their grand-daughter. They let Marta and Julio talk to Anatole on their own, to see if he could remember more about the other little girl in the car. Marta showed him a picture of Mariana, hoping it would jog his memory, but three years had passed and the picture said nothing to him. Later Marta wrote: 'Evidently this child had rung down a curtain over the past.' They noticed that when they mentioned they had flown to Chile, it seemed to frighten him; he said he had been in a plane once, but quickly changed the subject. Whenever they mentioned Uruguay or Argentina the little boy became anxious and tried to change the subject.

Marta and Julio stayed in Chile several more days hoping that the stories in the press would produce results. They did not. Frustrated, the pair returned to Rio 'with very little hope of finding our grandchild and our children', wrote Marta in her letter to Ester.

In Montevideo, Ester never stopped looking for Mariana. She had visited every government office, army HQ, and police department she could think of, swallowing insults, threats, and indifference in the hope of gleaning a piece of information.

The years passed without news. Then, on 26 January 1983, the Brazilian newspaper *O Estado de S. Paulo* published a full-page interview with an Argentine who claimed to have been a member of SIDE, the Argentine intel-ligence agency, until 1979. He said he had left Argentina because he knew too much, although he also said he regretted nothing.

For the first time, a member of the security forces gave graphic details of what had happened to the disappeared, confirming the rumours that had circulated. He said most military bases had incinerators for burning rubbish, and these were used for burning bodies. He said that the bodies of those who died under torture were either burned, thrown into the River Plate, or buried in the countryside. The interviewer asked him what had happened to the children who were detained and whose parents had died. He said he remembered the case of a Uruguayan couple. Their child had been adopted by a colleague from SIDE.

Marta did not normally see this newspaper, which was edited in São Paulo and sold at few newsstands in Rio. It was Maria, the Uruguayan exile in São Paulo who had brought us the news of Anatole and Vicky, who tipped her off. Marta hurried to Copacabana, where she knew the São Paulo papers were on sale, and bought a copy. When she read the interview, she was sure that the child mentioned must be Mariana. If it were true, it meant that Mariana had never left Buenos Aires; she had never been taken to Chile.

Marta decided that she had to speak to the SIDE agent. She wrote to the newspaper explaining who she was. Plinio Vicente, one of the journalists who had interviewed the Argentine, replied, promising to see what he could do. But the weeks went by, and she heard no more.

Yet neither she nor Julio nor their son Pablo, who had also settled in Rio, could let go of the idea that the mysterious agent had the key to Mariana's whereabouts. As they talked endlessly about the interview, they concluded that if one person knew what had happened to Mariana, then others must also know. With the military regime crumbling after the debacle of the Falklands, somebody might be prepared to talk. How could they find such a person?

Julio suggested putting an ad in *Clarín*, the most widely read Argentine daily. They decided that the *solicitada* ought to be placed prominently on a main news page, with a big photograph of Mariana, not tucked away amongst the small ads. The cost would be astronomical. They asked Clamor to help.

We mimeographed an appeal with a picture of Mariana, calling it 'Let's Find This Little Girl. She Was Kidnapped', and I distributed it around newsrooms. Over 200 journalists contributed to the fund. An old school-friend of mine in England, Susan Howatch, who had shot to success with a series of bestselling gothic novels, contributed a generous sum.

Eventually we raised the amount needed to pay for the advertisement. The text, the photograph, and the money were entrusted to two clergymen – Clamor's Jaime Wright and the WCC's Chuck Harper – to take personally to the offices of *Clarín* in Buenos Aires.

The *solicitada* appeared on 20 May 1983 at the top of the page, with a large photograph of Mariana and the headline 'DESAPARECIDA'. It gave the date of her disappearance and the names of her parents, and asked anyone who had any information to get in touch, either with the Abuelas in Buenos Aires or with Clamor in São Paulo. Strict confidentiality was promised.

In Montevideo, Rio de Janeiro, and São Paulo, copies of the paper were sought out by Ester, Marta, and Maria. Now we all began the anxious wait to see if it would produce a result.

Instead it was Marta's letter to the journalist Plinio Vicente that suddenly bore fruit, four months after she had sent it. Out of the blue, Plinio phoned and said he was coming to Rio and wanted to talk to her, alone. Not even Julio could be present, because it was 'very confidential'. Marta agreed to meet him at a cinema in downtown Rio, the Cine Paysandú. Julio and Pablo were not happy about her going alone, so they followed her at a discreet distance. The date was 27 May 1983.

From the cinema they went to have lunch at a restaurant in Cinelandia, a busy square in front of Rio's imposing neoclassical Municipal Theatre. There, at the Taberna Azul restaurant, Plinio told Marta that he was expecting another person from the newspaper who was bringing some papers which he wanted to talk to her about. In a letter she wrote to me afterwards, she said, 'He seemed very nervous, chain smoking and looking about him.' It was

1 p.m. and the restaurant's pavement tables were full of men and women having lunch, talking and laughing. Marta waited anxiously, wondering what the papers could contain. Then a man approached their table and Plinio said to her, 'This is the surprise I prepared for you.'

As soon as the man spoke, Marta realized that he was an Argentine, and that she was face to face with the ex-SIDE agent who not only knew where Mariana was but who probably knew what had happened to Emilia and Jorge, Mariana's parents. She could not stop staring at him, this man who was the first, tenuous physical link to her beloved son in the seven years since he had disappeared. He had long, curly black hair, a small beard, and a large moustache. He wore a black leather jacket and dark glasses. He seemed to be about 35 years old. He spoke like a well-educated person and his tone was calm, not aggressive.

He told Marta that he had worked in a place where many Uruguayan prisoners were held. He had interrogated them but he assured Marta that he had not tortured them – that was the work of others. He said he had talked to several of the Uruguayans, including a member of the family of the murdered senator Zelmar Michelini. Marta then opened her bag, took out a picture of Jorge, and handed it to the man. The agent looked at it carefully, then said he did not recognize him.

The agent said that the Uruguayan prisoners had been put on planes and flown to Uruguay, and that he had accompanied these operations. When Marta asked him the dates, he said he did not remember. He then told her that she should look for her children not in Argentina but in her own country, because they had all been returned to Uruguay.

At last Marta plucked up the courage to ask the question she had been burning to ask since she first saw him. All around them, *cariocas* (natives of Rio de Janeiro) were sipping ice-cold beers and eating salads and pizzas in the hot sun, oblivious to the drama in their midst as a frail, white-haired grandmother faced a man who had probably interrogated and possibly tortured her son and daughter-in-law. Marta reminded him that in the published interview, he had mentioned the child of a Uruguayan couple who had been adopted by a friend. What was the name of the child, and who had adopted her?

In her letter to me, Marta later recalled: 'He did not like the question. At first, he said he knew nothing about her, it had happened earlier, not at the same period that Emi and Jorge were being held. He was clever and slippery, and it was difficult to nail him down.'

Then Marta produced a copy of the *Clarín* newspaper with the advertisement, which had been published just a week before, and showed it to him. He read it, looking long and hard at the photograph of Mariana. 'His attitude changed. Now he admitted that the child he had mentioned in the interview could be Mariana, but said he could not be sure if the person who had taken her was still in Argentina. He could only discover this by returning to Buenos Aires, which was impossible.'

Then he told Marta, as though it would placate her, that if it were indeed the same child, she need not worry because Mariana was now doing just as well, or even better, than she would be with her grandmother. This remark infuriated the normally calm and collected Marta. She said that she could not accept this – the child should be with her family, and not with the murderers of her parents. Despite the heat around them, an icy chill descended over the table. The agent told Marta to forget the idea of recovering the child because she would never get her back. What is more, he would not reveal the name of the person who had Mariana, because that person was a friend and he would never betray or denounce him.

The difficult conversation continued. Several times, the agent asked Marta what she would do if the child were found. Would she take her away from the person who had looked after her up until now? Marta said that first she would have to see Mariana and see how she was, and then, depending on this, they would decide what to do.

The conversation lasted three to four hours. Marta ate nothing; she had no appetite. She tried to think of ways to enlist the agent's sympathy, to make him reveal at least something about the man who had Mariana, but he remained impassive, saying, 'All I can tell you is that she is well, so why don't you accept that?'

Eventually, Marta got up and left. She was exhausted. She felt defeated. Julio and Pablo, who had watched the meeting from a table in the next-door restaurant, took her home in a taxi, listening to her account of what the agent had said.

As soon as she got home, she wrote a long letter to Ester, giving her a blow-by-blow account of the frustrating meeting. She went over and over the interview in her mind and discussed it at length with Julio. Julio felt sure that the man wanted money for his information – he was not going to give her something so valuable for nothing. So Marta wrote again to Plinio Vicente, asking him if the agent wanted money in exchange for the answers they sought. Again, there was no immediate answer. Only nine months later, in February 1984, did she receive a reply, saying that the Argentine, who had been living in Brazil under a false name, had disappeared. There were rumours that he might have gone to Central America.

But now it was the advertisement in *Clarín* which produced results. Three weeks after it was published, an anonymous letter arrived at the Clamor office in the Curia. The pale blue envelope was postmarked Buenos Aires. Marisa was on duty the day it arrived, and she phoned me immediately with the news. I rushed to the Curia.

The envelope contained photocopies of two newspaper cuttings about the involvement of SIDE agent Miguel Angel Furci in a bomb attack. With them was a typed note which read: 'Since the date referred to by you a child with these characteristics is here and [Furci's] wife has never been pregnant. It is impossible that they have adopted her because of the abnormal life he leads and the risks that not only he and his family run but also all the inhabitants of this building.'

The anonymous sender gave an address, 3257 Calle Santo Tome, Villa del Parque; the name of the adopter, Miguel Angel Furci; and the name of the child, Daniela Romina Furci. Could Daniela be Mariana?

I began making phone calls. By a stroke of luck, Belela Herrera, the UNHCR coordinator in Chile when Anatole and Vicky were discovered there, now worked in the UNHCR office in Buenos Aires.

Everyone was excited – but at the same time, cautious. After all, we did not know for sure whether the anonymous tip-off was genuine or not. It could be someone with a grudge. If Mariana had been 'adopted' by a SIDE agent, he was still protected by the regime; he was one of theirs. Great care had to be taken in trying to confirm her real identity. Although the military had been demoralized by the Falklands defeat in 1982, they were still in power.

Once again, there was the same air of suppressed excitement that we had felt when we got the news about Anatole and Vicky – and that had been even more improbable.

The first thing was to try to see the child. The address given in the letter was a small block of flats, and it was the grandmothers who got the first glimpse of the little girl who might be their granddaughter. The two granny sleuths spent two or three days walking up and down the road outside the building and round the block, hoping to spot a child that looked like Mariana. Then Ester suggested that their best chance of seeing her was at lunchtime, when she would be arriving from, or leaving for, school. They stood on the other side of the road and pretended to be chatting, showing each other photos. The first child who left the block of flats was too big; it could not be her. Then a little girl with plaits came out who would be the right age, eight years old. With her, carrying her school bag, was a tall, dark-complexioned woman with short hair. Ester reckoned she was a maid.

The little girl sang as she walked along; she seemed happy. Marta hurried round the block so she could meet her from the other direction. Ester followed along behind the girl, and then passed her. Trying hard to keep the emotion out of her voice, she said, 'What a lovely song!' When the little girl looked up, Ester said to herself, 'It's Mariana.' Marta came round the corner, and they followed the girl to school. They waited around all afternoon, but they did not see her leave the school.

It was essential to get a photo of the little girl and confirm her real identity. Belela remembered Mónica Parada, a Uruguayan photographer who lived nearby. Mónica agreed to take on the risky assignment, and Belela gave her the last pictures of Mariana, taken when she was one and a half, just before she disappeared with her parents.

Seven years had passed – it was now September 1983 – and to Mónica it seemed a bit crazy, trying to locate a child with just the address and a very old photo. But she wanted to help the grandmothers, so she agreed to try. She walked up and down the street several times, then kept watch from her car, a Ford Falcon. She raised the bonnet, pretending that the car had broken down. She was very nervous; she was afraid it wouldn't work.

She was very aware of the irony of a refugee spying on a member of the security forces.

She was in luck – out of all the children entering and leaving the apartment block, only one was in Mariana's age group. The girl was accompanied by a young woman who seemed to be an employee, so Mónica decided to follow her to school, strolling along casually behind. They walked five blocks until they came to a convent school, run by nuns. When the child went in the school gate, Mónica followed her into the playground, her heart thumping. The little girl began playing with another child, and Mónica strolled up to them as casually as possible, clicking away with her camera and thinking desperately, as a mother herself, what would be the best way to approach her. She had to get a good picture of the girl's face, and she was aware that at any moment the bell might ring and she would lose her chance.

'Hello, what's your name?', Mónica asked. 'Daniela Furci', the little girl replied, without batting an eyelid. Mónica, her heart still pounding, said, 'Would you like me to take your picture?' When Daniela said yes, Mónica quickly took a picture of her with her friend, and then separately, and left the playground.

Now she had to develop the pictures. She realized that she had used a roll of film which already had pictures of her own children on it. Argentina's dictatorship was still in place – suppose they traced the picture back to her? She was afraid, but she went ahead.

When the film was developed, she made copies and sent them to Ester, Marta, and Maria. They compared the photos with those of Mariana's parents, Emilia and Jorge. Maria thought the girl looked just like Ester. Mónica also took copies to Robert Cox, editor of the *Buenos Aires Herald*, the English-language paper that had courageously published stories about the missing children. Cox – 'being very English', she said – put the photos side by side with the old photos of Mariana and measured the faces with a ruler. He decided that the girl was Mariana.

Convinced that they had found Mariana, the grandmothers asked for an interview with the mother superior of the convent school. She listened carefully as Marta and Ester explained the situation. Then she gave them photographs of Mariana's first communion and, from the school register, she supplied all the data she had about the little girl.

Armed with the girl's purported date of birth, Maria, who was still in Buenos Aires, went to the registry office and obtained a copy of the birth certificate of Daniela Romina Furci. She had been registered as the natural child of Miguel Angel Furci and his wife, Adriana González. The alleged date of her birth was 29 September 1975, six months after her real date of birth, 22 March 1975. It was given as a home birth.

She had been registered on 29 June 1977, eight months after being kidnapped with her parents, and to justify the delay Furci told the judge that he had been separated from his wife at the time and had only met the child when she was four months old. Adriana had given a different story – she said that Mariana had been a year old when her husband returned to the marital home. Later, Furci gave yet another explanation, saying that he had failed to register the birth because his wife was ill and he had to look after her. He claimed not to know that a birth could be registered by a third party. Whatever the excuse, it must have aroused suspicion. To maintain the fiction that she was six months younger than her real age, they treated her like a baby instead of a toddler. A photograph of her baptism showed Furci holding her like a baby, although she was already nearly two years old.

But what was the next step, now they were sure they had found Mariana? They decided to consult the Abuelas, who said the next step was to go to court and accuse Furci of appropriating Mariana illegally. As neither of them lived in Argentina, the grandmothers enlisted the help of Mónica's partner, Milton Romani, another PVP exile and a companion of Mariana's parents, to present the case against Furci to a judge. But judges were still reluctant to try cases involving members of the security forces, and it passed from hand to hand like a hot potato until it got to the court in San Isidro.

Ester made many visits to the court in San Isidro, but found the judge reluctant to act. She argued with him. The Abuelas were supportive, but it was only when a new judge, Alberto Piotti, took over the case that things began to happen. Over a year had passed since they had discovered Mariana; the military had gone, and Argentina was once again a democracy.

In January 1985, the judge ordered blood tests to determine whether the child was the Furcis' own daughter, as they claimed. The Furcis refused, saying that they would only allow Mariana to do the test. But in June 1985 the couple disappeared, taking Mariana with them.

In Uruguay, where democracy had been restored and the cases of Mariana and the other disappeared Uruguayan children had received huge publicity, there was indignation at the news, and a petition addressed to President Alfonsín was signed by 80,000 people. In July, Ester took it to the Casa Rosada.

The court, however, acted. An order forbidding Furci to leave the country was issued, and Interpol was informed, because Argentina shared long land borders with Chile, Paraguay, Bolivia, Brazil, and Uruguay.

A 'wanted' poster with the Furcis photos was distributed. It took another year before they were tracked down, not by the police but by the Abuelas, following an anonymous tip-off. They told the judge, but a few hours before the police arrived to arrest Furci, he fled with his wife and Mariana, having himself been tipped off again. This time they went to Asunción, the Paraguayan capital.

Although Furci was wanted by Interpol, General Stroessner, in power in Paraguay for 32 years, welcomed him with open arms, as he did several other ex-members of the security forces who fled from Argentina with kidnapped children to escape court orders.

Ester decided to go to the Paraguayan capital herself. Milton Romani went with her. They spent three days in Asunción, finding it unbearably hot.

They visited all the Catholic schools, calculating that as Mariana had been in a Catholic school in Buenos Aires, the Furcis would enrol her in one in Asunción. By now, she would be 12 years old. The schools allowed them to look at the lists of pupils, but they found nothing.

Then the court in San Isidro received a communiqué from the Interpol office in Asunción, informing the court that the Furcis had entered Paraguay illegally at the end of 1985 but were presumed to have left the country for an unknown destination in 1988.

However, in March 1988, Pastor Coronel, the feared head of the Police Investigations Department in Asunción, sent a memo to Stroessner about the Furcis. He said that Furci had never worked during his stay in Paraguay, from which they deduced that he was still being paid by SIDE. The memo said that Furci had stayed until the end of 1986, before returning with his family to Argentina, 'where he lives under the protection of SIDE'.

This memo was in the archives of the secret police, which were abandoned when Stroessner was deposed in 1989 and later, in 1993, transferred to the Supreme Court. As one of the first journalists to search through the archives, which had been unceremoniously dumped in an empty room and were scattered over the floor, I discovered the memo.

Whenever it was that the Furcis had really returned to Argentina, once again the grandmothers had no idea of the family's location. All they could do was hope for another tip-off. Time was passing, Mariana was growing up, and they still had no idea where she was.

One day a man appeared at Ester's door in Montevideo, saying that he was a friend of the Furcis. He talked about Mariana, recalling that he had been at their home when Furci brought her from SIDE. He said that she was a very intelligent little girl, very playful and cheerful, and that everyone liked her a lot. He seemed unaware of how painful it was for Ester to know that strangers now knew more about her granddaughter than she did.

The man had come with a message from Furci: if the grandmothers dropped their court case against him, he would allow them access. When Ester told the Zaffaronis about the offer, they all felt the same way about it. No deal was possible with the man who had stolen their granddaughter.

In 1991, the tip-off came. Furci's address in Buenos Aires and the name of the school attended by Mariana were passed to the Abuelas. She was now nearly 17 years old. Fifteen years had passed since she first disappeared, and six years had passed since she disappeared for the second time. The grandparents had missed out on her entire childhood.

In June 1992, a new judge at the San Isidro court, Roberto Marquevich, ordered the arrest of Miguel Angel Furci and his wife. Furci's defence was that by abducting Mariana, he had saved her life. He said that when Automotores Orletti, the clandestine detention centre where all the Uruguayan prisoners were held, was closed down in October 1976, the prisoners, including Mariana's parents, were transferred to Uruguay. The Argentine and Uruguayan officers were dividing up items like furniture and typewriters between them, and among the 'items' left over was a small child, Mariana. According to Furci, Major Gavazzo, the Uruguayans' boss, asked him: 'What shall we do with this child? Why don't you take her?' Furci's wife, unable to conceive, badly wanted a child, so he took Mariana as a present for her.

After hearing the witnesses called by both sides, Judge Marquevich announced his verdict on 18 March 1993. He said it was the most difficult case he had ever tried, worse than a murder trial. He rejected the defence lawyer's plea that, as the child had been well treated during her 'captivity', this was a mitigating circumstance. He also dismissed Furci's argument that he had abducted Mariana because his wife was sterile, saying, 'Since when does the fact of being sterile give you the right to steal children?'

The judge sentenced Furci to seven years' imprisonment for 'appropriation of a minor, substitution of her identity and falsification of a public document' (the birth certificate). His wife, Adriana, got four years for the same crimes. Furci was the first member of Argentina's security forces to be sentenced for the kidnapping of one of the disappeared children. But three years later he was pardoned by President Carlos Menem, along with the nine members of the military juntas who had ruled during the dictatorship.

The judge also ordered that Mariana should be issued with a new identity document containing her real name and date of birth.

The judge left the most difficult decision of all, whether she wanted to return to her biological family or stay with the Furcis, to Mariana to decide, taking into consideration the fact that she was now 18 years old. Mariana decided that she wanted to remain with the Furcis, and continued using her adopted name, Daniela, the name she had grown up with. For Marta and Ester, it was hard to reconcile this difficult teenager with the adorable child they had known before she disappeared. It was even harder, after their years of struggle to find her, to see her cling to the people who had stolen her.

It took several more years before Mariana, now a married woman with three children of her own, fully accepted her real identity, thanks to the careful, patient work of the Zaffaronis, who gradually drew her back into her biological family. Marta did not live to see this happen, but Ester, who died in 2012 aged 93, did. She was able at last to hug her granddaughter, who finally rejected her adopted name and became Mariana once more.

Clamor's role varied in each of the cases described in this book, but at crucial times, we were able to provide practical and financial assistance to help the search for the missing children. In each case, there was a successful outcome – but meanwhile, several hundred children remained unaccounted for.

CHAPTER 21
The survivors of La Cacha tell their stories

In 1983, as Argentina began to tread the painful road back to democracy and the human rights organizations became more vocal in their demands to know the destiny of the disappeared, the military began a rearguard action to cover its tracks. It introduced a law granting its members amnesty, denying any responsibility for their crimes, and declaring the non-existence of the disappeared.

Clamor decided to organize a meeting of survivors of one of the concentration camps, known as La Cacha, to challenge the military version of events and establish the fate of some, at least, of the disappeared. Thousands of people had disappeared into the clandestine camps, and very few had lived to tell their stories. This would be the first ever meeting of survivors.

Seven of the eight known survivors of La Cacha were now exiles living in Brazil, Italy, Mexico, and Sweden. The eighth still lived in Argentina. Clamor arranged flights to bring them to Brazil, accompanied by their partners and their six children. They stayed at a convent near São Paulo, where the nuns, helped by Alma, Jaime Wright's wife, looked after the children.

The four-day meeting, held in October 1983, took place in strict secrecy to ensure that no word leaked out before the participants had returned to their countries of exile. *Clamor Bulletin* No. 15 carried a full report, explaining that the name of the detention camp, La Cacha, was derived from a children's cartoon strip character called 'Witch Cachavaca' who had the power to make people disappear.

The survivors pooled their memories, remembering the names of other prisoners and of the guards. They recalled dates, dialogues, the tortures suffered, and many other details to produce a 35-page document. They said that torture at La Cacha followed a standard pattern:

> We were tied hands and feet to a sort of grid, known as the 'parrilla' [grill] … there were between eight and 15 torturers, including some women. I remember Fatty Lucrecia, Catalina and Marina. Then the prisoner was hit with rubber truncheons on the head, chest, and knees, and received electric shocks. They worked in synchrony for 15 minutes at a time, then paused a moment, before beginning again, three, ten, however many times were needed.

Other tortures were waterboarding and asphyxiation with pillows and nylon bags. The torture sessions were interrupted only to revive the person with water and begin again. When the prisoner fainted, he was given drugs to bring him round. This 'classic' treatment was combined with being hung by the hands, threats, and being tortured with family members.

After being tortured, the prisoners were 'chained to hooks fixed into the floor and thrown down on mattresses, plastic sheets or blankets. We were kept hooded all the time, being allowed to raise the hood as far as the nose only when we ate; this was twice a day.'

Although it was a clandestine centre in a civilian building, a disused radio station, 'all the equipment there belonged to the 7th La Plata Army Regiment because its crest and monogram were on jars, blankets, mattresses, etc. Some of the drugs used came from the Navy's pharmacy.'

Alcira Ríos was one of the survivors who described her ordeal: 'On 27th July 1978 at 1.30 a.m. our home in San Nicolas, Buenos Aires Province, was violently invaded by heavily armed men in civilian clothes and others wearing Army fatigues, their faces hidden by nylon stockings and scarves.' Luis Pablo, her husband, was hit on the head, causing a deep wound; he was then hooded, put in a car, and taken away. Alcira was held in the house while her mother, who was sleeping in the same room as her two small sons, was interrogated. Later Alcira, also hooded, was taken to the same place as Luis, who was already being tortured.

> We stayed there for two days being submitted to intense torture, the second day, on the night of 28th, we were transferred to a clandestine detention centre, which we learnt later was La Cacha … and thirty-six days later, on 1st September, we were taken out of La Cacha and abandoned in front of the La Tablada Regiment, handcuffed and gagged, in a car in which they had left guns. Military personnel took us into the army barracks where we were held for six days, and then took us to different police stations. We were held [at those stations] until 20th October, when we were transferred to the Villa Devoto prison, and recognised as legal prisoners. We were then tried by a war court, which declared it was not competent to judge us, and passed the case to a federal court, where the judge set us free on 13th July 1979.

They had been held for almost a year. As soon as they could, they fled to Brazil with their two small sons, who were deeply traumatized by the disappearance of their parents.

The survivors reckoned that 300 people passed through the camp during the time they were there. They confirmed that the whole operation, far from being the work of rogue elements as the military maintained, was highly organized and carefully recorded. A register of the detained was kept by the officers.

Among the prisoners were several pregnant women:

> Pregnant women received no special treatment because of their condition. In La Cacha the natural expectations of any pregnant

woman were brutally substituted by their fears for the birth and the future of their babies, as a result of torture and their situation as disappeared prisoners. The only affection and cheer they had was that supplied by their fellow prisoners. Perhaps this document can convey to public opinion both in Argentina and elsewhere an idea of the savagery and inhumanity which developed in all the clandestine camps, where not only adults but unborn and newborn babies had to bear all the horror and barbarity of the situation.

Several women gave birth at La Cacha. Laura, the daughter of Estela de Carlotto, who succeeded Chicha as president of the Abuelas, gave birth to a boy she named Guido. Estela learned of the existence of her grandson during a visit to São Paulo in 1980, when she met Alcira Ríos.

The survivors listed 80 men and women, with ages ranging from 19 to 60, who had been seen in La Cacha. They also listed the various sectors of the security forces that were involved in the running of the camp: the army, the navy, the prison service, and SIDE all provided officers and men for the various tasks, working as abductors, torturers, and guards.

At the end of the meeting, copies of the final document were sent to the WCC, which had helped to fund the meeting, and Amnesty International.

After the survivors had safely returned to their respective homes, the press were given details of the meeting. The Abuelas included the new information from the La Cacha survivors in their latest list, naming 70 children who had disappeared when their parents were detained or who were known to have been born in a camp. Another 90 were believed to have been born in captivity, but their genders and their names were unknown.

CHAPTER 22
The theology of loopholes

Five years after its creation in 1978, Clamor had added more members but was still basically just a small group of unpaid volunteers, without a formal structure or legal framework. The only exception was Jaime Wright, a minister of the United Presbyterian Church, who was freed to work for Clamor full-time while continuing to receive a salary.

Jaime liked to tell the story of visitors from abroad who arrived imagining they would find an organization occupying a seven-storey building with dozens of paid staff, instead of a small group meeting in each other's homes, and eventually in a small room in the basement of the Curia. In *Bulletin* No. 15, published in December 1983, he wrote:

> Those who have supported us will be happy to know that we have succeeded in avoiding institutionalization. Although we did finally receive a room of our own (Room 9) on our fifth birthday, and own two typewriters, we continue to have no employees. This bulletin is being produced – like others – by some of Clamor's seven members and friends on volunteer service or special assignment.

Over the years, the group had grown. The original three members were joined in late 1978 by Sister Michael Mary Nolan and Padre Roberto Grandmaison, and then in 1980 by two more members of the Curia's Pastoral Committee on Human Rights and the Marginalized, Thereza Brandão and Fermino Fechio. Thereza Brandão knew Chile well and had sheltered Paraguayan refugees, including Basilica and Miguel, in her home. Fermino Fechio was a lawyer who worked for local government helping to legalize the situation of São Paulo's many clandestine settlements and *favelas* (shanty towns).

The many exiles who had settled in São Paulo, Rio de Janeiro, or Foz do Iguaçu regularly brought us fresh information and new arrivals to be interviewed. They also helped to translate the bulletins. Between 1978 and 1984, Clamor published 16 bulletins, with versions in Portuguese, Spanish, and English, and dozens of press releases.

In Room 9 we received a constant stream of visitors: members of the human rights organizations in Argentina, Uruguay, Paraguay, Chile, and more rarely, Bolivia; representatives of international organizations, some of whom had become good friends, like Tricia Feeney from Amnesty International and Chuck Harper of the WCC. Clare Dixon of the Catholic Agency for Overseas Development (CAFOD), members of Swedish, German, and Dutch churches, and Margaret Wilde of Paraguay Watch, a Washington-based NGO whose newsletters were important sources of information, visited less frequently.

Jaime had begun to use the phrase *a teologia das brechas* – the theology of openings, or loopholes – to describe Clamor's unorthodox methodology; this was a theology that had 'grown out of our own dark days of repression (1968–1978) in Brazil'. The idea was that any opportunity – any chance, however unlikely, however unconventional – could be used if it benefited the cause of the people for whom we were fighting. Emilio Mignone of CELS wrote that 'the presence of Clamor [on a proposed committee] is a guarantee that [the committee] would not be limited to a theoretical and contemplative defence of human rights'.

The theology of loopholes became a Clamor catchphrase – one that would be put into practice in January 1981 when the Canadian prime minister, Pierre Trudeau, a candidate for the UN secretary general's job, made an official visit to Brazil.

We decided that this was a golden opportunity to ask Canada to accept more refugees from Latin America. The question was how to get a letter into Trudeau's own hands, rather than into the hands of an aide. When we discovered that he would be guest of honour at a lunch organized by the Brazilian–Canadian Chamber of Commerce at the Hilton Hotel in São Paulo, we decided that this would be the moment, and that Padre Roberto, a fellow French Canadian, would be the messenger.

Jaime bought five tickets for the lunch, and five of us – Jaime, Roberto, Sister Michael Mary Nolan, Luiz Eduardo Greenhalgh, and myself – arrived early in order to get seats near the top table. The other guests, businessmen in smart suits, looked askance at the odd group in their midst, especially the priest in his black cassock, and the minister in his dog collar.

The tables were laid with an impressive array of cutlery, indicating several courses. We decided that the best time for Roberto to deliver the letter would be just before the dessert. We waited, tense, for the right moment. When it came, Roberto got up and walked quickly in the direction of Trudeau. As he neared the top table, security guards began to move towards him and the room fell silent, surprised. Roberto quickly greeted Trudeau in French, identified himself, and said that he was a colleague of Father Corbet, a priest he knew was known to Trudeau.

By now Roberto was surrounded by guards, who were ready to drag him away – but Trudeau asked them to move aside. Roberto rapidly told him about Clamor, about the problem of the refugees, and handed him the letter we had drafted, then returned to our table, triumphant. The tension was over, and we all tucked into the lavish dessert. When Trudeau made his after-lunch speech, he mentioned the letter, which he had quickly read. After he returned to Canada, correspondence continued with Clamor.

The *teologia das brechas* had been applied before, notably when President Jimmy Carter visited Brazil in 1978 and invited Dom Paulo to ride with him in his car to the airport in Rio. It was the only chance to talk alone without eavesdroppers or minders. Dom Paulo asked Jaime to prepare a briefing for the conversation. We drew up a list of topics, including the disappeared in Brazil and the Southern Cone.

We suggested comments on the American ambassadors in countries of the region, praising the ambassador in Bolivia, because he had helped stop that country from returning to military rule, but criticizing the new ambassador in Paraguay, who had declared that he was there 'to defend US interests and not to worry about human rights' when he replaced Robert White, a stout defender of human rights and critic of Stroessner. In Chile we suggested praising the American government's support for justice in the Letelier case, saying that it had surely helped to reduce repression in Chile.

In 1981 the famous American protest singer Joan Baez came to Brazil and was invited to sing at TUCA, the theatre of the Catholic University. An hour before the show was due to begin, the auditorium was packed – but behind the scenes there was high drama. Federal Police agents had appeared and announced that the show was banned because Baez had entered the country on a tourist visa and was therefore not permitted to work. Clamor members were there in force, and Padre Roberto was called on to help negotiate a solution. He told the police that if Baez was not allowed to sing, there would be a riot. Eventually a compromise was reached: she would be allowed to sing two or three songs, standing in the front row instead of on the stage.

The first five years of Clamor's existence, from 1978 to 1983, when all the Southern Cone countries were ruled by dictators and thousands of refugees were fleeing to Brazil, were undoubtedly the most intense. At the beginning of this period there was no light at the end of the dark tunnel of repression, but by 1983 signs that the dictatorships were beginning to crumble were multiplying.

In *Bulletin* No. 15, which came out in December 1983, we looked back on those first five years in an article called 'Five Years of CLAMORing':

> Our bulletins have been more sporadic than periodic, but our dedication to the cause of human rights in the Southern Cone has been continuous. The coming into existence of CLAMOR was like the opening of a floodgate, as appeals and denunciations poured in. In these five years the terrible dimensions of the human rights tragedies in these countries have shocked, saddened, and angered us, and sometimes, led us to despair. But, at the same time, the incredible heights of courage, dignity, and solidarity to which we have seen people rise have inspired and encouraged us.
>
> During these years we have received hundreds, perhaps thousands, of letters, phone calls, visits from people in Argentina, Bolivia, Chile, Paraguay and Uruguay. 'Solidarity knows no frontiers' was the phrase we coined to explain that, if the forces of repression did not respect frontiers, invading neighbouring countries to violate

human rights, then why should not solidarity do the same in the defence of those same rights?

The phrase has a broader meaning, really, for it also means that – in addition to geographical frontiers – solidarity cannot be limited by political, religious, ideological, racial, social, economic, and linguistic barriers.

After five years of chronicling the depths of human suffering and cruelty, CLAMOR hopes that the floodgates are now closing.

For other organizations in the incipient field of human rights, Clamor's bulletins, with their eyewitness accounts and their detailed reports on a region which received little coverage in the mainstream press, were an important source of information.

For the purposes of this book, I asked members of human rights organizations about their memories of Clamor and its bulletins. For Jenny Pearce of Index on Censorship, 'Clamor was part of the first generation of human rights organizations; there weren't many then. It was part of the struggle to get human rights recognized. It was early days for human rights work – now it is hard to realize that. Disappearances were unknown, and the dictatorships in Latin America were supported by the West.'

'*Clamor* was user friendly, because it was in three languages and readable – [differently from] some bulletins which were tracts, long-winded, *Clamor* was well written', explained Julian Filochowski of the Catholic Institute for International Relations.

Other recipients, like the human rights group of the Dutch Reformed Church, were amazed by what they read: 'We were greatly shocked by the contents of *Clamor*', said one member of the group. 'We had thought we were well informed.'

At the end of 1983, Jaime Wright, physically and mentally exhausted after five years of non-stop activity, decided that it was time to move on. It was not an easy decision. From the very first moment, Jaime had thrown himself heart and soul into Clamor, working late into the night, writing articles, replying to letters, designing the layout of the bulletins, doing the accounts, dealing with the minutiae of the organization. He had received scores of refugees and exiles, human rights workers, clergy, and overseas visitors in his own home and had made many trips to Argentina, Paraguay, and Chile. He had developed a very close bond with Dom Paulo, who later referred to him as his auxiliary bishop. His close connections with Chuck Harper of the WCC and leaders of American and European churches, both Catholic and Protestant, ensured a constant stream of funding. He had formed an especially close relationship with the Abuelas and continued to visit them after he had left Clamor, as an adviser and friend. For many, Jaime had been the public face of the group.

By now the number of bulletins had dropped drastically, partly because we had become involved with Clamor's other publications – the List, the calendars of disappeared children – and partly because, as Brazil slowly moved to end the rule of the military and return to democracy, members were increasingly involved with other demands.

All the dictatorships in the region were coming to an end. Bolivia's military regime had collapsed and Hernán Siles Suazo, elected in 1980, had finally taken office in October 1983. Argentina held elections in October 1983 and Raúl Alfonsín became president in December that year. Uruguay held elections a year later, in November 1984, electing Julio Sanguinetti, who took office in March 1985. The refugees began to return to their countries, many of them after seven or eight years in exile.

Clamor was able to dedicate more time to Paraguay and Chile, where Stroessner and Pinochet still had a firm despotic grip on power, although the situation in Argentina was far from safe.

From 1984, as the number of refugees dried up, Clamor members took part in the growing number of congresses and seminars on human rights. The human rights organizations felt a strong need to understand what had happened and to think about how it could be prevented from happening again.

In February 1985 we decided to hold our own seminar in São Paulo to discuss the role of the organizations within the political, social, and economic situations that had developed in each country. Twenty-seven of them took part, and the results were published in a special *Bulletin*, No. 17.

In 1985, Dom Paulo was awarded UNHCR's Nansen medal in recognition of his work with refugees and on human rights. In his acceptance speech, he praised the work of Clamor.

In the 2000s, Argentina's President Nestor Kirchner revoked the amnesty laws, and Videla and other surviving junta members were put on trial again, this time for their 'systematic plan to steal babies and children'. Videla was sentenced to 50 years, but died in 2013. Trials followed of several hundred lower-grade officers who had worked at concentration camps like La Cacha and Automotores Orletti. But for most of the families of the disappeared, their fate remained unknown. One by one, the generals died without revealing their secrets.

By 2014, 116 grandchildren had been found, some of them seeking out the Abuelas themselves because they suspected they could be the sons or daughters of disappeared parents. Many of the Abuelas died without finding their grandchildren. In 2014, Estela de Carlotto, president of the Abuelas, found her grandson, whose existence she had first heard about in the Curia in São Paulo, when ex-prisoner Alcira Ríos told her that her daughter, Laura, had given birth to a son whom she called Guido.

CHAPTER 23
Argentina: The return to democracy

In 1983, Argentina's ignominious defeat in the Falklands war – with the loss of over a thousand young men, most of them raw recruits – came on top of worsening economic conditions in the country. There was growing international condemnation of human rights abuses. Argentina's military realized that its days were numbered.

The demand for answers to the question 'Where are the disappeared?' had grown as hundreds of thousands shook off their fear and marched through the streets shouting 'Con vida los llevaron, con vida los queremos!' (They took them alive, we want them back alive!)

For seven years the armed forces had acted with total impunity, kidnapping, torturing, and killing, certain they would never be held to account. Now they began to realize that the day of reckoning was approaching. The brave, solitary campaigns of the families, the Madres, and the Abuelas were turning into mass demonstrations. Their white headscarves had become symbols of resistance and courage.

In April 1983, junta president General Reynaldo Bignone, who had succeeded General Galtieri, architect of the Falklands fiasco, announced the military's answer. The 'Final Document of the Military Junta on the Struggle against Subversion and Terrorism', published on 29 April, was read out on radio and TV networks. It claimed that all those allegedly missing had either chosen to go into exile, or underground, or were to be considered as dead for legal purposes: 'The most typical case of a disappeared person is one in which the missing person opted for a clandestine life without informing his family, who in turn "filed a complaint" of a disappearance they cannot explain, or if they can, do not wish to.' The document stated that others had been killed in internal strife between the guerrillas themselves, but it gave neither numbers nor details.

The military accepted no responsibility for the disappearances, because whatever had been done was done in a situation of war. 'The actions of the members of the armed forces in the conduct of the war shall be considered as acts of service.'

There was to be no investigation, no trial. The junta essentially washed its hands of the situation, saying: 'Only history can judge and determine with precision who should bear the direct responsibility for the unjust methods used and the innocent lives lost.'

The junta's final statement was followed by a new law which laid the ground for impunity by stating that all operations carried out against 'subversion and terrorism' were executed according to plans supervised and approved by the high command of the armed forces.[1]

The final document aroused a storm of indignation, repudiation, and condemnation around the world, not only from human rights organizations but from the American, French, and Italian governments and the Vatican. In Argentina, the Madres asked whether 'to kidnap, torture, assassinate and lie without shame are acts of service?' In Brazil, Dom Paulo called the final document 'the final solution', while Clamor issued a strongly worded declaration saying:

> The Argentine government, already holder of the dubious record for political disappearances, has now shocked world opinion by declaring that all those named on the long and tragic lists of disappeared in Argentina must be considered dead for legal and administrative purposes.
>
> It is impossible to believe that after abducting thousands of human beings, forcing 500,000 of their own citizens into exile all over the world and finally calling elections to restore democracy to Argentina, the Argentine government can produce a document that is such an affront to the long-suffering families, to Argentine society and to civilization in general.

The group Families of the Detained and Disappeared for Political Reasons issued a response entitled 'Reply to a Cynical Document'. It read:

> Assuming a responsibility that the people never conferred on them, deforming the truth, falsifying deeds, hiding and justifying the horrors committed by the military, security and police commands, the present military Junta – the continuation of the military Juntas which have succeeded each other in power since 24th March 1976 – has issued a document, in reality an anti-constitutional Act with which they intend to place a full stop to the dramatic question of the thousands of detained-disappeared.
>
> They want to justify the unjustifiable, remove the investigation and trial of their illegal actions from the ambit of Justice ... and remit themselves to the judgement of God and history.
>
> Falsifying facts with the usual cynicism, they make our detained-disappeared into clandestine fugitives, dead in confrontations and unidentified beings.
>
> ... The repression did not commit 'errors'. It was perfectly structured and organized according to a pre-fixed plan. The terrorism of the state, implemented and emanating from the high commands, had as its aim the elimination of political and ideological opponents and the implantation of terror in order to immobilize the entire

population, without caring about victims who were not the targets of its actions.

This sinister plan of repression which led to the imprisonment, torture, murder, disappearance and exile of thousands of citizens, was necessary to put into practice the economic policy of submission to imperialism, with its consequences of hunger and unemployment.[2]

The junta's hope that, with its final document, it could turn the page on the disappeared showed just how out of touch it was. For the families, the fate of their loved ones, the anguish of not knowing what had happened to them, remained an open wound.

In August the military made another attempt to guarantee its own impunity by introducing an amnesty bill, in reality an auto-amnesty law, in the name of 'reconciliation'. Once again there was universal repudiation, not only from the human rights organizations and the political prisoners still being held in prisons all over the country, but also from political parties and public opinion in general. Presidential candidate Raúl Alfonsín, who was the front runner for the elections due to be held in October, promised that, if elected, he would revoke the military's amnesty law.

As the demoralized dictatorship neared its end, the Abuelas produced a pamphlet reading: 'The babies born in captivity are waiting for justice. They should be returned without delay to their legitimate families by the military government which knows where they are. If you know something ... help us to find them.'

Elected president on 30 October, Alfonsín took office in December 1983, repealed the amnesty law, and set up a commission to investigate the disappearances. Many Argentines had wanted a parliamentary committee of inquiry and criticized the new commission as a whitewash – but time would show that they were wrong.

Ernesto Sabato, a well-known Argentine writer, was chosen to head the National Commission on the Disappearances of Persons, CONADEP. Its members included lawyers, elected deputies of the new Congress, members of human rights organizations, and the Catholic bishop Jaime de Nevares of Neuquén, one of the few bishops who had supported the work of the Madres and Abuelas.

In January 1984, CONADEP invited Dom Paulo to join its ranks because of his work for the disappeared, but he declined, saying that the Commission's work was a task for the Argentines themselves.

CONADEP then asked Clamor to provide the index cards that we had used to make our List. After discussing whether we should risk sending the originals, we decided to do so, and carefully packed the 8,000 cards, plus copies of testimonies, into stout cardboard boxes. These were sent to CONADEP in Buenos Aires, with the promise that they would be returned as soon as they had been used.

CONADEP finished its work in September and published its report in November 1984. Its list contained 8,960 names, well short of Amnesty International's estimate of 16,000. Calculating that for every name on the list, another two people were also missing, Argentine human rights organizations reckoned that the real total of the disappeared was nearer to 30,000.

Nunca Más, the report based on the statements of thousands of relatives and scores of survivors, revealed to Argentines the full extent of the reign of terror that the armed forces had imposed on the country for seven years, supported by some sectors of society, the other countries of the Southern Cone, and during much of the time, the United States and other Western governments.

As a result of CONADEP's work, in April 1985 the members of the three juntas who had presided over the years of state terrorism were put on trial. It was the first time leaders of a dictatorship had been tried since the Nuremberg Trials after the Second World War. After harrowing evidence from concentration camp survivors and relatives of the disappeared, including the Abuelas, General Videla and Admiral Massera were sentenced to life imprisonment. The other junta members received long sentences.

For the Abuelas, the end of the military regime had brought a flood of information about the missing children shown on their posters. At last the identity question had been cracked with the development of the *abuelismo* test. In September 1984, the Abuelas presented a bill to Congress for the creation of the National Genetic Data Bank. They wanted blood tests to be made compulsory, instead of it being left to each judge to decide whether to order a test or not. The Data Bank would store the genetic data of the grandparents and the families who were searching for their children, ready for when the children were located. Supported by the American Society for the Advancement of Science and the New York Blood Bank, it would cost US$200,000.

The judicial system was now the Abuelas' major problem. The judges could be slow and unsympathetic, and in some cases even connived with the children's appropriators. President Alfonsín's promise that the cases of kidnapped children would have priority had not produced any concrete action, even though the *abuelismo* process was able to prove with 99.9% certainty the real identity of the child, including those born in captivity.

For the lawyers who worked with the Abuelas, it was difficult to keep up with all the cases now being heard in different courts. They suggested that a letter should be sent to the judges and appeal courts as a form of pressure.

When the Abuelas finally got their interview with President Alfonsín, two years after he took office, 38 of the presumed 500 missing children had been located. Three grandmothers, Chicha, Estela Carlotto, and the treasurer Rosa Roisinblit, went to the Casa Rosada and presented their demands. They asked the government to take up the cause of the disappeared children, to call on the public to collaborate in locating them, and for a special envoy to provide a direct contact between the president and the Abuelas. Last but not least, they wanted official support for the proposed National Genetic Data Bank. Alfonsín accepted all four requests.

It was not only in the cases involving disappeared children that the judges had failed to do their duty. In its *Bulletin* No. 16, dated November 1984, Clamor published a long article, based on a study prepared by a group of political prisoners in Rawson prison,[3] under the title 'The Sad Role of Justice during the Repression: Complacent, Conniving and Even an Accomplice'. It noted that the judges had been incapable of elucidating a single case of disappearance, although many such cases were very well documented: 'In January 1983, according to the data held by APDH and Clamor, the total of detained-disappeared in Argentina, duly documented, is 7,291.' The prisoners calculated that the real total was triple this number.

The article continued: 'Neither did the justice system investigate disappearances of prisoners which occurred in the "legal" prisons. No political prisoner was questioned about the circumstances in which their companions – later disappeared – were taken out of the prisons where they were "legally registered".'

The restoration of democracy in Argentina brought the return of thousands of political exiles, many after nearly a decade abroad. They came from France, Norway, Sweden, Spain, Mexico, Canada, and Brazil. Yet many political prisoners, members of left-wing guerrilla organizations, had still not been freed. In January 1984, Dom Paulo received a request asking him to intervene with the new Alfonsín government to obtain the freedom of over 100 political prisoners who were still being held.

In December 1986, President Alfonsín, under heavy pressure from the military, presented the Full Stop Law to Congress to limit the trials of members of the armed forces. It established a deadline for accusations – 22 February 1987 – after which no one else could be prosecuted. For the Abuelas and other relatives the new law at first caused despair, but then they began a determined effort to bring accusations to the courts against as many members of the military as possible before the deadline came into effect.

The military was out of power, but it remained restless and rebellious, determined to avoid further trials. After the 1987 Easter mutiny of discontented army officers, Alfonsín was forced to introduce the Law of Due Obedience, which provided immunity for crimes against humanity. The Abuelas produced a poster reading: 'We search for two generations. Those responsible for this horror should be tried and condemned. We reject the Law of Due Obedience.' The poster carried scores of photographs of disappeared babies and children and their parents, and couples whose babies had been born in captivity.

The Abuelas had hoped that once democracy was restored, the government would take energetic steps to resolve one of the worst ongoing legacies of the dictatorship: the appropriation of helpless babies and small children, and the denial of their families' right to bring them up. But the combination of an uncooperative judiciary and a democratic government still wary of the military had prevented rapid progress. It was still only the careful, patient detective work of the Abuelas themselves that brought results.

The Abuelas also criticized the attitude of the media which said, 'If the child is happy, then leave it alone.' They said this ignored the trauma of history; it ignored the future and looked only at the moment.

In November 1988 the Abuelas were again received by President Alfonsín at the Casa Rosada, where they asked him to demand the return of the kidnapped children – there were at least seven known cases – taken to Paraguay illegally by their appropriators to escape court orders demanding blood tests or restitution. They also asked the president to introduce urgent measures to speed up the localization of the hundreds of children still missing, including the designation of a special public prosecutor.

By now Alfonsín's government was being undermined not only by military rebellions but by the fast-deteriorating economic situation, including rocketing inflation, a foreign debt crisis, and growing unemployment and poverty. In reprisal for Alfonsín's decision not to continue supporting the Contras in their campaign of violence to destabilize the Sandinista government in Nicaragua, President Ronald Reagan refused to make economic concessions.

Elections were brought forward because of the crisis, and on 14 May 1989, Carlos Menem of the Justicialista (or Peronista) Party won a landslide victory. On 8 July, Alfonsín handed over power.

A year and a half later, in December 1990, Menem pardoned Videla, Massera, and all the other military prisoners. Fifty thousand marched through the streets of Buenos Aires in protest. The men who had been responsible for so much pain and grief were free again, without having revealed what they had done with the disappeared.

Over the years, many bodies had been found in clandestine cemeteries, buried as 'NN' – No Name. In 1985 the world-famous forensic scientist Clyde Snow came to Argentina to train a group of university students, and a year later they set up the Argentine Forensic Anthropology Team, which began the work of identifying the bodies exhumed from the unmarked graves. Snow, who also came to Brazil at the invitation of Clamor, said: 'Bones make great witnesses; they speak softly but they never forget and they never lie.'

In 1995, more light was shed on the fate of the disappeared when a naval officer called Alfredo Scilingo revealed to journalist Horacio Verbitsky that he had taken part in flights on which dozens of prisoners were thrown alive from planes into the ocean.[4] Arrested in Spain, Scilingo is currently serving a prison sentence there.

Notes

1. Duhalde, E. L. (1999) *El Estado Terrorista Argentino: Quince Años Después, una Mirada Crítica*, Buenos Aires: Editorial Universitaria de Buenos Aires, p. 293.
2. *Ibid.*, pp. 293–295.
3. Familiares de Detenidos-Desaparecidos por Razones Politicas. (1984) 'O Triste Papel da Justiça Durante a Repressão: Complacentes, Coniventes e Até Cumplices', *Revista Testimonios* 2.
4. Verbitsky, H. (1995) *El Vuelo*, Buenos Aires: Planeta.

CHAPTER 24

Uruguay: The military leaves power

By 1983 the Uruguayan military was under pressure from the population to restore democracy as the economy floundered and the regime became more isolated internationally. In neighbouring Argentina, elections had been set for 30 October 1983 as the increasingly bold human rights organizations took to the streets in mass marches, demanding to know what had happened to the thousands of disappeared. In Uruguay, by contrast, the human rights movement, centred around the families of political prisoners and the disappeared, was timid – but with support from the Montevideo branch of SERPAJ, set up in 1981, it was beginning to become more vocal.

Mayday 1983 saw the first major protest led by the unions. Thousands took part in a protest in the centre of Montevideo demanding an amnesty for all political prisoners; for the first time, the police did not intervene. In August 1983, a 15-minute banging of pots and pans while lights were switched off took the government by surprise. Days later, SERPAJ was closed down for denouncing the torture of a group of young people who had been arrested soon after the protest, and its offices were invaded by the police.

SERPAJ coordinator Luis Pérez Aguirre, a Jesuit priest, appealed to Clamor for solidarity, and we issued a note of protest under the title 'A Light Has Been Put Out. A Voice Has Been Silenced'. Undaunted by the SERPAJ's closure, Padre Aguirre and other members set up a new organization to carry on their work, called the National Commission for Human Rights.

Months later the Uruguayan capital witnessed its biggest ever protest rally, with an estimated 400,000 people filling the streets of the city centre, singing the national anthem, and calling for free and fair elections and the release of political prisoners. It was just days after the Argentines had voted in the elections that put an end to the dictatorship on the other side of the River Plate.

In May 1984, Clamor's Fermino Fechio, with the actor Ruth Escobar and Workers Party state deputy Paulo Frateschi, accompanied Tota Quinteros on her return to Uruguay after eight years of exile in France. Tota had fled in 1976 after her daughter Elena had been kidnapped from inside the Venezuelan embassy in Montevideo and disappeared. Still fearful of the Uruguayan authorities, she asked Clamor to provide an escort.

Fermino remembered the fear that still pervaded Montevideo, even as a return to democracy was being negotiated. In Montevideo, they were followed everywhere. When they visited Tota's family, they found that everyone was terrified, sure they would be arrested.

The next day they went with Tota to the Ministry of the Interior, where Tota demanded explanations about the fate of her daughter. The minister refused to see her. Tota then phoned up the chairmen of the political parties and asked them to come and see her. 'Sanguinetti came, not knowing what it was about, otherwise he wouldn't have come. He kept looking round in the hotel lobby, he was so scared', Fermino later recalled.

When the time came to fly back to Brazil, afraid that Tota would be arrested at the airport, they asked some of the foreign correspondents based in Montevideo to accompany them. There, Frateschi told Fermino, 'If they arrest her, you go through to tell the world what's happened. I'll stick with her. I am a congressman – I have more guarantees.' But Tota went through without problems, and from the tarmac she waved to the journalists.

'On the plane, Tota cried and cried', recalled Fermino. 'The cabin crew stewardess brought us a bottle of wine. We told her, "One day they will have to pay".'

Following its defeat in the 1980 plebiscite, the military had admitted the need for a transition back to civilian rule, but wanted it to be slow, gradual, and totally under the military's control. Initial talks with some of the political parties broke down over the question of an amnesty for members of the military who had committed human rights abuses.

In July 1984, secret talks were held at the Naval Club, though without the leaders of the more progressive parties who were in prison. The Frente Ampla's leader, General Liber Seregni, had been held for 9 years, while Wilson Ferreira Aldunarte, leader of the Blancos, after 11 years in exile, had been arrested on his return.

The military, uncomfortably aware of President Alfonsín's authorization of legal proceedings against the members of the juntas across the river in Buenos Aires, wanted guarantees of non-prosecution, avoiding any accountability for its human rights crimes. It had in effect turned Uruguay into a vast prison, with the highest rate of political prisoners per capita in the world.

A timetable was agreed, with elections to be held on 25 November 1984. Meanwhile, the release of political prisoners, many of whom had been held for over a decade and were suffering from chronic illnesses like cancer, began. But over 60 were still held, including Tupamaro leader Raúl Sendic, who, although already incarcerated for 12 years, was sentenced to another 45 years. Those released were presented with a bill for their accommodation and food during the time of their imprisonment, which had to be paid. This absurd and cynical practice, which Clamor had denounced in one of its bulletins, was only revoked after the military left power.

Julio Sanguinetti of the conservative Colorado Party won – unsurprisingly, as both leaders of the other main parties, Liber Seregni and Wilson Aldunarte, although now free, were banned from standing. Altogether, 5,000 politicians of the more progressive parties were excluded.

Taking office in March 1985, President Sanguinetti kept to the pact agreed at the Naval Club and refused to investigate the human rights abuses committed during the 12 years of military rule. However, members of the Frente Ampla and the Blanco Party set up two parliamentary committees of inquiry to investigate the 1976 kidnappings and murders of Senator Zelmar Michelini and former speaker of the House of Deputies Héctor Gutiérrez Ruiz, and the disappearances of other Uruguayans in Argentina. The Congress also quickly passed a bill to release all political prisoners, including the Tupamaros, and decided that the fees charged to earlier prisoners on their release would be repaid.

With the lifting of censorship, the press began reporting all the stories which for years had remained hidden from the general public, including the case of Mariana Zaffaroni and the other disappeared Uruguayan children. The fate of Mariana, aged 18 months when she was kidnapped, became a *cause célèbre*, and her picture appeared on posters everywhere. There was a mass protest in front of the Argentine consulate in Montevideo, and 80,000 people signed a petition addressed to President Alfonsín. In July, Mariana's maternal grandmother Ester took the petition to the Casa Rosada in Buenos Aires, asking Alfonsín to intervene and to restore Mariana to her rightful family. She was received by the minister of the interior, Antonio Troccoli, who promised her that action would be taken. *'Quedase tranquila, señora'*, he said. 'Rest assured, we will get to the bottom of this.' But she heard no more.

The clumsily named Law for the Proscription of Intended Punishments, or *Lei de Caducidade* (Law of Expiration), in effect an amnesty law, was rushed through Congress: this new law stated that no member of the police or military could be held responsible or punished for crimes committed during the dictatorship. It quickly became known as the Law of Impunity. Sanguinetti himself helped to spread the idea that if any member of the military were brought to trial, there would be another coup. So the new law guaranteed not only the impunity of those who had tortured and killed, but the continuation of the veil of silence about the fate of the Uruguayans who had disappeared after capture.

In 1987, preparations began for a referendum on the amnesty law. In order to hold the referendum, the signatures of 25 per cent of the electorate were needed. An amazing 634,702 signatures – 28.8% of the electorate – were collected, but the government claimed that many were fraudulent and wanted to cancel the referendum. Such was the outcry, however, that it had no option but to go ahead.

Ester Gatti, Mariana Zaffaroni's grandmother, was chosen to head the committee for the 'no' vote. She travelled all over Uruguay, giving talks, explaining why the people who had committed human rights crimes must be brought to trial. She found that many people knew nothing about the disappeared and had no idea of the terrible things that had happened under military rule, and the tour gave her a chance to talk about it. It was exhausting, but she felt confident they would win. When the results came in, they showed that the 'no' vote had won easily in Montevideo, but lost the overall vote. The families were deeply disappointed.

But Ester never gave up her campaign to get Mariana back. One day she heard that President Sanguinetti was opening a new school near the one she taught at in Colón, and she decided to try to confront him. When she arrived at the school, there was a crowd around the president. She shouted, 'What has President Sanguinetti done for the child called Mariana Zaffaroni?' Three or four advisers immediately surrounded her. One of them said, 'Señora! Why are you saying this? Every day we get a cable from the Ministry of Foreign Affairs about it! You can come to see us and we'll show you everything we have.' The next day Ester went to the presidential offices; she waited and waited, but the adviser was not there and she never learned any more from them.

Journalist Roger Rodriguez discovered details of the clandestine flights which had brought Uruguayan prisoners from secret detention camps in Buenos Aires back to Montevideo, most of them never to be seen again. In 2009, ex-Tupamaro guerrilla José Mujica was elected president of Uruguay, but not until 2011 was the Law of Impunity revoked by Congress.

CHAPTER 25

Paraguay: Stroessner is overthrown

While Brazil, Argentina, and Uruguay, with varying degrees of difficulty, had rid themselves of their military regimes, Paraguay was still locked in the grip of the aging dictator General Alfredo Stroessner at the end of 1985.

A million Paraguayans lived in exile. Any attempt at opposition was met with swift repression. Politicians, journalists, peasant leaders, academics, and unionists were thrown into prison for the slightest attempt at protest. Armed gangs known as *garroteros*, carrying clubs, electrified cattle prods, and sometimes shotguns, invaded opposition meetings and beat people up. Paraguay was virtually a one-party state. The official Colorado Party's perpetual candidate, General Stroessner, was re-elected every five years, when the permanent state of siege was lifted for 24 hours to allow voting. For international observers the election process was fraudulent and illegitimate, with the opposition being harassed and intimidated.

An armed civilian group called the Anti-Communist Action Group (*Grupo de Acción Anticomunista*, GAA), allegedly funded by Causa, the political wing of the radically anti-communist Unification Church of the Reverend Moon, had also appeared on the scene 'to give the Communists the treatment they deserve', according to the minister for justice, José Eugenio Jacquet. The Unification Church and the World Anti-Communist League had both been welcomed in Paraguay, where statues of Chinese nationalist leader Chiang Kai-shek and Nicaraguan dictator General Anastasio Somoza graced its squares.

In 1986, the GAA targeted a non-violent May Day rally in Asunción.

> Peaceful rallies have been attacked by the police, and gangs of thugs recruited by the Colorado Party have appeared on the streets. ... [They] invaded a hospital where staff were striking for higher pay, beat up protesters on the street, and wrecked the Nanduti radio station with stones and bullets. They chose the radio station, which has the biggest audience in Paraguay, because its owner, Humberto Rubin, was defying the unwritten laws of censorship to broadcast coverage of the protests. When physical violence failed to silence the radio, jamming began. The radio resorted to playing over and over again the slogan 'You can kill one rose, two roses, even three, but you cannot kill the spring. Radio Nanduti is still on air.'[1]

The only opposition paper, *ABC Color*, had been closed down two years earlier, in 1984. Its owner, Aldo Zulcolillo, and a skeleton staff of journalists still went into the offices every day, and among the silent typewriters and empty desks religiously filed away reports on the day's events. General Stroessner, now 75 years old, was about to go through ritual re-election for yet another five-year term in spite of his advanced age.

In the countryside, discontent was growing rapidly after thousands of small farmers were evicted from their land when it was sold over their heads to Stroessner allies. Many peasant farmers recruited to work on the giant binational Itaipu Dam, which straddled the border with Brazil, found themselves out of work when it was completed, and without land to return to. Less than 10 per cent of Paraguay's 100 million acres of fertile soil was in the hands of the peasants, while 12 transnational food companies owned over 80 million acres.

Paraguay also held the unwelcome record of having the world's longest-serving political prisoner. Army captain Napoleón Ortigoza had been sentenced to death in 1962 for murdering an army cadet, a charge he always denied, and for leading a conspiracy to overthrown Stroessner. His sentence was commuted to 25 years' imprisonment after a priest allegedly threatened to reveal the names of the real murderers if he was executed. Ortigoza was finally released in December 1987 on completion of his sentence, most of it served in solitary confinement. He was immediately placed under house arrest, but managed to escape and ask for political asylum at the Colombian embassy.

A personality cult that owed much to Maoist China saw the elderly president's face displayed everywhere. A giant oil painting of General Stroessner was the first thing visitors saw as they arrived in Asunción airport. Foreign journalists were given a book written in bad English extolling the amazing virtues and astonishing achievements of the great leader.

In 1988, Pope John Paul II accepted an invitation from the local Catholic Church to make a four-day visit to Paraguay. The opposition realized that Stroessner would do everything he could to use the papal visit to endorse his regime, but they also saw it as a unique opportunity to denounce the reality of life in Paraguay and the decades of human rights abuses while, for a few brief days, the country was in the spotlight of the world's press.

The visit came at a time when relations between the Catholic Church and the regime were strained because of the growing involvement of the Church in political and social problems. The year before, in 1987, the Church had organized a 'national dialogue', an attempt to bring trade unions, political parties, and student organizations together to discuss the transition to a democratic process, but the Colorado Party boycotted the initiative and it collapsed. Debates on human rights and political issues held in churches and in the Catholic university were broken up by paramilitary gangs.

In reply to this violence, the Church excommunicated those responsible and organized the ringing of church bells in protest. In October 1987, a mass march through the streets of Asunción was held. To avoid reprisals against the marchers, they walked in silence.

A month before the pope's arrival, Clamor sent Fermino Fechio and myself to Asunción on a fact-finding and solidarity visit. We found that the human rights situation had worsened, with over 400 opponents of Stroessner, from all sectors of society, in prison.

On the eve of the visit, Asunción was plastered with posters proclaiming 'Blessed are the peacemakers', under pictures of the pope and General Stroessner. *ABC Color's* Aldo Zulcolillo claimed that members of the government had been ordered to carry rosaries in their hands.

The Catholic Church wanted the pope to go to Concepción, the poorest and least developed part of the country, but the government vetoed it, claiming that the local airport was not safe for the papal plane. Then, three days before he was due to arrive, the authorities announced the cancellation of his planned meeting with the 'builders of society' – politicians, intellectuals, professionals, and labour leaders. After strong protests from the Vatican, the encounter was reinstated, but live radio and TV coverage was banned.

At the meeting, the pope told the 3,000-strong audience, which included all the leaders of the opposition, that 'real peace is incompatible with a society where the rights and even the existence of others depends on the arbitrary judgement of the most powerful'. This was interpreted as a reply to Stroessner's speech of welcome when he insisted that Paraguayans all lived in peace. The pope also praised the bishops' efforts to organize a dialogue between the different political parties.

As soon as John Paul II boarded his plane to leave, the police arrested five peasant leaders who had staged a hunger strike to call the pope's attention to the land situation. *Patria*, the official voice of the regime, accused the Church of politicizing the visit.

Yet in spite of constant persecution and harassment, the resistance to the dictator grew, and on 3 February 1989 I was awoken in the middle of the night by a phone call from Heriberto Alegre, a lawyer from the Churches Committee. Breathless and excited, he told me that a coup was under way to overthrow Stroessner. After several hours of suspense, with rebel forces bombing the presidential palace and police HQ, and fighting between rival army groups in the capital, regiments around the country declared their allegiance to the rebel leader, General Andrés Rodríguez, who was the father in-law of the dictator's own son. Over the crackly line from Asunción, Heriberto read me Rodríquez's declaration that he had overthrown Stroessner in the name of democracy. I immediately transmitted the news to the BBC.

Getting wind of the plan to retire him from active service, Rodríguez had acted while he still had troops under his command. The 35-year-long reign of Alfredo Stroessner had come to an end. Stroessner flew to Brazil and settled into a comfortable exile near the sea in Paraná. As I wrote in the *Guardian* in 1991, 'General Stroessner is now a geriatric exile, drooling over children's TV in Brazil.'[2] He had been Latin America's longest-ruling dictator.

Elections were held in May, three months after the coup, giving opposition parties little time to organize voter registration or set conditions for their participation. It was therefore no surprise that General Rodríguez won with over 70 per cent of the vote, but it was a victory marred by widespread and well-founded allegations of fraud and irregularities.

The former chief of police, Pastor Coronel, who was accused of personally torturing hundreds of political prisoners, was arrested and eventually sentenced to 25 years. The release of political prisoners was not immediate. Remigio Giménez, for whom Clamor had campaigned ever since his wife Dirce Mecchi had asked for our help in 1979, was still being held. In May, Clamor sent a telegram to President Rodríguez demanding his release. But it took another four months before this happened, and after over 10 years of unjust imprisonment, he was finally freed.

At least Remigio was still alive. The search for those who had disappeared during Stroessner's 35-year rule was aided by the 1993 discovery of the archives of the secret police, which revealed the fate of some of them. One was Agustín Goiburú, a doctor and member of the opposition Popular Colorado Movement, who disappeared after being detained in Argentina in 1978. I told his story in an article for the *Guardian* in 1993:

> Under the burning midday sun, two men dig holes in the soft earth of a field behind Asunción's military prison, the Guardia de Seguridad. It seems a bucolic scene. Horses graze nearby and pigs root about under the trees. But Rolando and Rogelio are looking for the remains of their father, Dr Agustín Goiburu, a Paraguayan doctor seized from exile in Argentina 15 years ago and never seen again.
>
> ... The Goiburu family now knows that the doctor was brought back to Asuncion for interrogation in the notorious police HQ known as Investigaciones, where thousands of political detainees were tortured, and many died.[3]

For over 35 years, everyone who had dared to oppose the dictatorship had paid a heavy price. Stroessner had relentlessly tortured, murdered, and locked up all those who wanted a better, fairer, less unjust country. Now Paraguayans were free at last to build that country.

Notes

1. Rocha, J. (1986) 'Paraguay Facing Up to the End of Stroessner', *The Guardian*, 16 June.
2. Rocha, J. (1991) 'Paraguayans Find Power Still Rests with a General', *The Guardian*, 4 February.
3. Rocha, J. (1993) 'Archives Yield Clue to Fate of Paraguay's Disappeared', *The Guardian*, 19 February.

CHAPTER 26
Chileans say 'no' to Pinochet

In Chile, after the 1973 coup and the crushing of the unions, the introduction of a market economy had produced the so-called 'economic miracle', which for a few brief years brought prosperity to the middle classes.

But by 1981 the miracle was over. Many companies went bust. Capital fled abroad. Wages and pensions were frozen, and unemployment reached almost 50 per cent in the poorer districts. Soup kitchens provided the only meal for thousands. The building industry collapsed. The once powerful unions were reduced to a handful of members.

In July 1985, Clamor's Thereza Brandão spent three weeks in Chile, talking to members of churches, social organizations, political parties, and trade unions. On her return, she made a long and detailed report on the situation.

Thereza noted signs that the unions were beginning to reorganize, as the economic situation worsened. The rural unions, which had suffered even worse persecution than the urban ones, were reported to be accumulating forces again. The National Confederation of Chilean Workers (Confederación Nacional de Trabajadores de Chile, CNT) was active in organizing protests.

The 1973 coup and its violent aftermath saw thousands of Chileans killed and disappeared, thousands more imprisoned, and several hundred thousand forced into exile or banished internally to the country's harsh northern region. Any form of protest, opposition, or criticism was violently repressed, but as the economic situation deteriorated, timid protests began.

In 1983, in the district of Pudahuel in greater Santiago, a group of six people from the local Catholic church, calling themselves the Sebastian Acevedo Movement, began staging lightning protests against torture. The actions were very quick, all over in three minutes, because people were still so scared. They sang, distributed pamphlets, and then got on the first bus that passed, disappearing into the crowds.

The protests took place first at the CNI (which had replaced DINA as the agency for repression and intelligence), then at the Mapocho railway station, and then at the *El Mercurio* newspaper, which was accused of collaborating with the regime. They denounced the places where torture was being practised. In her report, Thereza noted: 'The numbers grew to 300. At first it was seen only as a movement of priests and nuns, most of them foreign, but now SERPAJ and some political parties have joined in. They happen once a month, people are only told just before when and where.'

Several members of SERPAJ were arrested, tortured, exiled, or relegated to remote parts of the country for their non-violent work in favour of human rights. Nevertheless, they organized informal workshops to transform people's fear and train them in non-violent resistance, showing them examples of other successful non-violent campaigns. Over a thousand people were arrested, but the movement grew, creating new ways of protesting. Some of them were inspired by the film *Ghandi*, others by the solidarity movement in Poland.

Another tactic was slowdowns – on a designated day, people walked and drove very slowly as a sign of protest. This movement was impossible for the regime to repress. It showed people that the majority opposed the regime, empowering them and enabling them to overcome fear. At night, the banging of pots and pans as a form of protest began in Santiago, soon spreading to other regions. Courageous demonstrators marched through the streets singing 'He's going to fall, he's going to fall'. Pinochet was so annoyed by this that he banned public singing. Even Shakespeare was used against the dictator – when *Hamlet* was performed, the assassination of Hamlet's father by his brother Claudius to usurp the throne, which is normally just the background to Hamlet's tragedy, became the main theme of the play.

Not everybody believed in non-violence. At the end of 1983 the radical left formed a coalition and began a bombing campaign against the regime. Over 700 bombs were detonated against electricity pylons and the underground system. This brought an increase in repression. The opposition was divided, with those who believed that violence was not the answer creating a broad coalition of 11 parties, called the National Accord for a Transition to Full Democracy.

Thereza described how the non-violent movement had developed into larger protests, putting up barricades at the entrance to poor districts (*barrios*). The churches opened their doors for meetings, and as medical first-aid posts. But as the barricades grew, so did the repression. Thereza wrote:

> The repression became more and more violent. Many were killed, wounded, arrested, exiled or relegated.
>
> In Pudahuel alone, 80 died. From then on older people were afraid and stayed at home. Only the young took part, but they persuaded the older ones to leave their doors open. The groups of vanguard were very impatient. People got frightened when they arrived wearing balaclavas and offering guns. The mobilization lacked political leadership. If there had been clearer political leadership and less vanguardism maybe the situation would have evolved into insurrectional struggle.

While some young people chose armed struggle, many became alienated, turning to drugs, alcohol, and delinquency as an escape from the lack of work and of opportunities to study. The government's economic policies were causing an increase in hunger, malnutrition, and child prostitution, and a deterioration in health and education services.

Strikes began – first the copper miners, and then, in July 1986, the Chilean unions felt strong enough to call a national strike. The success of the strike, which was supported by exile groups in São Paulo, put the regime on the defensive, but just two months later, on 9 September, an unsuccessful assassination attempt on Pinochet's motorcade killed five bodyguards and gave him the pretext for reintroducing a state of siege.

The attempt was carried out by a far-left Marxist fringe group known as the Manuel Rodríguez Patriotic Front (*Frente Patriótico Manuel Rodríguez*, FPMR), and provoked a wave of reprisals: 11 members of the FPMR were hunted down and killed, and many who had nothing to do with the attack were arrested. The editor of the magazine *Análisis*, José Carrasco Tapia, was murdered. Radio stations were censored and alternative publications were closed down. Church lay workers and priests were persecuted. Maryknoll priests had their houses searched and their visas revoked. Some French priests were expelled.

In São Paulo, Clamor received regular correspondence from the Association of Families of Political Prisoners, asking us to campaign for their imprisoned relatives. They were very worried about the conditions of the 350 or so political prisoners, many of them sharing cells with common criminals and at risk of violence. Most of them had been tortured. Thirteen had been sentenced to death, including two women.

We also received appeals from the Association of the Families of the Detained and Disappeared. They listed 49 women who had disappeared in Chile between September 1973 and October 1977, plus another seven in Argentina. One of these was a paraplegic who had gone to Argentina to obtain new orthopaedic legs. Her eight-month-old baby, Claudia Poblete, disappeared with her.

The Catholic clergy were involved body and soul in the popular movement and were very critical of the position of the Church hierarchy. The cardinal who had become archbishop of Santiago in 1983, Juan Francisco Fresno, was much more conservative than his predecessor, Cardinal Raúl Silva Henríquez. The Church began to talk about reconciliation, but the more progressive bishops demanded that this should be conditioned by truth and justice. 'This created a loophole for the church of the poor and it seems that many of the bishops did not realise the reach of what they had signed up to', noted Thereza in her report.

Chile's Catholic Church had not at first openly opposed the regime, but was now providing a vital space for organizing and protecting victims of human rights abuses through the Vicariate of Solidarity. In April 1985, two of the Vicariate's collaborators, sociologist José Manuel Parada Maluenda and educator Manuel Guerrero Ceballos, who had been investigating an army death squad called the Joint Command, were kidnapped by members of it, tortured, and abandoned in a street with their throats cut.

In May 1985, families of eight murdered Chileans began a hunger strike at the Church of St Filomena in Santiago.

In December 1985, the Chilean magazine *Análisis* published an article on the notorious Caravan of Death, an army group which had toured Chile by helicopter soon after the coup executing political prisoners held in local jails. The article revealed that the second in command of the Caravan, Colonel Sergio Arredondo González, was living in Brazil and was said to be working for Codelco, the Chilean state copper company. This news reached Brazil at the beginning of 1986, and a reporter at the newspaper *Folha de S. Paulo* discovered that Codelco's offices were located in the centre of São Paulo and that their director was indeed Colonel Arredondo.

Clamor invited Carmen Hertz, the widow of one of the men executed by the Caravan, to come to São Paulo for a press conference. Carmen's husband, Carlos Berger, had been the director of a local radio station called *El Loa*, in Calama, in the north of Chile. His name was on one of the death certificates of 21 men executed on 19 October 1973 in Calama, held in Clamor's archives. They were aged between 18 and 55, and the cause of death was identical in each case: 'destruction of the thorax and cardiac region by shooting'.

After the conference, held in the Curia, a crowd of journalists went straight to the Codelco offices to confront Arredondo. Believing they had come to question him about copper prices, the unsuspecting colonel invited the journalists in and plied them with coffee. Clovis Rossi, the *Folha's* experienced and well-informed reporter on Latin America, then challenged the colonel, quoting statements made in Chile by the son of General Arellano Stark and by Colonel Eugenio Rivera, the military governor of the region where the executions took place, to which Arredondo had no convincing reply.

The Salvador Allende Committee of Political Refugees in São Paulo issued a declaration accusing Arredondo of 'direct participation in the torture and death of over 70 political prisoners during the month of October 1973'. The declaration continued: 'Arredondo, as an Army Colonel and second in command of the Death Squad, knows where the bodies of over 70 murdered Chileans are to be found. The families of those who were executed have the right to know where the bodies of their beloved ones are buried.'

Clamor and AALA then petitioned the Ministry of Justice demanding the expulsion of Arredondo, and protests were held in front of the Codelco offices in São Paulo. The request was denied, but soon afterwards the colonel returned to Chile.

In April 1987, the pope made a six-day visit to Chile and spoke to a crowd of thousands in the National Stadium, the same place that had become an infamous centre of torture and death for hundreds of Chileans immediately after the coup. He acknowledged the 'sadness' of the place but exhorted young Chileans not to resort to violence.

The pope told the bishops that they had a right to pass moral judgement in political matters, but preached the need for reconciliation and unity. He defended democracy and welcomed the promised plebiscite. FASIC produced a list of all the known political prisoners, including their sentences and the prisons at which they were held.

The following year, the Chilean government organized the plebiscite, confident of victory. Clamor sent Thereza Brandão and Padre Roberto Grandmaison to Chile to collect information on the preparations for the vote to approve or reject Pinochet's plan to stay in power for another eight years. Declared 'Supreme Leader of the Nation' in 1974, Pinochet had no intention of relinquishing power.

The grassroots non-violent movement organized the 'no' campaign. They were allowed daily time on TV of 15 minutes, and used it to reveal the many abuses of human rights that had taken place.

On 5 October 1988, to Pinochet's surprise and fury, the 'no' vote won by 56 per cent to 43 per cent. A bad loser, Pinochet tried to stage a coup, imposing martial law – but other military leaders resisted, having seen that the writing was on the wall. In 1989, a referendum approved a new constitution. General elections were held, and Patricio Aylwin of the Christian Democratic Party, leading a coalition of left and centre parties, emerged victorious. But Pinochet continued as commander-in-chief of the army until 1998, when he became a senator for life, guaranteeing immunity and impunity in Chile. The same year, he was arrested in London.

In his 17 years as president, Pinochet had destroyed democracy and murdered and tortured an entire generation of Chileans with the support of the United States and his military colleagues in the Southern Cone. He was the last of the region's dictators to leave power. With his exit, Clamor's work was finished.

CHAPTER 27
Clamor closes its doors

In 1990 the last of the Southern Cone dictatorships, Chile, inaugurated a civilian president, and the years of military rule that had blighted the region, killing, torturing, and disappearing thousands, sending hundreds of thousands into exile, ruining economies, and mutilating societies, came to an end. Democracy, however limited and imperfect, had been restored, and therefore the raison d'être for Clamor's existence had disappeared.

The return of civilian governments did not always bring truth and justice; in some countries, this would take decades to achieve. Only some of the dictators and their henchmen were brought to trial.

In Argentina, the nine leading members of the various military juntas, including Generals Videla and Viola and Admiral Massera, had been tried and given life sentences. In the 1990s they were amnestied by President Carlos Menem, but in the 2000s, under Nestor Kirchner's government, they were tried and condemned for their 'systematic plan to steal the children and babies of political opponents'.

In Bolivia, General Luis García Meza, his interior minister Luis Arce Gómez, and 54 others were tried and convicted by the Supreme Court in Sucre for their crimes.

Paraguay's dictator, Alfredo Stroessner, had escaped into a comfortable exile in Brazil, but the dreaded head of the secret police, Pastor Coronel, was in prison awaiting trial.

In Uruguay, an amnesty law prevented anyone from being tried for human rights violations until it was finally repealed in 2011.

In Chile, for many years an amnesty law protected Pinochet and members of the armed forces and police from being held responsible for their crimes. But after his death in 2010, prosecutions began.

At Clamor, the refugees who had once crowded round the back door of the São Paulo Curia while children played and babies cried, exchanging news and making plans, had disappeared. The number of phone calls and visits had dwindled. After 12 years of frenetic activity, it was time to wind up our affairs, and for our members to go their separate ways.

The group's membership had grown slowly over the years. Maria Auxiliadora Abrantes, or Dodora, a psychologist, joined the group in 1982. She was a member of the Brazilian Amnesty Committee (*Comitê Brasileiro de Anistia*, CBA) and the newly created Brazilian Solidarity Committee (*Comitê Brasileiro de Solidariedade*, CBS). Married to Aldo Arantes, a leader of the clandestine Communist Party of Brazil, whose members were hunted by the military after the 1964 coup, she had been arrested with her two small children in Alagoas, where she was taking part in literacy campaigns among rural workers. After being held in prison for several months, Dodora went into exile in Uruguay.

In 1983, Cida Horta, who had married Luiz Eduardo Greenhalgh, joined. She had spent several years in Cuba as a political exile, after fleeing Brazil soon after the 1964 coup. She was able to help with interviewing refugees at the Curia. Later she was joined by Inge Schilling, who had spent 16 years in exile, first in Uruguay and then in Argentina, with her husband, economist and left-wing politician Paulo Schilling.

In 1988, two more people joined the Clamor team – Dominican João Xerri, parish priest of the São Domingos church in Perdizes and later provincial of the order, who came originally from Malta, and Lilia Azevedo, a human rights activist of the Catholic Church.

As so many meetings were held in our homes, even our children became involved. Jaime's daughter, Anita, a primary school teacher, showed the Abuelas a drawing by one of her pupils which they liked so much that they adopted it as their logo. My young son and daughter, Camilo and Ali, played with the children of Argentine and Uruguayan refugees who came to the house, communicating in a mixture of Portuguese and Spanish. Their large collection of Lego was a big attraction.

Clamor was a small group, and it always counted on the collaboration of a large number of individual volunteers and organizations in Brazil. There was a general atmosphere of sympathy in Brazil towards the refugees who had begun to arrive in large numbers in the second half of the 1970s.

Among the organizations with which Clamor worked most closely was AALA. This association was set up in 1980 by a group of professionals led by São Paulo lawyer Belisário dos Santos Jr, to create a regional network collaborating on human rights issues. AALA helped to debrief defectors and made joint visits to Paraguay with members of Clamor to campaign for the release of Remigio Giménez.

Another was the MJDH, based in Porto Alegre. Set up by lawyer Jair Krischke in March 1979, it was active in denouncing the 1978 kidnapping there of the Uruguayan PVP members Lilián Celiberti and Universindo Díaz, and Lilián's children. Located in the capital of Brazil's southernmost state, Rio Grande do Sul, which shares an extensive land border with Uruguay, it became the first port of call for many Uruguayan exiles and refugees.

The CBS was a solidarity movement set up in 1980 by a group of Brazilians and exiles. Coordinator Hamilton Octavio de Souza, a journalist, recalled in an interview with me that, after the amnesty in 1979, Brazil was moving towards democracy, and it became the space in South America where violations of human rights could be denounced. 'Many more would have been killed if it weren't for Clamor's activities', he noted.

When we decided that it was time to close our doors, the question remained of what to do with our voluminous archive, including the many letters we had received over the years from families and organizations and the eyewitness accounts of disappearances, torture, clandestine camps, and repression provided by refugees arriving in São Paulo. The archive was eventually taken in by São Paulo Catholic University's Centre for Documentation and Investigation, and a few years ago was selected by UNESCO as one of its Memory of the World archives.

Clamor was fortunate to count on generous funders right from the start, especially the WCC. Our close association with Dom Paulo encouraged many churches and church organizations, both Catholic and Protestant, to support our work. These included Swedish Free Churches Aid; Algemeen Diakonaal Bureau in Holland; CAFOD and Christian Aid in the UK; and Trocaire, the Irish Catholic overseas development agency, in Ireland. Grants also came from the National Catholic Church in the United States, and the United Church of Canada.

The donations were used to pay three part-time helpers in the office during the last seven years, to print and post our bulletins free of charge all over the world, for the preparation and publication of the List of disappeared in Argentina in 1982 and for the 1983 and 1984 calendars of disappeared children, and to pay the printing costs of pamphlets, postcards, and newspaper ads for organizations in Argentina. They helped to pay for our investigations into missing children in Bolivia, Chile, and Argentina and for fact-finding missions to Paraguay, and to pay travel expenses for relatives or members of human rights organizations coming to Brazil or to other countries.

They also funded the publication of two books, Patricia Lorca's *El Día que Nos Cambió la Vida* (The Day that Changed Our Lives), about Chile after the 1973 coup, and Cácia Cortez's *Brasiguaios: Os Refugiados Desconhecidos* (Brasiguaios: The Unknown Refugees). Cacia's book described the painful return to Brazil of thousands of small farmers who had moved over the border into Paraguay when their land was flooded for the giant Itaipu Dam on the border of the two countries. They had successfully settled and built up thriving communities, but when large-scale soy farmers decided they wanted to expand their lands, a wave of persecution was unleashed against them by Stroessner's police and army, and they fled back to Brazil with nothing, becoming literal refugees in their own country.

None of our achievements would have been possible without the uncompromising support at all times of Dom Paulo, Cardinal Arns, the archbishop of São Paulo, who inspired and encouraged not only us, but all those who came into contact with him.

Over the years the members of Clamor had sought to live up to our symbol, a candle flickering in the darkness, offering light and hope, and to our motto 'Solidarity knows no frontiers', to counter the terror unleashed by the regimes of Operation Condor. But now it was time to put out the candle, so we did.

APPENDIX 1
List of Clamor bulletins and press releases

Between 1978 and 1985, 16 issues of the *Clamor Bulletin* were published in English, Portuguese, and Spanish.

No.	Date	Content
1	June 1978	Argentina: published to coincide with the World Cup held there.
2	July 1978	Editorial comparing the horrors of detention camps in Argentina and Uruguay with the horrors of Second World War concentration camps. News of arrests, kidnappings, and disappearances in all five Southern Cone countries.
3	October 1978	A long article about national security not respecting frontiers, with examples of cross-border abductions and disappearances. The confessions of a Chilean ex-DINA agent about how he tortured and killed prisoners.
4	December 1978	Launched the phrase 'Solidarity has no frontiers', which became Clamor's motto. Described the kidnapping in Porto Alegre of the Uruguayan exiles Lilián Celiberti and Universindo Díaz. Also listed 17 small children and 22 adolescents who had been forcibly disappeared in Argentina.
5	May 1979	Reported the growing pressure on members of human rights organizations by Southern Cone governments and began publishing the section 'Where Are They?', listing cases of disappeared people.
6	August 1979	Report on the number of forcibly disappeared pregnant women the fate of whose babies was unknown, prepared for the visit to Argentina by the OAS Human Rights Commission.
7	September 1979	Paraguay: the human rights situation, detentions, torture, deaths, censorship, secret trials, human rights organizations, and Stroessner's unpopular decision to offer asylum to Nicaraguan ex-dictator Anastasio Somoza.
8	November 1979	Details of the visit by the OAS Commission to Argentina and of the special ecumenical mass held in São Paulo by Cardinal Arns to denounce the potential genocide of 12,000 disappeared people following the Argentine government's announcement that they would be declared dead if they did not reappear within 90 days.
9	March 1990	Article on the cynicism of the regimes, with examples, and the fact that the OAS Human Rights Commission found that of the nine countries which most violated human rights in the world, four were located in South America (namely Argentina, Chile, Paraguay, and Uruguay). Also covered the visit to Paraguay by a Brazilian congressman, at Clamor's request, to obtain the release of imprisoned journalist Alcibiades Delvalle, president of the Journalists' Union.

No.	Date	Content
10	August 1980	Uruguay: the political, trade union, and Church situation, and the inhumane conditions of political prisoners. Reports on Uruguayan exiles who had disappeared in Argentina, Brazil, and Paraguay, and more details supplied by Army deserter Hugo Rivas on the kidnapping in Porto Alegre of Lilián Celiberti, her two children, and Universindo Díaz.
11	September 1980	Bolivia: the recent coup and the violent repression unleashed by the military, especially against the miners and the churches.
12	December 1980	Prison conditions in Southern Cone countries, the visit of Pope John Paul II to Brazil, and the approval of a new Foreigners' Law in Brazil, seen as threatening to exiles.
13	March 1981	Discovery in Chile of human remains at Yumbel, believed to be those of people executed after the 1973 coup.
14	December 1981	Discussed trade unions and workers after the various military coups in the region. Listed workers disappeared and killed.
15	December 1983	Recounted the five years of Clamor's existence, with details of activities, publications, and achievements.
16	November 1984	Round-up of the region: the return to democracy in Argentina had not solved the question of the thousands of disappeared, but a solution had been found for the identification of the babies born in captivity and adopted. In Uruguay, Paraguay, and Chile, opposition to the authoritarian regimes was growing while economic conditions worsened.

In addition, Clamor issued many press bulletins for the Brazilian and international media. Some examples:

Date	Content
26 September 1978	'Repression in Paraguay in 1976: Hunger Strike'
31 July 1979	'Children Found in Chile'
31 July 1979	'Self-Kidnapping?' (the strange disappearance of Uruguayan exiles in Porto Alegre)
14 August 1979	'Confiscation of Lists of Disappeared' (Argentina)
20 March 1980	'The Revolt of Paraguayan Peasant Farmers'
27 March 1980	Launch of the World Campaign for Disappeared Children
21 July 1980	'Fifth Anniversary of the List of 119 Disappeared' (Chile)
11 September 1980	'The Duty to Denounce'
9 October 1980	'Repression after the Death of Somoza' (Paraguay)
13 August 1981	'The Case of Remigio Giménez: Same Problem, Different Solutions'
10 August 1983	'Paraguayan Political Prisoners on Hunger Strike'
6 September 1983	'A Light Has Been Put Out' (the closure of SERPAJ in Uruguay)
17 April 1985	Covered the international seminar organized by Clamor on the role of human rights organizations in the new political, social, and economic situations in the countries of the region.
5 September 1985	'Children Kidnapped in Argentina ... Disappear Again'

APPENDIX 2

Clamor past covers and images

ANO I
Nº 1
Junho 1978

CLAMOR

Comitê de Defesa dos Direitos Humanos para o Cone Sul, Vinculado à Comissão Arquidiocesana de Pastoral dos Direitos Humanos e Marginalizados de São Paulo

Apresentação

Com o presente damos início as atividades do Comitê de Defesa dos Direitos Humanos no Cone Sul CLAMOR – órgão vinculado à Comissão Arquidiocesana de Pastoral dos Direitos Humanos e Marginalizados de São Paulo.

CLAMOR tem por objetivo a defesa dos direitos humanos na América Latina, especialmente nos países do Cone Sul. Com a finalidade de dar a conhecer suas atividades, periodicamente editará o presente boletim com informações.

É interesse do CLAMOR estreitar vínculos com orgãos congêneres para cooperação mútua.

A perspectiva do CLAMOR é cristã, ecumênica, sem filiação partidária e seus objetivos são humanitários.

Este primeiro número do boletim, saindo às vésperas da Copa do Mundo, quando a atenção do mundo está voltada para a Argentina, é dedicado exclusivamente àquele país.

Endereço para correspondência:

CLAMOR
Av. Higienópolis, 890
01238 - São Paulo - SP - Brasil

"Inclina os teus ouvidos ao meu clamor.

(Salmos 88, 2)

Figure 1 Clamor 1 cover

1. Report on disappeared Women who were pregnant at the time of their arrest. (Prepared by the "Asamblea Permanente por los Derechos Humanos" - Buenos Aires, Argentina.)

2. Press Bulletin, 7.31.79.

3. Press Bulletin, 8.14.79.

Figure 2 Clamor 6 cover

CLAMOR

Nº 10
Year II
August/1980

"Bend an ear to my clamor." (Psalms 88,2)

Committee for the Defense of Human Rights in Southern Cone Nations
of São Paulo's Archdiocesan Commission for Human Rights and the Marginalized

CLAMOR
Avenida Higienópolis 890, sala 12
01238 - São Paulo, SP
Brasil

Figure 3 Clamor 10 cover

CLAMOR

"Inclina tu oído a mi clamor." (Salmos 88,2)

Comité de Defensa de los Derechos Humanos en el Cono Sur
Comisión Archidiocesana de la Pastoral de los Derechos Humanos y Marginados de São Paulo

Avenida Higienópolis 890, sala 12
01238 - São Paulo, SP
Brasil

<u>Clamor</u> Nº 11
Año II
Septiembre/1980

EL GOLPE Y LOS DERECHOS HUMANOS EN BOLIVIA

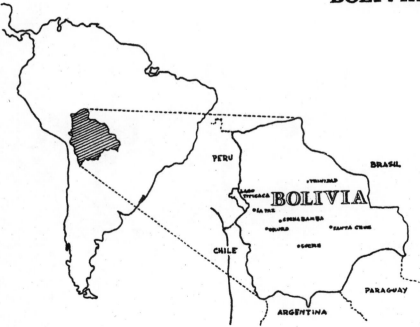

Figure 4 Clamor 11 cover

CLAMOR

"Inclina tu oído a mi clamor." (Salmos 88,2)

Comité de Defensa de los Derechos Humanos en el Cono Sur

Comisión Archidiocesana de la Pastoral de los Derechos Humanos y Marginados de São Paulo

<u>Clamor</u> Nº 13
Año III
Marzo/1981

Avenida Higienópolis 890, Sala 19
01238 – São Paulo, SP
Brasil

LOS DERECHOS HUMANOS
EN
CHILE

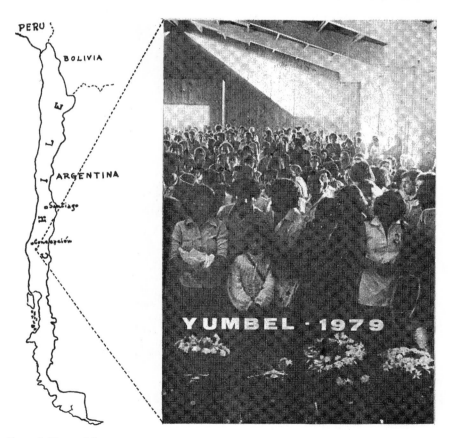

Figure 5 Clamor 13 cover

CLAMOR Clamor Nº 14
Year IV
December 1981

"Bend an ear to my clamor." (Psalms 88,2)

COMMITTEE FOR THE DEFENSE OF HUMAN RIGHTS IN SOUTHERN CONE NATIONS OF SÃO
PAULO'S ARCHDIOCESAN COMMISSION FOR HUMAN RIGHTS AND THE MARGINALIZED

MILITARY REGIMES AND TRADE UNIONS IN THE SOUTHERN CONE

CLAMOR
Av. Higienópolis 890, sala 19
01238 - São Paulo, SP
Brazil

Figure 6 Clamor 14 cover

DESAPARECIDOS

ᴇɴ ʟᴀ ARGENTINA

[DISAPPEARED IN ARGENTINA]

CLAMOR - Pág. nº

Nº	APPELIDOS Y NOMBRES	NA	ED	DOCUMENTOS	E.CIV.	PROFES.	FECHA Y LUGAR DE DETENCION	FAM.DESAP.	OBSERVACIONES
3158	GROISMAN, Omar					Via	23.03.76		
3159	GROPPER, Daniel José		19	DNI 12.660.46		Est	11.08.77 - Capital Federal		
3160	GROSSI, Carlos					Obr.met	23.05.77 - Córdoba		
3161	GROSSI, Charles del Carmen	AR	45	LE 4.084.626	Cas/2	Obr.met	05.08.77 - Va. Madero - Bs.As.		Sindicalista Obr. DURATOMIC
3162	GROSSO, Carlos	AR	21			Est	16.05.78 - Capital Federal		
3163	GRUJIC de CORONEL, María Teresa	AR	24	DNI 10.412.786	Cas/3	Est	27.01.77 - La Plata - Bs.As.		
3164	GRUMBERG, Claudia Inés	AR	25	CI 7.293.725		Emp.ofc	11.10.76 - Capital Federal		Emp. SAGAZOLA
3165	GRUNBAUM, Roberto	AR	28	LE 7.866.744		Ing	16.06.77 - Capital Federal		
3166	GRYNBERG, Susana Flora	AR	29	LC 5.711.833		Lic.fis	20.10.76 - Bs.As.		
3167	GUACARDO RECCA,								
3168	GUAGLIONE, José Luis	AR				Emp.pub	19.08.77 - Resistencia - Chaco		Se encontraba en
3169	GUAGNINI, Diego Julio	AR	25	CI 6.550.158	Cas/1	Est.obr	30.05.77 - Capital Federal	a 6923	V. "Club Atlético "Banco"
3170	GUAGNINI, Luis Rodolfo	AR	33	CI 4.438.135 LE 10.896.357	Cas/2	Per	21.12.77 - Capital Federal		
3171	GUALDERO de GARCIA, María del Carmen	AR	21		Cas/e	Emp.ofc	08.06.76 - Bs.As.	c 2763	
3172	GUALDONI MAZON, Juan Carlos	AR/ES	27			Emp.ban	26.06.76 - Capital Federal		Delegado
3173	GUANCIROLI de GENOUD, Lía Maria-na Ercilia	AR	22	DNI 11.991.225	Viu/1	Est	03.80 - Bs.As.	a 2867	
3174	GUARDIA, Hugo								
3175	GUASTA, Eugenio Antonio	AR	36	CI 4.734.981	Cas/2	Com	23.11.76 - Zárate - Bs.As.		Carnicero

Figure 7 Booklet, *The disappeared in Argentina*, 1982. Cover and a page from the list of names

Figure 8 The author, Jan Rocha, in 1992

Figure 9 An early Clamor meeting, 1978. Left to right: Michael Mary Nolan, Roberto Grandmaison, Jan Rocha, Jaime Wright

Figure 10 Lunch for Clamor members at Jan's house, 1988. Left to right: Mariana (daughter of Cida and Luiz), Cida Horta, Luis Paulo (son of Cida and Luiz), Roberto Grandmaison, Thereza Brandão, Michael Mary Nolan, Jan Rocha, Bruna Rocha (daughter of Jan and Plauto), Luiz Eduardo Greenhalgh

Index